LOCAL GOVERNMENT ADMINISTRATION

LOCAL GOVERNMENT ADMINISTRATION

by

ALAN GRIFFITHS
F.C.I.S.,
lately Director of Administrative Service,
West Wiltshire District Council

SECOND EDITION

LONDON:
Published by
SHAW & SONS Ltd.
Shaway House, SE26 5AE
1987

First *Published* ....November, 1976
Second *Edition* .... September, 1987

ISBN 07219 0712 1

CONTENTS

PUBLISHER'S NOTE

This work was originally designed as a work of reference for Chartered Secretaries engaged in Local Government and as a text book for students taking the examination of the Institute of Chartered Secretaries and Administrators. In practice, however, it was found to be acceptable to a much wider range of reader and has become established as a manual dealing with the practical work of a Local Authority used by both members and officials alike. In particular it has proved especially useful in the training of new entrants in Local Government.

The new edition has been considerably improved by re-arrangement of the Chapters into a more logical sequence and has been brought fully up to date in the light of the current role and function of Local Authorities

POSTSCRIPT

In this age of equal opportunities, the reader for whom this book is intended might equally well be a woman or a man. The English language does not always provide a satisfactory method of being fair to both sexes, without loss of readability. So, in most cases we have used the masculine gender, but in all instances, it is intended to apply to either sex.

We rely on the reader to make a sensible interpretation for himself, or herself.

CHAPTER 1

THE LOCAL GOVERNMENT SYSTEM

INTRODUCTION

"Local Government is the concern of everyone."

This sentence was used by another author thirty years ago as the introduction to an earlier book on the subject[1] and it could scarcely be bettered. He might well have gone on to explain that in all recorded history civilised communities have found it necessary to establish some form of machinery for the efficient administration of their local affairs.

There was, by way of illustration, the disturbance at Ephesus when, it is recorded, "the town clerk quieted the crowd". The story can be found in Acts of the Apostles, Chapter 19, where the intrepid town clerk is reported to have said, "If Demetrius and his craftsmen have a case against anyone, assizes are held and there are such people as proconsuls; let the parties bring their charges and countercharges. If, on the other hand, you have some further question to raise, it will be dealt with in the statutory assembly".

Need for local authority

This well-known biblical story is repeated here because it clearly establishes the essential nature of a lawful local authority. It is also plain that people naturally favour an assembly in which each can have a say but it is often necessary to appoint magistrates or officials of some kind to act in the name of the community.

[1] Local Government in England and Wales. W. Eric Jackson.

The practice of electing an individual to be the local authority tends to be popular in those countries accustomed to the Presidential system in national affairs. Communities in France and the U.S.A., for example, have mayors with considerable personal power and influence. The "city manager" system, where the executive business of local government is carried on by a paid, appointed official is used in many countries, notably the Republic of Ireland.

In Great Britain, with its long history of parliamentary democracy, the local authority is invariably a local parliament or "council", democratically elected, operating within the law and subject to the control and direction of the central government in matters of national importance but otherwise enjoying considerable autonomy in the management of local affairs.

Need for paid staff

Whatever form the local authority takes, unless it is an extremely small one with very few powers, it invariably finds it necessary to employ a team of full-time paid officials and staff to carry its policy decisions into practical effect. A key position in the paid structure of any local authority is occupied by the chief executive and administrative officer. Formerly this was almost always the same man, the functions being absorbed into the former statutory office of town clerk or clerk of the council. Since the reorganisation of 1974 this is not necessarily so. Many authorities have divided the two functions and now have a chief executive in overall charge of their paid staff but without departmental responsibility and a separate principal officer in control of the administrative machine.

In adopting this system, local authorities are following recommendations made in the Report of the Study Group on Local Authority Management Structures (commonly called the "Bains Report"), published in 1972. In this report it is suggested[1] that the head of the central administrative

---

[1] Chapter 7.34.

department is rather analogous to the secretary of a company and the title of County (or District) Secretary is put forward as an apt one.

THE EVOLUTION OF MODERN LOCAL GOVERNMENT

The student of constitutional history may care to examine the ancient forms of local government in this country which preceded the reforms of the early Victorian era. It is sufficient for our purpose to say that they were inadequate for the needs of a developing society following the Industrial Revolution. Often they were also corrupt and inefficient.

The pattern of local government that emerged may not appear to our generation to have been wholly successful. At any rate, further drastic reorganisation took place fifty years later. But it is probably fairer to say that the local government of the mid-nineteenth century, in its day, represented a considerable advance on what had gone before. It is questionable whether the reforms of the past decade will stand up to critical scrutiny over one hundred years hence.

The objective of the early Victorian reformers was to provide a separate elected local authority for every required service. Thus a single township might have a Board of Guardians, a school board, a burial board, a Board of Highways, a sanitary authority and so on. Each had the power to levy its own rate and to conduct its own elections. The areas for which each board was responsible did not necessarily coincide. A measure of central control was exercised by higher authorities such as the Central Board of Health and the Poor Law Commissioners.

The result was a hotch potch. Control from the centre was not uniformly exercised and must at times have been resented by members of local boards. One cannot imagine the reaction of a largely uneducated public to have been anything but complete bewilderment. Nevertheless the system appears to have worked tolerably well for a time. Graft was largely eliminated and, although the services provided by these authorities nowadays appear to have been crude and paltry, they were no doubt considered adequate and efficient by the standards of the time.

Local government in the late nineteenth century

By the later years of the century it had become obvious that the system needed to be simplified and improved. This time the legislators devised a system that was to survive in outline, though extended and improved in detail, for about a hundred years, and which is still the essential basis on which local government is based today.

This reform dates from the creation in 1871 of the Local Government Board, a new Government department responsible for the oversight of all local government matters. Measures were then taken to introduce a logical pattern of local authorities each responsible for providing a wide and varied group of services in its locality.

Certain places, such as the City of London, were permitted to retain ancient privileges of self-government, but over the greater part of the country the local boards were abolished and replaced by local councils of the kind we know today. Apart from the historical authorities already referred to, there were six kinds of local council. In the larger cities and towns a single authority, known as a County Borough Council, was made responsible for all services. In the more sparsely populated regions the functions which were thought to need organising on a large scale were allocated to county councils and, in the smaller towns, the remainder was allocated to a Borough (or Town) Council. The laudable objective was apparently to secure that decisions were taken at the most local possible level consistent with the provision of an adequate and efficient service. Accordingly a three-tier system was evolved for rural districts. In these districts the county council exercised rather more power than in the boroughs (notably in respect of the roads); a small number of functions was performed by Parish (or Village) Councils and the rest by a Rural District Council, formed by amalgamating a number of villages for the purpose. The sixth kind of local council was named an Urban District Council. This status was given to the larger villages and small towns which were able to exercise on their own account the combined powers of a Rural District Council and a Parish Council but which did not qualify for Borough status. With the passage of time many urban districts were to grow into sizeable towns and were granted additional powers so that, in recent times, it became almost impossible to distinguish them from the borough councils except in the matter of local tradition.

The method of financing the new local authorities was, as formerly, a local tax or "rate" levied on the occupiers of property. On the reasonable argument that taxation and representation went hand in glove, the franchise at local elections was originally limited to ratepayers.

Changes in sociey in the twentieth century

The success of the new system may be assessed by the fact that a full hundred years elapsed from the date of the formation of the Local Government Board until the structure was finally dismantled and rebuilt by the Local Government Act 1972. In those hundred years, society underwent a fundamental change. The functions of the local authorities were increased and extended and it can fairly be claimed on behalf of the old councils that they coped with their wide range of responsibilities exceedingly well.

They had originally been charged with the upkeep of roads built for the use of the horse and cart; they eventually came to be responsible for broad motor highways. Before World War I, housing had been provided almost exclusively by private enterprise; the responsibility of the local authority was seen to be the improvement of their sanitary condition. After that war local authorities were first called upon to provide municipal housing for the working classes, mainly as an essential element in a slum clearance programme. Following World War II, the provision of rented municipal accommodation for all social classes became public policy and something like one person in three now lives in a house rented from the local council.

Town and country planning, which had had limited practical effect before World War II, burst into prominence with the passing of a major Act of Parliament in 1947 and has since steadily expanded into a major local authority activity. The Welfare State, as it is commonly called, has made enormous demands on local authorities to provide social services for the aged, the infirm and the handicapped, and for children.

By contrast, and by a stroke of irony, several services formerly provided by local authorities, such as gas and electricity, hospitals and, recently, water and some health services have been transferred to the control of purpose-formed boards. However, these are not locally elected boards on the nineteenth-century pattern but are regional authorities usually appointed by a Secretary of State and are not democratically elected, in the generally accepted sense, at all.

The increase in the statutory duties of local authorities placed a strain on their financial resources which the rate yield alone could not bear and substantial grants from the national exchequer became essential. Consequently, the franchise at local government elections was extended to all electors with a local qualification whether or not they were also ratepayers.

Demand for new local government system

In spite of efforts to contain the situation, the demands made on the public purse both at national and local level have continued to grow year by year. Pressures for drastic reform of the local government system began to build up after World War II. A series of White Papers on the areas, functions and financial resources of local authorities were published in the 1950s and there followed some regrouping of local authorities, mainly in London and the Midlands, which can hardly be said to have made any dramatic effect on the local government system as a whole. Sadly, an official report on new sources of local authority finance ("the Allen Report") proved to be completely unproductive.

In 1966 a Royal Commissioin was set up under the chairmanship of Sir John Maud, shortly afterwards to be created Lord Redcliffe-Maud, to "consider the structure of local government in England, outside Greater London, in relation to its existing functions; and to make recommendations for authorities and boundaries, and for functions and their division, having regard to the size and character of areas in which these can be most effectively exercised and the need to sustain a viable system of local democracy; and to report."

London government reorganisation, which had taken place a few years earlier, had provided for municipal services in the capital (other than the City) to be divided between two authorities, the Greater London Council on the one hand and one of a number of new London Borough Councils, each having a population of around 300,000, on the other. This organisation was evidently considered satisfactory, or it was not considered opportune to disturb it again, and the Royal Commission was not, therefore, concerned with it. Nor was it concerned with Scotland for which a different Royal Commission was appointed.

Recommendation of Redcliffe-Maud

The main recommendation of the Royal Commission was to replace the existing local authorities by new all-purpose authorities, which it called "unitary authorities", on the model of the County Borough Councils. This could have been done, effectively, by transferring the powers and duties of the boroughs, the urban and rural district councils and the parish councils to the corresponding county council.

For some reason, presumably of a political nature, the recommendation did not find favour with H. M. Government and the Local Government Act 1972, which followed, provided for a dichotomy on the London pattern. With the exception of the parish councils, which emerged from the exercise completely unscathed, all the old authorities, including the county boroughs, were abolished although a few, principally among the county councils, reappeared in a new form scarcely different from the old.

Local government boundaries

Local Government Boundary Commissions (not to be confused with the Royal Commission) sat to redraw the local authority map of England and Wales. Some new county councils were created and the boundaries of some of the old ones significantly changed. New district councils were formed, in most cases somewhat larger than the old ones. The first elections were held in 1973 and the new local authorities took over their responsibilities on 1st April, 1974.

In and around the major provincial cities the London model was copied rather more closely than was possible in the rest of the country. The new counties centred on the principal connurbations were named "metropolitan counties" and their districts were "metropolitan districts". Metropolitan district councils were allocated rather more powers and duties than their non-metropolitan counterparts.

From April, 1986 these metropolitan counties were abolished and their responsibilities were passed either to the Metropolitan Districts, (for *e.g.* the G.L.C. to the London Boroughs) or to ad hoc committees responsible for specific functions *e.g.* Fire.

Local authority functions

The main functions of non-metropolitan county councils are social services, personal health services, education, highways and transport planning, consumer protection, police and fire services and some town and country planning (principally the preparation of structure plans). All district councils are responsible for housing, most town and country planning (especially local plans and development control), environmental health, refuse collection, leisure services and rating. In addition, metropolitan district councils are responsible for social services, personal health services, education, highways and consumer protection. Metropolitan Districts (and outer London Boroughs) thus come closest to the concept of the "most purpose" authority.

THE LEGAL FRAMEWORK OF LOCAL GOVERNMENT

At this point it may be convenient to consider the legal limitations on the activities of local authorities. All local authorities are statutory corporations having a name, perpetual succession and an official seal. That is to say each has a legal existence quite separate from its members, officers, ratepayers or whoever may be said to comprise its constituent members.

Action lawfully taken in the name of the council binds the council and not the individuals who took the action on its behalf; likewise the benefit of such action accrues to the council and not to its members. By the same token, the council cannot accept the responsibility for action taken otherwise than in its corporate name.

But action taken unlawfully and knowing it to be wrong, becomes the personal responsibility of members voting for such a cause of action.

A local authority, acting in the usual way by a majority vote, may embark upon a certain course of action. Following an election, members holding different views may secure a majority of seats on the council. They may, if they so wish, rescind the previous decision but they cannot repudiate responsibility for action already taken in the council's name. In other words, the council has perpetual succession even though its members do not.

The official seal is, as it were, the signature whereby the will of the council is authenticated. Formerly a local authority could not take any formal, legal action otherwise than by the use of its seal but nowadays the signature of an authorised officer or agent, clearly subscribed for and on behalf of the council in its corporate name, will be sufficient except in a deed when the use of the seal is obligatory by law.

The doctrine of "ultra vires"

Although a statutory corporation enjoys a legal existence of its own like any individual, its position differs from an ordinary person in one vital respect. Whereas an individual may lawfully do anything he likes as long as it is not expressly forbidden by law, a body corporate may not do anything at all unless it is expressly authorised by law to do so. Anything which is not so authorised is said to be beyond the powers of the authority and the rule is universally known as the doctrine of *ultra vires*.

The doctrine is strict but it has been held[1] by the Court of Appeal that

> the doctrine ought to be reasonably, and not unreasonably, understood and applied, and that whatever may fairly be regarded as incidental to, or consequential upon, those things which the legislature has authorised, ought not (unless expressly prohibited) to be held, by judicial construction, to be *ultra vires*.

For example, an authority has the statutory power to provide and manage houses for letting. It might fairly be regarded as having the power to insure the property, including the tenants' effects, but not to provide a wide variety of fringe benefits for its tenants.

Remedies for unlawful expenditure

As a body corporate a local authority may sue and be sued in the courts and an aggrieved ratepayer, who considers some expenditure to be *ultra vires*, may commence an action in the High Court to secure redress.

Action may also be taken by the local authority auditor, an official whose duties include the auditing of local auth-

---

[1] *AG v Great Eastern Railways* (1880) 5 AC 473.

ority accounts. It is his duty to check the statutory authority for all expenditure and, income. If he finds none and that as a result of some illegality, financial losses have been made, then he can apply to the court for a declaration that the expenditure or loss of income is contrary to law. If the court makes the declaration asked for it may also order the persons concerned to make good the illegal expenditure from their own pockets and, if any person concerned is a councillor and the unlawful expenditure exceeds £2,000, he may be disqualified from serving as a councillor for a specified period.

In addition, if the auditor considers that a loss or deficiency has been caused by any person he or she may issue a certificate of surcharge requiring that person to make good the loss or deficiency. If the sum involved exceeds £2,000 and the person concerned is a councillor he or she is disqualified from serving as a councillor for five years. There is a right of appeal to the courts against a decision by the auditor to make a surcharge.

A further check occurs wherever the consent of a Government department is required. This was particularly effective a few years ago when a specific sanction was required from a Government department for every loan raised by a local authority. The present system of block loan consents for many kinds of expenditure has reduced the effectiveness of this check.

JUDICIAL AND CENTRAL GOVERNMENT CONTROL OF LOCAL AUTHORITIES

We have already seen that there is legislative control of local authorities by reason of their status as bodies corporate and the effect of the doctrine of *ultra vires*. Parliament can impose new duties on local authorities or it can take some of the old ones away.

There are, however, a great many ways in which Ministers of the Crown can exercise effective control of local authorities through the central administrative machine. Not the least of these is what has been cynically called government-by-circular. Circulars are issued by Government departments giving advice to local authorities on the exercise of their functions. Many of these do no more than offer helpful advice, to be assessed and used by local authorities at their discretion. Some circulars also have the backing of the law and may be issued as a subsequent part of or as detailed clarification of the main Act.

Exchequer grants

Some of these relate to specific services, eg, police, and thus give an element of central control over the local authority spending. Grant is only paid as a percentage of approved expenditure.

Similarly, grants towards housing are associated with some element of central control over spending levels.

However, the majority of grant assistance to local authorities is applied through the mechanism of a block grant, which relates to all services. The calculation of this grant is extremely complex, being based on the Government's assessment of the local need for various services – referred to as the Grant Related Expenditure Assessment – and also to an overall limit of expenditure that the Government proposes to pay. Both these figures can vary from year to year, as does the distribution of grant between classes of authority. The system is further complicated by a penalty procedure which penalises those authorities that spend more than the Government thinks they should. There is a final control mechanism called "rate-capping" where central government can fix the overall rate levy for an individual authority that has not been deterred by the grant penalty provisions.

The system in detail is understood by very few people, and is regarded by local government, and more latterly by the Government itself, as being very unsatisfactory and in need of radical change. The important question is when.

Control of Borrowing

Another facet of central government control relates to control over borrowing. Capital spending on items such as school buildings, houses, roads, etc, although capable of being financed out of day to day spending, is invariably so large in amount that money for this needs to be borrowed. The same considerations as apply in private life to the purchase of a house, or an expensive acquisition which is spread over a period of years, apply equally to local authorities.

But there are restrictions placed upon day to day spending, and local authorities have to borrow money for much of their capital spending but are only entitled to do so broadly within the limits fixed by central government.

Central government, dependant on whether it wishes to increase or decrease capital spending, can therefore influence significantly the spending of local authorities by virtue of the amounts allocated to them for borrowing purposes. Even where local authorities can generate capital receipts by the sale of assets, they are further restricted on the proportion of these that can be used for new capital spending.

Audit

Another form of administrative control is provided by the audit service. The accounts of local authorities are subject to audit by an auditor appointed by the Audit Commission. The auditor has a duty to satisfy himself that the accounts have been prepared in accordance with any regulations made and in compliance with the law and good accountancy practice. The legislation establishing The Audit Commission also imposed additional duties on the auditor regarding the achievement of value for money. Auditors must now satisfy themselves that authorities have proper arrangements for securing economy efficiency and effectiveness on the conduct of their affairs. The auditor must publish a report on any matters arising whenever he considers this is desirable in the public interest, whether it relates to irregularities in the accounts or value for money issues, – good or bad. If any item is contrary to law he has the power to bring the matter before the court.

Ministerial powers

Many Acts of Parliament now empower ministers to make regulations prescribing ways in which the object of the statute shall be achieved; others give them the right to determine appeals by aggrieved persons against decisions of a local authority. Recently, appellate jurisdiction has been extended to officers of Ministerial departments.

In the education, police and fire services, inspectors are appointed by H. M. Government. Local bylaws do not take effect until they have been "allowed" by the responsible minister; compulsory purchase orders and other local schemes of this nature require the confirmation of the Secretary of State. Planning applications of a contentious nature may be "called in" for the decision of the Secretary of State. In the event of wilful refusal by a local authority to perform an essential duty, the Minister may himself take over the duty and may appoint another person to carry it out on his behalf.

Commissioner for local administration

A new innovation in this country is the office of Commissioner for Local Administration, whose function is similar to that of the Parliamentary Commissioner for Administration (the Ombudsman). A person who considers himself aggrieved by alleged maladministration of a local authority may lodge a complaint with the Commissioner. He should do this through a member of the council although, if no councillor will act as the intermediary, he may do so direct.

The Commissioner must formally enquire into the complaint and, if he finds it proved, he must send a copy of his findings to the local authority for publication. He may also ask them what steps they propose to take to remedy the injustice.

Control by the courts

Local authorities are, of course, subject to the jurisdiction of courts of law like any other person or body corporate. They are as liable to be made parties to actions under statute or common law as anyone else. But as public authorities they are specifically liable to certain forms of action. We have already noted that an auditor may bring a matter before the court. Specifically he may ask for a declaration, that is to say that he may ask the court to find that the law has been infringed and to order a remedy. This course of action is not, of course, limited to the auditor. Another remedy that may be sought is an injunction, whereby the defending party may be required to do, or to refrain from doing, some specified act.

The court also has power to make orders of *mandamus*, prohibition and *certiorari*. Briefly, an order of *mandamus* compels the performance of a public duty; an order of prohibition prevents the completion of an illegal act already begun; an order of *certiorari* compels an authority to review, and if necessary to quash, an earlier decision.

CHAPTER 2

LOCAL GOVERNMENT AND ITS METHODS

Having defined the present structure of local government, its historical basis and the controls within which it operates, it is now appropriate to examine the way in which it sets about the performance of its allotted tasks. In doing so, we shall pay particular attention to the special skills likely to be required of professional officers engaged in its administration.

THE CONSTITUTION AND ORGANISATION OF LOCAL AUTHORITIES

Local government in England and Wales is largely based on the provisions of the Local Government Act 1972, which gave effect to the proposals for local government reorganisation contained in the White Paper[1] and the consultative document for Wales[2] and which replaced the principal Act of 1933 almost in its entirety and provisions in a good many other Acts as well. It also incorporated and amended provisions originally enacted in the London Government Act 1963, although the Act of 1972 was not intended to have any fundamental effect on the structure of municipal government in London. The Local Government Act of 1985 abolished the GLC and the Metropolitan Centres with effect from 1st April 1986.

---

[1] "Local Government in England: Government Proposals for Reorganisation" Cmnd. 4584.
[2] "The Reform of Local Government in Wales."

Counties and districts

As we have already observed, the two countries were divided into areas named counties and districts. In England, six metropolitan counties were created (which have now been abolished) and 39 non-metropolitan counties. Wales was divided into six counties and 37 districts. The Act also provided for England to be divided into districts and the principal local authority functions were divided between the new county and district authorities. Provision was also made for England to be divided into parishes and Wales into communities for certain very limited purposes of which perhaps the most important is the right to be consulted about planning applications affecting land in their localities. The legislature had been assisted by advisory bodies which were, as had been intended all along, created permanent statutory bodies, the Local Government Boundary Commissions for England and Wales. Whereas previously the initiative in proposing boundary changes had rested with the local authorities, the Act provided that the Boundary Commissions were henceforth to keep the situation under continual review. The English Commission, in fact, had to make a hurried start to their statutory responsibilities. The Act did not define the English districts and the English Commission was charged with carrying out this responsibility in time for the first elections in 1973.

Appointment of committees and staff

Previous legislation imposed a number of restrictions on the freedom of local authorities to order their own affairs. For example, they were required to set up statutory committees for certain purposes and to appoint suitable people to various statutory offices. The new local authorities have been given the opportunity to be much more flexible. No one has suggested that committees can be dispensed with or that there is any means of getting things done without employing staff and workpeople for the purpose. But it is now left to the local authority itself to decide what committees and sub-committees it wants and what powers they shall exercise. Similarly they are at liberty to appoint whatever staff they like for the adequate performance of their functions. They can, if they so wish, delegate powers to committees or to officers; they may come to arrangements for other authorities to act as their agents or they can undertake agency responsibilities themselves and they can engage suitable persons as consultants.

Election of chairman

Every principal council — which means to say every county or district council — must elect a chairman annually from among its own members and he continues in office until his successor is able to replace him. Previously a local authority had the power to elect an outsider to the Chair and this gave it the opportunity to honour a local personage of some distinction who might be well suited to the ceremonial duties of the office but who did not currently hold a seat on the council. The power was rarely used in recent times. Like the ancient office of alderman — a member who used to be elected to the council by the councillors themselves and not by the electorate at large — it was scarcely in keeping with the modern interpretation of democracy and both have now been abolished.

The election of a chairman must be the first business to be transacted at the annual meeting of a council and is to be followed by the election of another member as vice-chairman, an office that is now obligatory for all principal councils. For borough councils, principally, those authorities serving urban areas the office of mayor is substituted for that of chairman.

Election of councillors

As a result of these changes in the law, all members of a local authority must now be councillors elected by the local government electors for the area. For the purposes of such elections, every county is divided into electoral divisions each returning one member, metropolitan districts are divided into wards each returning three members or a multiple of three and non-metropolitan districts are also divided into wards each returning whatever number of members is provided for by order of the Secretary of State.

County council elections take place every fourth year, the whole council retiring together. Similar provisions apply to London Boroughs. An election for metropolitan district councillors takes place every year, except in the year of the county council elections, and one-third of the council retire by rotation. Non-metropolitan district councillors may either retire simultaneously or by thirds, according to the terms of the appropriate order.

Parish councils

Every parish in England has a parish meeting for the purpose of discussing local affairs and, in addition, if a parish had a parish council on 1st April, 1974, it continued to have one after that date. If it did not, the district council is obliged to establish one as soon as the local government electorate reaches 200 or, if the parish meeting so requests, once the electorate is over 150. There is nothing to prevent a parish meeting from asking for a parish council to be established at any time, even though the electorate may be less than 150 but in the latter case the power is exercisable at the discretion of the district council. Likewise the power is discretionary if the parish is already a partner in a group having a common parish council. Most of the small towns that were formerly boroughs and urban districts now have parish councils with special privileges as to the use of their traditional nomenclature. If the electorate of a parish falls to 150 or less, the parish meeting may call upon the district council to dissolve the parish council if one exists. The power of the district council appears to be discretionary but it seems hardly likely that the district council would refuse. Two or more parishes may ask the district council to group them under a common parish council but it is provided that all partners in the proposed group must be willing. An existing group may ask the district council for an order dissolving the arrangement.

Election of parish councillors

A parish council is a body corporate and the provisions for its election and the election of its chairman and vice-chairman are broadly the same as those applying to principal councils. The number of members of the parish council is decided by the district council; it may never be less than five but there is no statutory maximum. A parish meeting, which comprises all local government electors of the parish, is not a body corporate. Responsibility for parish property resides in the "parish trustees" who are the chairman of the parish meeting and the "proper officer" appointed by the district council.

In Wales the district council must establish a community council if the community meeting so request irrespective of the number of local government electors in the community. This does not apply if the district and community boundaries coincide. There are no community trustees; the community property vests in the district council.

THE WORKING ARRANGEMENTS OF LOCAL AUTHORITIES

Local government differs from most other forms of human activity — even from many other branches of the public service — inasmuch as two separate groups of people are intimately concerned in its detailed management. These are the councillors, or elected representatives of the public, on the one hand and the professional officers and supporting staff on the other.

The attitude of the councillor

Councillors take the view, not unnaturally, that they have been elected to office through the ballot box. They have been chosen to do a job and, if they do not do it to the satisfaction of the electorate, they will be thrown out of office at the next election. They expect, therefore, to know all that is going on and to have a say in any decisions of importance, particularly those decisions affecting the member's own ward or electoral division. The position of the councillor differs from that of the national politician.

A Member of Parliament is an elected representative also but he is not necessarily a member of the Government even though he may be a supporter of the party in power. A councillor, on the other hand, certainly considers himself a member of the ruling body, even though he may belong to the minority political group. Her Majesty's Ministers head great departments of state and are responsible for the formulation and implementation of major national policies; they do not expect to concern themselves with the details of income tax assessments and social security benefits or any of the other routine matters under their jurisdiction. The councillor, however, is very much concerned with the choice of tenant for a particular council house or the decision on a simple planning application. These small things are matters that may assume some importance in the locality that he represents.

The attitude of the professional officer

The professional officer, however, tends to see problems as a test of professional skill and judgement. Having spent years in studying to obtain a degree and or professional qualifications and perhaps another twenty in acquiring the experience for senior office, it is not pleasant to see recommendations laid aside and replaced by instructions that offend professional judgment.

There is here the root of potential conflict and it is much to the credit of those who participate in local government that conflicts rarely arise in practice. This is because the vast majority of councillors show respect for the professional expertise of their officers and do not lightly set it aside. The officers, for their part, respect the democratic process and also, recognise the honest intentions and good sense of most members. However, conflicts must arise from time to time where political considerations are judged to be more important than others.

The relationship between members and officers

The old textbook explanation of the difference in the roles of members and officers used to be that members were responsible for policy and the officers for administration. This long-accepted view was challenged by the Maud Committee on Management in Local Government and was later repudiated in the Bains Report in these words:[1]

> Officers must accept that members have a legitimate interest in the day to day administration of cases involving their constituents and that it is frequently only a lack of information which causes them to pursue such matters into the administrative machine.

> Members must equally realise that the skilled professional officer is not just a servant who is paid to do as he is told. We do not dispute that the major policy decisions must be taken by the elected members but the officers have a role to play in the stimulation and formulation of policy and in seeing that members have available the necessary advice and evaluation to enable them to make the best decisions.

The committee system

The council, comprising the full complement of elected members, is the statutory local authority and bears the ultimate responsibility for all its decisions. But, by long tradition, local authorities do their work through committees consisting, usually, of a minority of members.

The functions of any local authority are many and varied. By dividing up the total membership of a council into a number of relatively small committees, each having control of a particular service or group of services, members are enabled to concentrate on making themselves very familiar

[1] Chapter 3.

with the work done by the committees of which they are members.

Most people can make a more effective contribution if they specialise within a limited field rather than by trying to become jack-of-all-trades. It also seems to be true that the fewer people who are to be involved in the decision-making process, the quicker a decision will be reached. It does not follow, of course, that a better decision will be achieved; the so-called "committee of one" would reach decisions quickly but not necessarily for the best. But there is usually an optimum number which is sufficient to ensure that every point of view is fairly expressed and adding to it only tends to get the business bogged down.

A further advantage of the committee system is that the work of the council is sifted before it comes before the full body of members. The common practice is for each committee to meet regularly to consider in some depth and to report on matters arising within its own sphere of responsibility. The minutes or reports of each committee are then laid before the full council and its recommendations may be adopted, amended, rejected or referred back for further consideration. Under this system, any councillor has the opportunity to intervene in matters which come before committees of which he is not a member. As might be expected, it is not a frequent occurrence for councils to reverse the recommendation of a committee but it does happen often enough to keep committee chairmen on their toes. It is the knowledge that their report can be challenged that encourages committees to explore their problems from every angle.

Delegation to committees

It is now a widespread practice to give plenary power to a committee to make firm decisions on many of the matters coming before them and to translate those decisions into immediate action. The minutes of the committee (or, if they are very lengthy, a suitable synopsis) are still presented to the council for information but members of the council who are not on the committee concerned can do no more than ask questions to elicit further information and can do nothing to reverse or vary the decision of the committee.

A common complaint against the policy-making process in local government is its slowness and, it must be admitted, this complaint is not ill-founded. The system may be democratic but it is certainly not quick. The company secretary will often be able to bring an important matter before his board at very short notice and implement their decision immediately they have made it. The local authority secretary has a lot to do by way of agenda papers, reports and minutes, co-ordination, consultation and confirmation before being in a position to dispose of the matter. Delegation to committees, and even to officers, does have the advantage of producing speedier results.

It used to be argued that the old system allowed for second thoughts insofar as recommendations had to be ratified by the full council. This is not so where committees enjoy delegated power but the system of ratification is still in wide enough use for the point to remain valid.

It might also be said that the new practice defeats the democratic process inasmuch as a councillor who has been elected to serve the interests of constituents may be unable to influence a decision which is of importance to many of them. It does depend on councillors placing trust and confidence in each other to consider the rights and preferences of all their inhabitants — not merely those in their own wards or parishes — and to ensure that proposals that are really controversial are not decided until all councillors have had a chance to make their views known. In fairness it should be added that the same argument can be applied against the political party system since members of the minority groups cannot do anything effective to upset the policy of the controlling group.

The political group system

When a council is composed on political party lines — and this is not always the case even today — it is customary for the councillors who are members of the same political party to meet regularly as a group to agree upon a "party line" in respect of the problems with which the council has to deal. If one party has an overall majority of members on the council, it can and invariably does use its voting strength to make sure that it has a working majority also on every committee. It is then in a position to ensure that the party line is translated into the official policy of the council. The majority party is often said, accurately, to have "control" of the council and its leader is usually described as "leader of the council".

The group system is not, strictly speaking, part of the working arrangements of local authorities. Group meetings are private gatherings; normally they are not attended by the council's officers and any minutes that may be kept form no part of the council's records. But where the party system is in operation, to ignore the existence of the group meeting would give a completely false picture of the manner in which local affairs are conducted.

Appointment of chief officers

Save in the very smallest parish or community councils, the work of a local authority is so voluminous and widespread that it cannot possibly be done entirely by councillors. Committees meet and decide what shall be done but the implementation of their decisions has to be left to permanent salaried staff and workpeople. The invariable practice is to appoint a limited number of chief officers who are almost always highly qualified and experienced professionals. Some of them are chosen for their expertise in a particular field of local authority activity. Examples are the Chief Education Officer and the Chief Housing Officer. Others, such as the Chief Financial Officer and the Secretary, are chosen for their mastery of a particular essential technique. At one time, certain officers had to be appointed by law. Local authorities now have discretion as to the officers they appoint but, in practice, it is recognised that the appointment of suitable chief officers is essential.

Appointment of supporting staff

It is also necessary to provide chief officers with the back-up staff needed for the workload. This workload will depend upon a number of factors, principally the size of the county or district but also the nature of the locality (whether, for example, it has a large urban renewal problem), the policy of the council (for instance, whether it has agreed to receive overspill population from another area), the directives from H. M. Government and the legislation emanating from Parliament and the public demand for local services. The supporting staff will usually include other professionals appointed as principal or chief officers to take charge of important sections of the work, younger officers, perhaps newly qualified or still working at their examinations, in middle-management posts, and the required number of clerks, typists and miscellaneous staff. Thus the employees of local authorities are divided into departments and it is an unfortunate by-product of the system that the loyalty of many employees tends to be their department rather than to the authority as a whole. This is not altogether surprising since many employees rarely see a councillor or an officer of another department and they soon fall into the habit of looking upon the head of their department as their true employer. Local government is commonly criticised for excessive departmentalism; it is often said that departments of some local authorities behave as though they were separate entities and not, as they should, as parts of a greater whole. Where, as sometimes happens, terms of reference of committees coincide with the responsibilities of particular departments, there may be a temptation for a committee chairman to look upon himself as the political head of the corresponding department and rivalry develops with other committee chairmen, particularly if departments are in competition for the allocation of scarce resources. When this happens openly it is difficult to rebut the charge of excessive departmentalism.

THE BUDGETING PROVISIONS OF LOCAL AUTHORITIES

No description of the arrangements for managing local authorities is complete without reference to the way in which the money is shared out. There is never enough money to do all the work that really ought to be done; on the other hand, expenditure can never be reduced to the point which the rate-payer feels he can really afford. Consequently every local authority budget is a compromise.

Annual estimates

Because rate demands are made annually, local authorities make annual estimates of their expected expenditure and income (including the income from Government grants) and calculate the rate that they will require to levy accordingly. In the case of a county council or other precepting authority, it calculates the precept that it will have to submit to the district council — which is the authority responsible for making the rate — but the principle is the same.

At the appropriate time of year, the committees responsible for the provision of services — in this context often called "the spending committees" — make schedules of the work they hope to carry out in the financial year under consideration. In accountancy terms much of the "work" in question may involve capital expenditure. It may include the acquisition of land for future development or the initial stage of a construction programme timed to last for several years. Expenditure of this kind is usually financed by loans. The money needed in the first year may be quite small but the ultimate commitment may be considerable. Other expenditure, paradoxically called "revenue expenditure" or, in lay terms, the running costs of services and renewals of equipment, falls to be met entirely within the one year.

Because charges required in service levels take longer than a year to implement and capital spending also is spread over longer periods, many local authorities have three year programmes of capital spending, while others give a general indication to committees of spending levels expected over the next two to three years.

Scrutiny of proposed expenditure

The likely cost of the committee's programme is then assessed by the responsible officers in collaboration with the council's financial staff and detailed estimates are presented to the committee. In all probability, the estimated expenditure will prove to be unacceptably high and will have to be pared down. The amended estimates are then presented to the Finance Committee or whatever committee is responsible for the control of the council's expenditure. This committee has the advantage of scrutinising the estimates of all the spending committees and it is very likely that the proposed aggregate expenditure will still be considered too high. In this case, estimates will be sent back to spending committees for further pruning. Only when the Finance Committee is satisfied that all feasible reductions have been made will the revised estimates be placed before the council with a recommendation as to the rate to be levied in the succeeding year.

Some Councils pre-determine the level of committee spending in advance, by fixing a cash limit within which committees are expected to keep. The end result might be the same, but this method does allow the central policy committee to concentrate on the shape and overall pattern and level of spending leaving service committees to sort out the operational details.

Monitoring of actual expenditure

During the course of the year, possibly quarterly, statements of revenue and expenditure are normally presented to the responsible committees as a safeguard against overspending. There will, of course, be unforeseen expenditure to be incurred during the year. Committees faced with such expenditure are usually required to submit a supplementary estimate for the consideration and approval of the Finance Committee. Fortunately, it is almost always the case also that some expected expenditure is not needed after all, perhaps because a current scheme has run into delays and difficulties, and a little money can therefore be diverted to other essential purposes.

CHAPTER 3

THE COUNCIL AND ITS MEMBERS

All members of a local authority must be councillors elected by the local government electors for the area. The statutory provisions which govern the holding of such elections are to be found in the Local Government Act 1972, and the Representation of the People Act 1983. The term of office of councillors in England and Wales, is four years.

County council elections take place every four years, the whole council retiring together. In metropolitan districts one-third of the councillors retire at a time and an election is held every year except when a county council election is taking place. A system of simultaneous retirement applies in some non-metropolitan districts; elsewhere the same system applies as in metropolitan districts. Simultaneous retirement is also the rule in the London Boroughs.

QUALIFICATIONS AND DISQUALIFICATIONS

Every candidate for elected office must have certain qualifications before becoming a member of a local authority. There are also certain disqualifications which members must avoid if they are not to invalidate candidature or lose membership.

Rules relating to qualifications

A candidate is qualified to be elected as a councillor if he is a British subject or a citizen of the Republic of Ireland and on the day on which he is nominated (and also, if there is a poll, on the day of election) he has attained the age of

21 years, and also has at least one of the following additional qualifications:

(*a*) he is on the day in question, and thereafter continues to be, a local government elector for the area of the local authority concerned, or

(*b*) he has during the whole of the twelve months before that day occupied, either as owner or tenant, any land or premises in that area, or

(*c*) his principal or only place of work during that twelve months has been in that area, or

(*d*) he has during the whole of those twelve months resided in that area.

In the case of a parish or community council it is sufficient to have lived during the whole of the twelve months within three miles of it.

It is worth remembering that, because of the time lag involved in the work of revising the Register of electors, a person will continue to be a local government elector for some time after leaving the area. This period may be as long as sixteen months or so and as long as his or her name appears on the current register the elector is entitled not only to vote but also to stand as a candidate. Furthermore, even though a councillor may have ceased to be a local government elector for the area, he will be entitled to complete his term of office if he qualified by reason of his work, residence or occupation of property.

The law does not require that a candidate shall have worked in the area for the whole of the twelve months preceding the election and, in the case of a candidate who may have changed jobs or normal place of work during the year, it is by no means clear what is meant by the term "principal place of work".

The term "resided" seems to suggest that the candidate's normal or principal home should have been in the area during the year in question, even if temporarily absent from time to time and temporarily resident elsewhere. Residence is a matter of degree but the word does imply a degree of permanence (*Fox v. Stirk*, (1970), 2 Q.B. 63).

As the word "land" is defined as including any interest, easement or other right in relation to land, occupation of land or premises can be given a very wide interpretation.

Rules relating to disqualification

A person who has one of the prescribed disqualifications is not only disqualified from seeking election, but is also disqualified from continuing to be a member and is obliged to vacate his seat. A person is disqualified by any of the following disabilities, that is to say, either:

(*a*) he holds a paid office or employment other than the office of chairman, vice chairman, or deputy chairman, under the auspices of the local authority or any joint committee joint board or joint authority on which the authority are represented, or

(*b*) he has been adjudged bankrupt or has made a composition or arrangement with his creditors, or

(*c*) he has during a period commencing five years before his election been disqualified by the High Court for wilfully incurring expenditure contrary to law.

(*d*) he has during a similar period been convicted of an offence for which he has received a term of imprisonment of not less than three months, whether suspended or not, or

(*e*) he has been disqualified by the court either for corrupt election practices, such as bribery, or for being concerned in financial irregularities relating to the expenditure of public funds.

The provision relating to the disqualification of officers and servants is quite wide. It extends to teachers in maintained schools and to members and employees of a coterminous Passenger Transport Executive but it does not extend to the chairman or vice-chairman of the council even though he may receive a payment in respect of that office. There are, however, several exceptions relating to teachers.

The disqualification of a bankrupt ceases immediately the bankruptcy is annulled either on the ground that he ought not to have been adjudged bankrupt or on the ground that his debts have been paid in full. In other cases, the disqualification ceases at the end of five years from the date of discharge unless the discharge is accompanied by a certificate to the effect that bankruptcy was caused by misfortune without any misconduct on the bankrupt's part. Where such a certificate is given, disqualification ceases on the day of his discharge.

Where a person has made a composition or arrangement with his creditors the period of disqualification will end after five years or immediately all debts are paid in full, whichever is the sooner.

ACCEPTANCE, RESIGNATION AND VACATION OF OFFICE

Acceptance of office

Every person elected to an office of a principal local authority, whether it be that of chairman, vice-chairman or councillor — must make and deliver to the proper officer a declaration of acceptance of office. The declaration must be in writing and is required to be made before either two members, the proper officer, a justice of the peace or a commissioner for oaths. Until the declaration is made, the person elected must not (except for the purpose of making the declaration) act in the office, otherwise he may lay himself open to penalties. If the declaration is not made and delivered within two months of election the office falls vacant at the end of that period.

The term "the proper officer" relates to the officer appointed by the local authority to perform that duty. In many authorities, the Secretary will normally be the proper officer for this purpose. Before the first meeting is held following an election it may be found convenient to organise a little ceremony at which each of the successful candidates can make and deliver their declarations. This reduces the possibility that a new member may inadvertently act in the office before he has completed the necessary formality.

In the case of a parish or community council the procedure is slightly different. The chairman is normally required to declare his acceptance at the meeting at which he is elected, a councillor before or at the first meeting following his election. To allow for absentee members, the council may in either case permit the matter to be postponed to a later meeting. The declaration is to be made before a member of the council or the proper officer and delivered to the council itself at the prescribed meeting. In no case may a parish councillor act as such until his declaration has been made and if he fails to deliver it at the proper time the office becomes vacant.

Resignation of office

The holder of an office may resign at any time without penalty. In a principal local authority this is done by written notice to the proper office. A parish or community councillor will deliver the notice to the chairman and, if the chairman wishes to resign, he will deliver his notice to the parish council or meeting, or the community council, as the case may be.

Resignation takes effect immediately notice is received by the appropriate person and it follows that it cannot subsequently be withdrawn.

Vacation of office

If a member of a local authority fails throughout a period of six consecutive months to attend any meetings of that authority he will (unless the failure was due to some reason approved by the authority before the expiry of that period) automatically cease to be a member. Attendance at a committee or sub-committee meeting, or a meeting of a joint committee, is for this purpose counted as attendance at a meeting of the authority, and absence is not counted if it is due to service in war or other emergency in the armed forces or on other national service which the Secretary of State considers an adequate reason for absence.

Attendance at any meeting as a representative of the local authority is deemed for this purpose to be attendance at a meeting of the authority itself.

The provisions give considerable latitude to the less conscientious member. Attendance at almost any meeting handling local authority business once in every six months is enough to prevent forfeiture of membership and, even if this modest target is not achieved, the council can excuse the member by approving the reason for absence. However, if such approval is to have effect it must be given before the period of six months expires, othewise forfeiture of membership will occur automatically. The period runs from the date of the member's last attendance.

It is the member's own responsibility to notify the council of his reason for absence and, if necessary, to seek their approval but the capable Secretary will certainly make sure that the council are informed when the six months period is nearing its end and will probably make an attempt to discover the cause of absence. If there are reasonable grounds for supposing that the absentee member is unaware of his peril it is fair that the officers of the council should take steps to warn him in good time so that he can either attend the next meeting or seek approval for his absence. Such circumstances may occur in the relatively rare instances when meetings of the local authority are infrequent. It may happen that, where an authority meets at quarterly intervals, the meetings may be so spaced that, if a member fails to attend only one, an interval of six months will elapse between his last attendance and the next meeting he is entitled to attend. A normally conscientious member might, by reason of a relatively short absence on business or holiday, miss one whole cycle of meetings and thereby fail to attend for six months. It might well not occur to him to obtain approval for his absence; it is right that the authority, through the vigilance of its officers, should protect him from the loss of his membership.

CASUAL VACANCIES

Where a member of a local authority ceases to be a member before his full period of office has expired steps must be taken to fill the vacancy so caused. The point of time at which a vacancy actually arises is important for it is from that date that the procedure for filling the vacancy is set in motion.

This point of time is determined in the following manner:

(i) on failure to make and deliver the declaration of acceptance of office, at the expiration of two months from the date of election;

(ii) on resignation, at the receipt of notice of resignation by the proper officer;

(iii) on death, at the date of death;

(iv) on disqualification by reason of a High Court declaration, conviction or corrupt election practices, at the expiration of the time allowed for appeals or on the date when the appeal is withdrawn or decided;

(v) in all other cases, at the date on which a vacancy is declared by the court or the local authority itself, as the case may be.

Declaration of vacancy

The local authority is required to declare a member's seat vacant when he ceases to be qualified to be a member or he forfeits his membership by failure to attend meetings. They must also declare the office vacant if he becomes disqualified otherwise than by reason of High Court declaration, conviction or corrupt election practices unless a declaration has already been made by the court.

When a casual vacancy arises, public notice must be given

by the local authority as soon as practicable; where they themselves declare the office vacant they must give notice immediately after the declaration. They must do this by posting the notice in one or more conspicuous places in their area and in such other manner as they think desirable. In most cases the notice, signed by the Secretary, will be fixed to the public notice board at the local authority's offices.

Election to fill vacancy

An election to fill a vacancy declared by the High Court or by the local authority must be held within 42 days from the declaration. In any other case no steps are required to be taken until notice of the vacancy has been given in writing by two local government electors for the area to the proper officer of the council. The election is then to be held within 42 days of that date. The date of the election is chosen by the returning officer — in practice he will choose the most convenient day of the week for polling but will otherwise allow the maximum time for the election campaign. Where less than six months of the former member's term of office remains unexpired no steps will be taken to fill the casual vacancy unless the total number of unfilled vacancies on the council exceeds one-third of the entire membership. A person elected to fill a casual vacancy is only elected for the balance of the former member's term of office and the seat will be available to be contested at the ordinary election at the end of that term in the normal way.

The unsatisfactory nature of the law on casual vacancies

The law in relation to casual vacancies seems neither logical nor consistent. Vacancies of which the local authority must be perfectly well aware (for example, on the death of a member) are not to be filled until notice is given by two electors. It may be argued theoretically that it is for the electorate and not the authority itself to decide whether it wants an election. But it is quite easy for two councillors to declare the vacancy if they wish; in practice the seat is left vacant only when there is a tacit agreement among the remaining members and the public at large is insufficiently interested.

On the other hand there are other instances when the local authority is compelled by law to declare the vacancy and hold an election whether the electorate want one or not. Yet these are the very cases which depend on circumstances which the authority cannot be sure of knowing. For example, a member might receive a suspended prison sentence from a court in another part of the country without his colleagues becoming aware of the fact.

Normally an officer of a local authority finds it difficult to make enquiries about a member's personal position. It is a good rule not to concern himself about a member's qualifications unless allegations are deliberately brought to his notice or the facts are such as he ought to have known, without special enquiry, in the ordinary course of his duties. There is no penalty on him if the statutory requirements are not strictly complied with.

Casual vacancy in office of chairman

An election to fill a casual vacancy for a council chairman must be held not later than the next ordinary meeting which is held after the expiration of 14 days from the date of the vacancy. In other words, the local authority can wait 14 days (whether or not they hold a meeting in that time) and then arrange to fill the vacancy at or before its next ordinary meeting. But there is no need to wait if an election can be held earlier. The meeting at which the election is to be held may be convened by the proper officer.

In a parish not having a parish council, a parish meeting is to be convened forthwith for the purpose of filling a vacancy in the office of chairman.

VALIDITY OF ACTIONS

The proceedings of a local authority are not invalidated by the existence of any vacancy among the membership, nor by any defect in the election or qualification of any member. Although a person may be liable to legal proceedings for acting as a member of a local authority when not entitled to do so, the acts which he performs as a member remain valid and effective. this rule prevents opponents of a measure from challenging any expenditure or decision on the ground that not all the council at the time were validly elected.

Legal proceedings can be taken, either in the High Court or a Magistrates' Court, against any person who acts as a member of a local authority when not entitled to do so. The High court may fine the offender a sum not exceeding **£50** for every occasion on which he so acted, and the Magistrates' Court may impose a fine not exceeding **level 3** on the standard scale for each occasion on which he so acted while disqualified or, if they think fit, refer the matter to the High Court which has additional powers to declare the seat vacant and to grant an injunction restraining the defendant from acting as a councillor. Proceedings can only be taken by a local government elector for the area of the authority and cannot be taken more than six months after the date on which he acted. An action can likewise be commenced in the High Court against anyone who falsely claims to be entitled to act as a member of a local authority.

The circumstances in which a person is not entitled to act as a member of a local authority are as follows:

  (i) when he is not qualified,

  (ii) when he has been disqualified,

  (iii) when he has failed to make and deliver the statutory declaration of acceptance of office,

  (iv) when he has resigned,

  (v) when he has forfeited his seat by failure to attend meetings.

INTEREST IN CONTRACTS AND OTHER MATTERS

It is most important that a councillor should not use his office, or appear to be using his office, for his own personal gain or advantage and the law therefore requires that any member having a direct or indirect pecuniary interest in any contract or other matter must disclose that fact as soon as possible. He must not then take any part in the discussion or cast any vote in relation to the matter. To avoid any suspicion that he is using his influence unduly it is a good practice for him to leave the meeting entirely until the particular business is complete, and the standing orders of many local authorities require their members to do so.

The term "pecuniary interest" is not defined and it is for the member himself to judge when such an interest exists. He can scarcely be too careful, however, and if in doubt should opt out. Disability does not arise from a mere sentimental interest or solely from the member's interest as an inhabitant or ratepayer. He may well have a pecuniary interest, however, if he is an employee or partner of a person having an interest in the contract, or if he is married or otherwise related to such a person. It is enough to give a member a pecuniary interest that there is a remote chance of his receiving some advantage or disadvantage and it is no defence for him to show that he cast his vote against his own interest.

If a member fails to disclose such an interest or he takes part in the proceedings in such circumstances he renders himself liable to a fine upon a prosecution instituted by the Director of Public Prosecutions, unless he can prove that he did not know that a matter in which he had an interest was the subject of consideration. A councillor can fall innocently into a trap, for example, if a contract is made with a solicitor whose client, unbeknown to the member concerned, is a business partner of a councillor.

The proper officer of the authority (usually the Secretary) is required to record in a book kept for the purpose, which is to be kept open at all reasonable hours for inspection by members of the authority, particulars of all disclosures.

There is nothing to prevent a member from entering into contracts with the council so long as he makes the necessary disclosure and does not vote or otherwise take part in the proceedings whilst the matter is under discussion.

It may happen that the number of members who would be disabled from taking part in a particular discussion would be so great as to impede the transaction of business. This could be the case, for example, if the majority of members were employed by one major local employer. In these circumstances the Secretary of State can remove a disability, subject to such conditions as he thinks fit. A district council has the same power in relation to the disability of parish councillors.

ATTENDANCE ALLOWANCE AND FINANCIAL LOSS ALLOWANCE

Councillors now have the right to receive payment in the form of an attendance allowance for the performance of any approved duty. Other members of local authorities and certain other local bodies, such as co-opted members of committees and sub-committees, are entitled to claim a financial loss allowance in respect of any actual loss of earnings. Since the attendance allowance is claimable as of right it ranks as earned income for tax purposes.

Every member of a local authority is also entitled to make a claim in respect of travelling and subsistence allowance but subsistence allowances are only payable in respect of duties performed at more than three miles from the member's usual place of residence.

"Approved duty" will normally include meetings of the council, committees and sub-committees, and the performance of such duties as visits of inspections, consultations and conferences about the work of the authority. Attendance at political party meetings and social functions do not properly count as approved duty since they are not concerned with the performance of the council's functions and any allowance paid in respect of them would probably be disallowed by the auditor.

The Secretary of State has power to make regulations providing, in particular, for the avoidance of duplicate payments (where, for example, a member represents more than one authority), the specification of claim forms and the publication of details of such payments. It is, however, generally for the authority to define "approved duty" and to fix the scale of allowance subject to maxima fixed by the Secretary of State. The council is also free to choose what conferences shall be attended and the number of members authorised to attend. It may also defray the reasonable expenses of courtesy visits, whether at home or oversea, and the reception and entertainment of distinguished visitors, including representatives of local government and the public services. The prescribed maxima for travelling and subsistence allowances do not apply to approved duty outside the United Kingdom.

A parish or community councillor is not entitled to an allowance except in respect of duties performed outside the parish, community or group area.

SPECIAL RESPONSIBILITY ALLOWANCE

In addition to attendance and financial loss allowance, Councils have the power to pay special responsibility allowances to specific members, who have particularly onerous duties to perform, for example the leader of the Council or a chairman of a particularly demanding committee which takes up a considerable amount of time.

The sums that can be paid are prescribed by regulations issued by the Secretary of State. They vary by class of authority and are not large in amount given the size of the task carried out by such members. However, it would appear that not many authorities exercise the right to pay such allowances.

CHAPTER 4

THE ROLE OF THE ELECTED MEMBER

A perennial source of discussion is the part which the elected member ought to play in the management of the local authority. Much time and space has been devoted to this and, indeed, the debate continues still.

The strict legal position may be stated shortly. Power vests with the council as a whole and, although the former rules which circumscribed the actions of local authorities have been somewhat ameliorated, it is still necessary that the council shall conduct its affairs in accordance with democratic principles. The role of the councillors, acting in concert, is therefore paramount. The individual councillor, however, has no statutory authority whatsoever. He may not enter into contracts in the council's name, and must not, without the council's authority, attempt to give orders to council employees.

It may be supposed, therefore, that the average councillor is nothing more than a voting robot, perhaps making an occasional speech and voting when the time comes. Very few councillors see their role in that light and, of course, the majority is right. The duties of a councillor are very much wider than that.

Motivation of elected members

The ways in which a councillor can best be of service will vary according to temperament. Councillors differ widely, which is just as well, and are motivated by different ambitions. Some are prominent in political life and wish to play a leading part in pursuing their party's aims and objectives. A few may see local government as a stepping stone to Parliament. Others not interested in party politics may nevertheless have a burning ambition to achieve certain reforms or developments in the locality. Some may have a great interest in a particular activity, like education or housing, which they see as an opportunity to pursue through membership of a local authority.

There are councillors who are simply interested in being the voice of their ward or parish and are not greatly concerned about happenings in other parts of the area. Some are mouth-pieces for particular organisations, such as a Council House Tenants' Association. Some just want to try to keep the rates down. Because councils are usually a cross-section of the public they serve there are members who stand for public office because they like to see their name in the local paper or to hear the sound of their own voice. Regrettably there have been a few, a very few, who have joined local councils for their own pecuniary advantage. The point to be made is that it is usually the councillor's own motives in standing for election that dictate how useful he can be as an individual councillor once he is elected.

The member and his constituency

The member who is solely concerned with matters affecting his own electoral division or, as he is sometimes called, "the constituency member" is not to be despised. He is elected to look after the interests of his constituents and, so long as he does that conscientiously, he is faithfully discharging his duty as he sees it. If his ambition does not spur him on to wider activity, so be it. Presumably his electors can measure his performance and if they are disappointed they will in due course have the opportunity to replace him. Of course the local authority would be gravely weakened if every member took so limited a view of his responsibilities but, human nature being what it is, it is highly unlikely that all members would refuse positions of responsibility and prestige on the council. The Secretary would be well advised to recognise the interest of every member in matters affecting his constituency and to try to ensure that he is informed — or at least has the chance to acquaint himself — of matters which are of some importance to electors in the locality. For example, if it is decided to postpone the building of a new library planned for a certain town or to close an existing one, it should be recognised that the local councillor will be bombarded with questions from potential or current library users and it is unfair if the councillor is kept in the dark as to the reasons. If he must, he will make himself a nuisance until he gets the information his constituents require. It is far better to see that he gets it promptly and with the minimum of trouble to himself and to those who have to supply the information.

The member and pressure groups

In the case of a member who is the spokesman of a particular external pressure group the situation is less straightforward and may call for the exercise of some skill and judgment. The general rule is that, unless information has been officially classified as confidential, a member is entitled to receive it and in the normal way an officer should see that he gets it on request. It must be remembered, however, that the purpose of supplying the information is to assist the councillor to discharge his duties as a member. If the officer has good reason to believe that a member is asking for the information for some private purpose which may be contrary to the council's interest and of which the majority of members would disapprove, he would be foolish to disclose it unless expressly authorised to do so. Such circumstances should, however, be considered very exceptional.

The supply of confidential information

Of course in the matter of supplying information to members, any officer must always use his good sense. The progress of negotiations for the purchase or sale of a particular property, tenders for work to be done, evidence to be offered in a court of law are examples of matters which are confidential by their very nature. It could be very much against the council's interest (and therefore the public interest) if such information got into the wrong hands and it should therefore be strictly confined to those whose duty makes it necessary for them to know it. A request for such information from anyone else, be he a councillor or otherwise, should be treated as highly suspect.

The member and public opinion

Another valuable function of a councillor, and one which has not received as much attention as others, is that of being an essential channel of public opinion. Leading members and officers of local authorities do not live in ivory towers. They ride in trains, eat in restaurants, drink in bars, and they overhear what people are saying about the policies of their local council. But they clearly cannot be everywhere and the ward councillor can play a vital part in feeding back the views of the man in the street so that committees know whether or not their policies are meeting with approval in all parts of their area.

The formulation of policy

The primary role of the elected member, however, has always been considered to be the formulation of policy and decision-making in the fundamental areas such as the identification of needs, the setting of objectives, the establishment of priorities and the allocation of resources. This remains broadly true although we have already examined the modern concept that such matters cannot be completely separated from matters of implementation and administration and, consequently, the limits of a councillor's role cannot be sharply defined. The Report of the Royal Commission on Local Government in England[1] referred to evidence that many councillors so concerned themselves with small decisions that they tended to lose sight of their

[1] Cmd. 4040.

more important duty to formulate policy. The report stated unequivocally that "there must be much more extensive delegation of executive business to officers". This recommendation was qualified in the following important passage:[1]

> Councillors must be prepared, we believe, to trust officers' good sense and ability to identify and pass upwards for instruction cases which though apparently of a routine nature suggest a need for reconsideration of policy, which involve a point of principle or which have become politically sensitive. A proper degree of delegation will not be easy to achieve. Much of local government consists in carrying out decisions which those affected may regard as unfair, obstructive or wrong-headed. Moreover such decisions often involve compulsion or restraint. So though in principle delegation in local government is of the same nature as in other fields, in practice it calls for an exceptionally high degree of mutual trust and understanding; in particular, the officer must have the skill to recognise the exceptional case and refer it to elected members for decision.

The member and committees

The vehicle whereby councillors will normally contribute to the formulation of policy is the committee system. A member can usually expect to serve on two or three committes and a number of sub-committees — much will depend on the number and size of committees and the number of members to be accommodated — and, if he has a strong preference for a particular committee, it is probable that he will be accommodated although a newly-elected member can hardly expect a vacancy to be created for his immediate benefit. As to committees of which he is not a member, he can still help to shape their policies by commenting, or possibly moving an amendment, when their minutes come before the full council for confirmation or report. If Standing Orders permit — as they usually do — he can also put down a question to the chairman of any committee. A skilfully worded question can have the effect of putting pressure on the committee. If the power is widely

[1] Para. 499.

used, committee chairmen will take the trouble to insist that the rough edges of committee policy are properly rounded off rather than face the possible humiliation of an embarrassing question in council.

Policy and resources

It is, of course, for each local authority to decide for itself whether to introduce a Policy and Resources Committee after the Bains model. Probably it will do so if it also accepts the desirability of a controlling, strategic policy and corporate issues. In this case, ambitious councillors will seek to be appointed to a seat on the committee and those who are unsuccessful in the first instance (assuming that they are supporters of the prevailing political view) may well agree to serve an apprenticeship on one of the supporting sub-committees which will have oversight of the three major resources of finance, manpower and land. The opportunity for such members to influence policy may thus vary in pattern from that to which councillors had become accustomed; there is no reason to suppose that that opportunity will be less effective.

Committee chairmen

Ultimately, the councillors who wished to use his position as an elected member to influence the policies of his council to the maximum extent will hope to be elected chairman of one of its major committees. In law the chairman of a committee has no greater personal authority than any other councillor but in practice the position is somewhat different. As such he will be recognised by his fellow-councillors as one of the senior and more influential members of the council to be listened to with respect, particularly concerning the sphere of his own committee on which he will be looked upon as the council's expert. Members of his committee who, it may be supposed, will mostly be less experienced than himself will look to him for guidance and thus his personal views will very frequently prevail. As a consequence, officers of the council will ask him to make minor — but none the less often important — policy decisions between meetings. They will do this because experience has taught them that a decision made by the chairman in this way is virtually certain to be endorsed by the committee at the first opportunity.

The leader of the council

Finally, in those councils which are controlled by a political party, the key position is held by the leader of the council, who is chosen by the majority party and is usually its leader. Where a fully political system is in operation all effective decisions are taken at meetings of the party groups held before the council meeting. Councillors who are not members of the majority group have no effective influence on those decisions and the officer may safely assume — provided the majority is watertight — that any instructions he receives from the leader of the council will be formally ratified at the next council meeting.

CHAPTER 5

THE COUNCIL AND THE COMMITTEE SYSTEM

It has already been stated that most local authorities make widespread use of committees in the administration of their affairs. The committee system has many advantages. It is generally accepted that a small number of people can deal with any job more effectively than a large unwieldy number. Parliament itself work on the committee system. The full House may debate a major issue but the shaping and amendment of any Parliamentary Bill is done in committee. Almost any organisation which may be mentioned works on the same principle, if it is an organisation of any size. A general meeting of all members is usually held annually, or with such frequency as may be necessary, but the real work of running the organisation is done by its committee.

Distinctive features of local authority system

Local authorities work on much the same principle but there are features which distinguish the local authority system from many others. Instead of appointing one committee to run all its affairs, a local authority normally appoints several, each with a particular function or group of functions to perform. The members are, as a general rule, allocated to two or three committees each, which gives them the opportunity to familiarise themselves with details of the services administered by their own committees. The system allows a small number of people to consider details of proposals and to present the more important or politically sensitive ones in a form that can be readily assimilated by other members of the council and these members, can bring fresh, independent minds to bear on the problem, or allow a much wider consideration before a final decision is taken. In this way every member of the council can contribute to the council's aims and objectives without having to familiarise himself with every detail of the council's work.

Statutory and non-statutory committees

A local authority has almost unlimited discretion as to what committees it will appoint (if, indeed, it wishes to appoint any at all), the work it will give each committee to do and the extent to which it will delegate authority to a committee without requiring it to report or to secure the approval of its recommendations by the full council. It can also please itself as to the size and personnel of committees and the frequency of their meetings. At one time, local authorities were obliged by law to establish statutory committees for certain purposes. This obligation was largely removed by the Local Government Act 1972, but it is still mandatory to appoint committees in connexion with education, police, sea fisheries, children, regional planning, social services, superannuation and national parks. The discretion of local authorities included a right to establish any committee or sub-committee or joint committee with another authority, or an advisory committee including persons who are not members of the local authority. The local authority can, if it so wishes, delegate any of its statutory functions to a committee and, contrary to the common law on the subject, the committee can delegate in turn to a sub-committee or to an officer, unless expressly forbidden by the council to do so.

Reappointment of committees

The normal practice is for local authorities to appoint their committees annually although there is nothing to prevent their doing otherwise if they so wish. In those cases where all councillors retire simultaneously there are sound arguments on grounds of continuity for appointing committees to serve for the full period between one ordinary election and the next but, in the event, this is rarely done. In the case of those councils where members retire by thirds, an annual reshuffling of committee membership is a practical necessity. The political control of the council may change hands at an election or the balance between the parties may significantly shift. Even if there is no change in political emphasis, there is likely to be some change in personnel so that, for example, someone who has specialised in education may be replaced by a new councillor whose great interest is the environment. For one reason or another, the composition of committees needs to be reconsidered after every ordinary election.

Continuity of committees

In the interests of efficiency it is desirable, so far as possible, to avoid breaks in the continuity of a committee's activity. Work has to go on, even during an election campaign, and notwithstanding that it may be difficult to get the members to meet at such a time the opportunity of doing so, if needs be, should be retained. By law, a councillor's term of office does not expire until a few days after polling day so that every councillor who is re-elected continues in office without any interruption in his membership. Even a retiring member who is defeated does not cease to be a councillor until a few days later and can technically be called to a council or committee meeting after the poll. Whether he could be persuaded to turn up is quite another matter.

Selection of committee membership

For obvious reasons it is very desirable that the gap between the election of new members and the appointment of the new committees should be as short as possible. Most authorities appoint the personnel of their new committees at their statutory annual meeting which is held, in an election year, between eight and 21 days after the retirement of the old council.

In order that the council may be able to do this, it is

desirable to settle in advance who are to be the members of the various committees. If the full council tries to do the work itself, without any advance preparation, the task is likely to prove long and possibly acrimonious. The period between polling day and the date of the annual meeting is short and speedy action is required. It can, however, be a delicate matter if there is a change of political control or a substantial change in membership of the council, and needs to be handled with tact and common sense. It must be remembered that the task is to prepare the way for the full council to make its appointments at the annual meeting and it would be a complete waste of time to put forward recommendations that are not likely to receive the council's approval. If the council is organised on political lines, and most are, the selection procedures are carried out by the political parties. There may be some where this is not possible in which case it may be necessary to have some form of selection committee.

Membership of selection committee

The selection committee very often comprises senior members of the council representing all shades of political opinion. Strictly speaking, all members of a council are equal in the sight of the law but, on most councils, there are those who are recognised by their colleagues as having a certain seniority. They may be the leaders of their political groups; they may be chairmen of important committees; they may simply be members who, by reason of their long experience and wise counsel, have gained the reputation of elder statesmen. Such members usually command the confidence of their colleagues to do a fair job but it has to be recognised that the new council, particularly if there has been a political change, may not be happy with the arrangement. If there is any doubt about it, the Secretary should seek new instructions from the chairman or leader of the council.

Selection procedures

As soon as possible, and subject to any instructions from leading members, the Secretary may be expected to send to every member of the new council a list of the proposed committees with a request that he should indicate his order of preference as to those on which he would like to serve. The task is likely to be much more difficult since it is common for a high proportion of members to express a preference for the same important committee and for an insufficient number to volunteer for a committee whose work is thought to be less interesting.

The selection process will have to consider how many members should be recommended to serve on each committee. The local authority, generally speaking, may appoint however many people it likes but frequently the size of committees is laid down in the council's own standing orders and the selection committee must draft its recommendations accordingly. It will also take into account the political balance of each committee. This will normally be the subject of agreement between the party groups. It is probable that proportions on committees will be approximately the same as the proportion on the council as a whole but it is quite possible that the controlling group may wish to strengthen its position by increasing its majority on each committee. If such a group allows itself only a small majority on each committee and some of its members are taken ill or are otherwise unable to attend, an unsatisfactory situation may arise in which recommendations are made by committees contrary to the prevailing political philosophy of the council. This hampers the performance of the council's business since such recommendations are bound to be reversed by the full council. Where committees have delegated power, there is absolutely no chance of the majority group permitting such a situation to arise.

In nominating the personnel of each committee, the selection process may take into account not only the individual preferences of members but also the balance of each committee apart from politics, for example the proportion of experienced members to newcomers.

If the council is organised wholly on political lines, the allocation of members to committees will be arranged by the party managers with membership normally in proportion to members of each party on the council as a whole.

Powers and duties of committees

A local authority may refer or delegate any of its functions to a committee, except its power to levy a rate or precept and its power to borrow money. By doing so it does not prevent itself from exercising the function itself whenever it so wishes. It is very important that the council should regulate, by standing order or otherwise, the powers and duties of each of its committees. No room should be left for doubt as to what a committee may or may not do. There should be no overlapping between committees. It should be absolutely clear what responsibilities have been delegated to a committee — that is to say the matters it can settle on the spot — and what things have merely been referred to it for consideration and report. Formal terms of reference should be drawn up for each committee and kept up to date in the light of new legislation and changing circumstances. It may be found convenient for the terms of reference of each committee to be formally renewed at the annual meeting of the council each year when the new personnel of the committee is approved. Model terms of reference to committees and a model scheme of delegation to committees and officers may be found as appendices to this volume.

Cycle of meetings

Whilst, to a limited extent, the day, hour and frequency of meetings can be left for decision by the members of the committee themselves, the local authority's business will be greatly facilitated by the production of a definite programme of meetings of committees, of sub-committees and of the full council.

Admission of public and press

Any meeting of a local authority or of a committee, sub-committee, joint committee or advisory committee appointed by one or more local authorities is required by law to be open to the public. That means it must be open to reporters who are, after all, themselves members of the public and they may publish a report of proceedings in their newspapers. The council or committee may, however, by resolution exclude the public (including the Press) whenever publicity would be prejudicial to the public interest by reason of the confidential nature of the business to be transacted or for other special and relevant reasons which must be specified in the resolution.

Governments have frequently appealed to local authorities to be as open and frank in the conduct of their affairs as possible and to exclude the public, only when that course is really necessary in the public interest. Circumstances in which the public may reasonably be asked to leave include consideration of reports on the progress of negotiations for the sale or purchase of property, the personal circumstances of problem families and certain matters involving the private affairs of employees. Experienced and responsible reporters recognise these items for themselves and most of them can be relied upon to respect an embargo on publication even if the meeting is not officially closed to the public. If the subject is one of great delicacy and confidentiality, however, there may be no alternative to the exclusion of everyone other than members of the committee and the officers dealing with the matter.

CHAPTER 6

THE COUNCIL AND ITS MEETINGS

Everyone who participates at the highest level in the administration of a local authority, whether as an elected member or chief officer, has to acknowledge that the council and committee meeting is the focal point of all his activities. The Council Chamber and the committee rooms are, as it were, the engine rooms of every County Hall and Town Hall. This is where the crucial decisions are taken and where the more important instructions are given and received. A councillor may be a good and conscientious constituency member but it is the contribution he is able to make in the course of discussion that determines the impact he makes in public life. A chairman may have social gifts but if he cannot conduct a meeting properly he must be classed as a failure in that office. Every chief officer, no matter how great his technical or professional skills or however well he may organise his department, must display competence in his association with the council and its committees. Of no officer is this more true than the Chief Executive and the Secretary. Whereas others must reveal some ability, none is required to be an expert on the law and conduct of meetings. Even the chairman, who needs to be more expert than most, may properly feel that he is entitled to help and guidance from the officer who is the council's chief professional administrator. His contribution is vital to the sound administration of his council's affairs. Only the highest standards of professional competence at all times will suffice.

The law relating to meetings would fill a book itself, and has frequently done so. In this chapter we shall only concern ourselves with practical points relating to the conduct of local authority meetings, particularly those upon which the Chief Executive or the Secretary will need to be well versed.

The chairman or Mayor

The election of the chairman or Mayor is the first business transacted at the annual meeting of the council. There is no rule relating to the appointment of chairman of a committee but, since it is not possible to conduct the business of the committee until the Chair is occupied, it is generally found convenient to follow the precedent set by the council and to elect a chairman of each committee as the first business at the first meeting of the committee in the new municipal year.

Who presides at his election?

If the chairman of the Council or Mayor in a Borough is present — and many councils provide in their standing orders that the chairman of the council or Mayor shall be a member of all committees *virtute officii* — it may be appropriate for him to take the chair temporarily for the purpose of presiding over the selection. This assumes he is not himself a candidate. Alternatively the retiring chairman or Mayor, if he is not seeking re-election, may preside over the choice of his successor. If no suitable member is able and willing to preside as a temporary measure, the usual practice is for the senior officer present to call for nominations. This is not altogether satisfactory since the officer is not a member of the committee and, if there is a keen contest for the office, the officer could find himself in an invidious position. He does not, of course, have a vote of any kind and consequently cannot exercise a casting vote in a case of equality. Fortunately, such a situation is rare. It is recommended that, if an officer were to find himself in that position, his best course would be to adjourn the meeting until a later hour – say for 15 minutes — on the ground that no chairman was available to conduct the proceedings. Since it is unlikely that members would allow that impossible position to continue indefinitely, it is highly likely that when the committee reassembled to resume the meeting a compromise solution would have been found.

Appointment by full council

Sometimes the selection of chairmen of committees will be made by the full council, possibly as a package to ensure a balanced share of such offices between members of different political persuasions or representing different territorial areas. There is nothing to prevent this but it is submitted that it would be advisable, if only for the record, that each committee should take formal notice of the appointment of its chairman. If it can also express its approval, so much the better since this adds considerably to the chairman's stature and authority.

Selection by rota

There is nothing to prevent a committee from selecting a different chairman from one meeting to the next but, generally speaking, this is a bad practice. To achieve efficiency, some continuity is necessary in the conduct of the committee's business and it is often essential, between meetings, for officers to obtain some guidance as to a committee's likely attitude towards some emergent point. Only a chairman who enjoys the complete and continuing confidence of his committee can presume to speak for them. The practice of rotating the chairmanship is, fortunately, rare. It is largely confined to joint committees where it is sometimes thought inadvisable to give any one of the constituent members the considerable advantage of the regular chairmanship.

Duties of the chairman

The basic duties of the chairman of any meeting are so universally recognised that they scarcely require definition. They are to preserve order, to ensure that the proceedings are properly conducted according to law and according to the standing orders or rules of the body concerned, and to take care that all shades of opinion are given a fair hearing, so far as practicable, and the wishes of the majority are accurately ascertained.

Importance of impartiality

In the performance of this duty the chairman should be absolutely impartial. Disorderly conduct, when it does arise, is often attributable to the fact that some members do not think the chairman is giving them a proper chance to express their point of view. It is sometimes argued, but not always admitted, that the chairman of a local authority committee should concentrate on supervising the debate and should express no point of view himself. The opposing argument is that the chairman is himself a councillor owing a duty to the people who elected him and, if he does not make his contribution to the discussion, he is to a certain degree distorting the true sense of the meeting. The truth is that there is nothing improper in the chairman giving his own point of view as a councillor; what he should not do is to give undue prominence to his own opinion by speaking longer or more often than anyone else or allowing those who share his opinion to enjoy the indulgence of the Chair.

Powers of the chairman

The powers of a chairman are not prescribed by law but every local authority has power to make standing orders to control its own proceedings, including those of its committees, and these should at least establish the basic authority of the chairman. To the extent that they do so, and to whatever extent other powers are expressly invested in him (for example, by the circumstances of his appointment), the chairman derives his authority from the council. The remainder of his authority he derives from the committee itself. This is plainly so where the committee has made or ratified his appointment. Even where they have not done so, the committee have by their action in assembling under his leadership impliedly agreed to his having the conduct of the meeting and thus, by natural inference, have given him the necessary authority to do so. If his authority is seriously challenged, no chairman should hesitate to use whatever powers he has to suspend the sitting until tempers cool sufficiently to allow orderly business to proceed.

STANDING ORDERS AS TO PROCEDURE AT MEETINGS

Almost all local authorities have standing orders which include standard rules of debate for council meetings. The purpose of having such rules is to give the chairman the authority he needs to control the proceedings. Specimen standing orders relating to procedure at meetings are given in Appendix One to this volume.

Strictly speaking, rules of debate apply also to committee meetings but it is the custom in most authorities to relax the rules for committee meetings. Committee members are customarily allowed to sit when speaking and to speak more than once. This enables discussion in committee to develop on more intimate and informal lines than is possible at a larger gathering and it is not uncommon for a committee chairman to assess the intention of a meeting, quite accurately, without requiring either a formal proposal or a vote. The debate, nevertheless, must proceed in an orderly fashion, which means that certain rules must still be observed. For example, only one member should be permitted to speak at a time, all must be required to address the Chair when speaking and the rulings of the chairman must be respected. If the informality of the meeting is abused, the chairman must exercise his authority and, if necessary, impose the full rules of debate laid down in standing orders. It is unlikely that he will have to do so since the committee itself is likely to object to having its proceedings disturbed by misbehaviour but, unless the chairman has the courage to take action in the last resort, his meetings may well degenerate into a shambles.

SIGNATURE OF MINUTES

Unless there is statutory business to transact, such as the election of a chairman, the first business at a meeting of any local authority, or one of its committees, is the signing of the minutes of the previous meeting.

The Local Government Act 1972, requires that minutes shall be drawn up and entered in a book kept for that purpose or upon loose leaves and shall be signed either at the same meeting (if that is practicable) or at the next following meeting by the person presiding. Any minute purporting to be signed in this way shall be received in evidence without further proof.

This procedure is sometimes called "the confirmation of the minutes" but this description is incorrect. Minutes of a committee sometimes require the confirmation of the full council before they become effective but they do not need to be signed before they can be acted upon. The purpose of signature is to provide evidence that they are a correct record of what the council or committee decided. Once they are signed it is not necessary for the chairman or anyone else to be called as a witness in legal proceedings to testify as to their accuracy. It is customary for the person presiding to ask the meeting to approve the minutes as a correct record of the previous meeting before he signs them. Strictly speaking there is no need for him to do so. It is his responsibility to satisfy himself that they are correct but it is a common courtesy to ask the other members whether they agree.

If the minutes are kept on a loose leaf system, the pages must be consecutively numbered and separately initialled when the minutes are signed.

VOTING

All questions coming or arising before a local authority are to be decided by a majority of members present and voting thereon at a meeting of the authority.

Second or casting vote

In the case of equality, the person presiding at a meeting has a second or casting vote. It is sometimes argued that a chairman cannot exercise a casting vote unless he voted positively in the first instance. This is not so. It is perfectly proper for the chairman to abstain, if he wishes, on the first count and subsequently to cast his deciding vote one way or the other in order to resolve the matter in a case of equality. What he must not do is to reserve his position in the first instance and subsequently seek to cast two votes to reverse a narrow majority. In effect, abstention is as much a vote as is voting for or against the motion. The first vote must not be used belatedly to contrive an equality that does not really exist.

Reference to the chairman out of meeting

The statutory requirement that all matters must be decided at a meeting of the local authority does not prevent delegation to committees or to officers, both of which are specifically authorised, but it does cast doubt on the legality of the common practice whereby questions arising between one meeting of a committee and the next are decided by the chairman. This is a valuable device which enables many matters to be dealt with expeditiously without an excessive number of meetings having to be called. It must be realised, however, that the chairman of a council or committee has no dictatorial powers. In effect he is only anticipating the decision of his committee and the legitimacy of the practice depends upon the willingness of the committee to ratify the things done in their name by their chairman. A chairman who cannot command the confidence of his committee is in an impossible position and would usually be well advised to make way for someone else.

Member voting must be present

It will be observed that, in order to cast his vote, a member must personally be present. There is no provision for proxy or postal voting. A simple majority of those voting is sufficient. The result is not invalidated by the absence or abstention of any member so it follows that the majority does not have to be a majority of the full council or committee. There are exceptions to the general rule; for example a resolution to promote or oppose a local Bill in Parliament must be passed by a majority of the whole number of members.

Methods of voting

So far as principal councils are concerned, the manner of voting is not now prescribed by law but frequently the matter will be governed by the council's own standing orders. In committee, a formal vote is often dispensed with and non-contentious items are approved in silence or with a murmur of assent. Otherwise a show of hands is most common. The vocal method, whereby members call out "Aye" or "No", can be employed but this method is imprecise and should be avoided unless the majority is overwhelming. A ballot is sometimes held, particularly on the election of a member to office such as that of chairman. Councillors who are required to choose between two or more colleagues may naturally prefer to do so in secret to avoid hurting the feelings of those they feel unable to support. A few local authorities possess mechanical equipment for casting and recording votes and some may find it convenient to call a division on the Parliamentary model but these methods are rarely used.

Recording of votes

Standing orders may provide that, upon the requisition of any member, the manner in which each member voted should be recorded in the minutes. In this case the names of all members present should be listed, including those abstaining, with a note of the way in which each used his vote. The simplest way of doing this, if the council is not too large, is to ask each member voting in a particular way to stand or to raise his hand and to remain in that position until the committee clerk calls out his name as having been duly recorded. If the council is larger and does not possess any mechanical means of recording voting, members may be invited to mark and sign a piece of paper indicating the use they made of their vote.

Voting at parish councils etc.

Voting at a meeting of a parish council or a community council is always by show of hands unless standing orders provide otherwise. Matters arising at a parish meeting or community meeting are settled by a simple majority of those present and voting, unless a poll is demanded. It is not prescribed how such a vote shall be taken but presumably it would normally be by show of hands.

RECORD OF ATTENDANCE

A record of those members attending a meeting of a local authority and the length of time they are present must always be kept. Now that councillors are entitled to claim attendance allowances there would be legitimate public criticism if an official record of their attendance were not kept and there is little doubt that the auditor would have hard words to say. If a committee is small, the committee clerk may be entrusted with the job of noting those present but it is better if all members are called upon to sign an attendance register. The names of those present are usually recorded in the minutes. This gives members a chance to check that their names have not been overlooked and some also like the evidence to show to their constituents that they are being assiduous in their public duties.

FREQUENCY OF MEETINGS

Principal councils are allowed considerable latitude in determining the frequency, hour and place of their own meetings. They are obliged to hold an annual meeting in every year on a date of their own choice in March, April or May. In an election year, the date of the annual meeting is more narrowly prescribed but a limited discretion is still permitted. Councils may also select the hour at which the meeting is to start but, if they do not do so, the meeting will begin at noon.

In addition to the annual meeting, the council may also hold such other meetings as it wishes at such date and times as it may determine. An extraordinary meeting (or, as it is sometimes called, a special meeting) of the council may be called by the chairman at any time and, if he refuses or neglects to do so upon a request by five members, the meeting may be called by any five members. They may do so immediately if the chairman refuses or, otherwise, upon his failure to act after seven days. The notice of the time and place of the intended meeting which must be published at the council offices in accordance with the statutory procedure must be signed by the members calling the meeting and must specify the business proposed to be transacted. The other statutory requirements for summoning a council meeting must all be complied with.

Meetings can be held anywhere the council may choose, whether within their area or not.

No business may be taken at a meeting of a council unless it has been specified in the summons with the exception of items which are required by law to be transacted at the annual meeting and other items which standing orders may allow to be dealt with as a matter of urgency. For the avoidance of dispute, it is desirable that everything to be done at the meeting shall be clearly stated in the summons.

The rules relating to parish and community councils are somewhat similar but there are differences of detail. For example, a parish council (but not a community council) must hold at least four meetings a year, including the annual meeting. In either case the time for starting the annual meeting, if not otherwise fixed by the council, is six o'clock in the evening. Meetings must not be held on licensed premises unless no suitable alternative is available and two members may requisition an extraordinary meeting.

ORDER OF BUSINESS, SPEECHES AND QUESTIONS

Each local authority may, by its own standing orders, determine the normal order in which business shall be taken. This practice enables the agenda paper to be prepared in an orderly and recognised form but there is no reason why the order should not be varied, if desired. It is the responsibility of the chairman to conduct the business of the meeting expeditiously and, if he thinks that object may best be achieved by changing the order of business, he would be justified in doing so. A good chairman will try to make sure that he has the consent of the meeting to any change. If it is known that some members have to leave early for another engagement, it might be advisable to take the more important items first; on the other hand it would be reprehensible to do so if some members are unavoidably delayed in arriving.

Precedence for unopposed business

In the normal way, it is customary to take formal and uncontentious business first. It is difficult to estimate the time that discussion of controversial business may take. Leaving it to the end does make sure that, whether the business of the meeting is completed or not, at least those matters not in dispute are settled and can be proceeded with.

The practice in dealing with reports of committees to council varies. Some councils take them in strict chronological order; some vary the order from meeting to meeting so that different chairmen get their turn to speak first when the council is at its most alert. Some deal with each report in turn whether it gives rise to debate or not. Others, following the precept already discussed, run through the full agenda giving formal approval to all unopposed business. A member can prevent the confirmation of an item at this stage by simply rising and saying "I object". This item will then be returned to and fully debated later in the meeting.

Respect for the Chair

It is the universal practice at any kind of meeting to insist that speakers should speak one at a time and should address all their remarks to the chairman. This enables the meeting to be conducted in an orderly fashion. If members are permitted to argue directly with each other or to converse when someone else is speaking, the meeting can quickly degenerate into a state of confusion.

Length of speeches

At council meetings it is customary to require the speaker to stand and to speak once only on any item. Standing orders usually impose a time limit on speeches since otherwise debates might become intolerably long. Five or ten minutes are enough for most purposes provided the council is sensible about permitting limited extensions for good reason. For instance, the Chairman of the Finance Committee would almost certainly need longer to present the annual Financial Report and Budget Speech.

Informality in committee

In committee, business is usually conducted much more informally. To encourage the free interchange of ideas, members are permitted to sit when speaking and to speak more than once. However, it is still essential that they speak to the chairman and only one at once. All speeches must be relevant to the subject under discussion. If irrelevant matter is introduced, the speaker must be called to order or the thread of the debate will be destroyed.

Questions on committee reports

When reports of committees are presented to the council, it is normal to allow any member to ask a question without notice on any item in the report. It is presumed that, before a topic becomes the subject of a report to the council, it has been so thoroughly discussed by the committee that the chairman of the committee should be able to answer questions about it without trouble. Sometimes, however, questions have only a marginal reference to the report under discussion and courtesy demands in such circumstances that advance notice should be given of the question.

Questions by notice

If a councillor wishes to ask a question which does not relate to an item on any committee report, standing orders often permit him to do so after giving due notice in writing, provided the question refers to some topic that is the legitimate business of the Council. The period of notice allows the chairman of the responsible committee, with the aid of the officers, to ascertain the answer but standing orders usually permit him to decline to answer if he finds it inconvenient to do so. Questions can only be put for the purpose of securing information. Discussion is not usually allowed and the questioner is not permitted to use his question as an excuse to make a speech of his own.

PRESENTATION OF REPORTS AND ESTIMATES

The bulk of correspondence sent to a local authority is properly addressed to the Chief Executive, or to the Secretary, or to the chief officer whose department is dealing with the matter. It is no part of a councillor's duty to enter into correspondence on the council's behalf and the occasional letter that is sent to the chairman or to some other member is best referred to the responsible officer for acknowledgement — the compliments of the member concerned can be politely woven into the letter of acknowledgement — and appropriate action. This convention relates, of course, only to official council business; there is nothing to prevent a councillor from writing to a voter who asks for advice on a personal problem. Indeed, in the larger authorities a members' secretariat may be provided.

Officer reports to committees.

It is also the responsibility of the officials to give professional advice to the council as to the execution of its statutory functions and to make progress reports relating to the effective performance of the council's policies. For these reasons, the agenda of local authority committees consist predominantly of reports by officers. A report may comprise of no more than a letter which the officer or his representative will be invited to read aloud and explain if he needs to. On the other hand, a professional report on some projected scheme may be written at some length and sent to members with their agenda paper several days beforehand. This gives councillors a fair chance to assimilate and consider the various problems involved. A more straightforward matter might be the subject of a verbal report.

Committee reports to council

It is not the normal practice for officers to report to the full council except for formal business such as the result of a by-election. Reports of committees form the main part of the council agenda. These reports deal with action taken by the committee under delegated powers, in respect of which the confirmation of the council is not required, and also with action recommended by the committee but which does need the council's approval.

Another method of submitting committee reports is to present their full minutes for scrutiny, and for approval where necessary. It is essential to distinguish between action taken under plenary powers and recommendations needing ratification, and much confusion can be caused if this is not clearly done.

Narrative reports

An alternative practice, favoured by some larger authorities, is the presentation of committee reports in narrative form similar to the written reports submitted by officers to committees. In fact, the officer's report, suitably adapted, might well form the basis of the committee's report. This method is particularly suitable when more than one committee is called upon to report on the same subject — for example, reports by both the Education Committee and the Finance Committee on the possible provision of a new school — since the relevant reports can be placed in juxtaposition on the agenda paper and considered simultaneously. It is an appropriate practice when the greater part of a committee's work consists of delegated business which needs to be reported to the council in synopsis only.

The practice has its uses in smaller authorities when a committee is appointed to investigate and report to the council on the benefits and drawbacks of a particular proposal. In such a case, a mere recommendation for or against the project is not sufficient. But in authorities that give their committees only limited delegation, particularly smaller authorities with modest staffs, the additional work involved in this method would probably be more than the Secretary could handle.

Budget reports

Only the council can fix the rate. The formal motion, whereby it is invited to do so, is customarily set out in full on the agenda paper; a copy of the budget, as approved by the Finance Committee, is sent with the agenda paper to every councillor. In presenting the budget and moving the motion to make a rate, the chairman of that committee frequently takes the opportunity to review the council's policies and the financial provision made to implement them. This is frequently referred to as "the budget speech" and standing orders are usually suspended to permit the chairman to speak for longer than the time normally permitted.

MOTIONS AND AMENDMENTS

Motions

A corporate body, such as a local authority, expresses its collective will by decisions taken at meetings of the authority. These decisions are arrived at by considering, and voting upon, motions which, if approved, become resolutions of the council or committee. A motion is therefore a proposal put forward by a member in the hope that enough people will support it for it to be adopted as a decision of the authority. At common law a motion does not need a seconder but, to discourage frivolous motions, the practice of requiring motions to be seconded is universally used and it is the general practice of local authorities to provide in their standing orders that every motion shall be seconded before it is thrown open for discussion.

Some chairmen allow the mover to speak to his motion in the hope that he will be able to find a seconder by the force of his argument but the majority require that the motion shall be formally seconded before permitting any speech on the subject. If the proposer cannot find anyone willing to second the motion, the chances of persuading a majority to vote for it must be thin and a lot of the meeting's time can be taken up by abortive speeches if the chairman is lax in such matters.

Amendments

A motion as originally proposed may not be acceptable to some members of the committee who would, nevertheless, be willing to support the proposal in a slightly amended form. When the motion has been moved and seconded and before it has been put to the vote, any member may move an amendment which, if duly seconded, should be put to the meeting for immediate discussion. An amendment must comprise a suggestion to leave out certain words, to insert or add words, or a combination of both. Anything which would have the effect of introducing a new proposal, different in substance from the original motion, or which amounts to the direct negative of the motion should be rejected by the chairman since neither is a genuine amendment.

Substantive motions

If an amendment is accepted by the meeting, the original motion is varied accordingly and is automatically put before the meeting for consideration as the "substantive motion". If the amendment is lost, discussion on the original motion continues. In either case, further amendments can be proposed but not such as to revive any proposal already rejected by the meeting.

Only one amendment should be before the meeting at any one time and the chairman should dispose of the current amendment before he allows anyone to move another. If the meeting tries to decide several things at once, nothing but confusion is liable to result.

Amendments to committee reports

A motion is normally permitted to be put forward at a meeting of a local authority committee without notice or other formality, provided it is relevant to an item on the agenda, such as a report or letter which is under consideration. For council meetings, however, a greater degree of formality is required. Most of the business probably comprises the consideration of committee reports, the approval of which is normally moved by the chairman of the committee concerned. To reject the motion would be to disapprove the report of the committee in its entirety which, in most cases, is unthinkable. The usual practice, therefore, is to propose an amendment (if so desired) deleting the particular recommendation which does not find favour with the mover of the amendment. Should the amendment be successful it is necessary to specify how the item of business shall be dealt with. There are three possibilities. The first is to substitute an alternative course of action for the one recommended by the committee. The second is to refer the item back to the committee for their further consideration. The third is to decide that no further action shall be taken on the matter at all. The latter is not a direct negative since the same result cannot be achieved by simply voting against the chairman's motion. It is very important to remember that the motion before the meeting is that of the chairman that the committee report be adopted. The member who is suggesting a different course of action on one particular matter is merely moving an amendment to the report. Failure to grasp this fundamental point is probably the greatest single source of confusion in the conduct of council meetings.

Notices of motion

Standing orders usually provide a method whereby a member can submit a motion in his own name, as distinct from the report of a committee, but this has to be done by notice and standing orders usually provide that the motion shall not be discussed by the council, otherwise than in cases of urgency, until a report of the relevant committee is available. Notices of motion are normally required to be given in writing to a nominated officer, possibly the Secretary, by whom the fairly elaborate procedure often prescribed by standing orders must be carefully followed.

Certain motions may be moved without notice. These are usually of a procedural kind and are listed in standing orders.

INTERRUPTIVE AND CLOSURE MOTIONS

There is a number of ways of interrupting a debate with the object of preventing further consideration of the matter under discussion or even of bringing the whole meeting to an end. Some of them, such as the guillotine and kangaroo procedures used in Parliament and the archaic device called "the previous question", are not applicable to local government. Those that are applicable are not much used but the Secretary must be familiar with them so that he is aware what to do when the need does arise. At any time when a member considers that a debate has gone on long enough he may intervene (even if he has already spoken) to move one of a number of available motions, commonly called interruptive or closure motions. Provided the motion is seconded and the chairman is satisfied that the business has been sufficiently aired and the motion is therefore reasonable, he should put the interruptive motion to the meeting at once. It is then for the meeting to decide whether the debate is to proceed or not; if the motion is defeated, the debate will continue as though nothing had happened.

Common forms of interruptive motion

The more common forms of interruptive motion appropriate to local government are as follows:

(i) "That the meeting do now adjourn". This is appropriate when the hour is late and implies that the meeting will resume at a later date. The date and hour for reassembly should be decided at the time of adjournment. It is not legally necessary to give notice of an adjourned meeting but the Secretary should ascertain whether the members would appreciate receiving a reminder as a courtesy. It is not advisable to use the adjournment, as Parliament does, merely as a form of protest. Local authorities have much practical business to transact and many people are liable to be inconvenienced and angered if work is put off simply to draw attention to a single complaint.

(ii) "That the debate do now adjourn." This is appropriate when it becomes apparent that discussion is likely to go on longer than time permits. The difference from the foregoing motion is that the remainder of the business is cleared up before the members go home; the way is then clear to concentrate on the one contentious topic at the resumed meeting.

(iii) "That the question be now put." This is appropriate when the mover feels that the topic has been sufficiently well ventilated. The object is to have the matter put to the vote forthwith so that the meeting may go on to the next item on the agenda.

(iv) "That the meeting proceed to next business.' The

inference is that the current debate is to be brought to an end and no vote taken. It is inappropriate when a motion is before the meeting, having been properly moved and seconded, but the form is sometimes used to prompt a chairman who seems to be permitting an aimless discussion to get out of hand.

Amendments should not be permitted to interruptive motions as they defeat the whole object of the exercise which is to give the meeting the opportunity of deciding whether it wants the debate to continue.

POINTS OF ORDER AND EXPLANATION

It is invariable practice to allow a member to interrupt the debate if he considers that standing orders are not being followed or if he himself is being misquoted or misrepresented by another speaker. The speaker who is interrupted is expected to give way until the point is cleared up. The chairman should insist that the point is made briefly and he should give his ruling on it promptly and firmly and should brook no further argument.

The system is much abused by unscrupulous members who take advantage of a weak chairman to make second speeches and generally to destroy the thread of their opponents' arguments.

RIGHT OF REPLY

The right of reply is normally given to the mover of an original motion immediately before the vote is taken. The idea is to give him the opportunity to answer the questions and objections that have been raised during the debate so that the arguments for and against the motion can be rounded off. The mover must not be permitted to introduce new arguments at this stage; this would be unfair since his opponents will not have the opportunity of attempting an answer.

The mover of an amendment is not, as a general rule,

given a right of reply. Even if his amendment is successful so that he becomes, in effect, the author of the substantive motion, the right of reply remains with the mover of the original motion.

It is imperative to remember that it is the chairman of the committee, as the mover of his committee's report, who has the right of reply on any question arising on the report.

QUORUM

Before a meeting can lawfully transact any business the prescribed minimum number of members must be present. This mininum number is called the quorum. The statutory quorum for a council meeting is one-quarter of the whole number. There is no statutory quorum for committee meetings but standing orders, as a matter of common sense, invariably prescribe such a minimum, which may often be one-quarter of the membership of the committee. At common law, if no quorum is prescribed, every member must be present, a rule which could render the transaction of business virtually impossible.

If a quorum is not present, the meeting should be adjourned to a date and time selected by the chairman or, if the chairman and vice-chairman be absent, by those members who are present. It may often be sensible to adjourn for only a few minutes until a quorum is made up since, assuming that the absentees have not previously apologised for absence, the explanation may be that members are held up in traffic on their way to the meeting. If the meeting is adjourned to a later date, it makes sense to send a fresh notice to every member, notwithstanding the absence of any legal compulsion. Not to do so would be likely to lead to a situation where no quorum was present on the second occasion also.

CHAPTER 7

CORPORATE PLANNING
AND MANAGEMENT

When local authorities were first established to take over the various functions of the former local boards, it was a natural development that many of them should set up separate committees to administer the different functions for which they had become responsible. With the active encouragement of the government, which has from time to time required local authorities to set up statutory committees for sundry purposes, the system has broadened and taken firm root. But the rigid departmentalism of many local authorities, with departments often closely coupled to a particular committee, has also helped to narrow the vision of some members and officers so that they have become more closely concerned with the immediate needs of a particular service rather than the longer-term objectives of the authority as a whole.

The system of annual estimating — too often handicapped by doubts concerning the exchequer contribution as Governments have shifted their position to adapt themselves to national economic difficulties — has also frustrated many local authorities from attempting some systematic social and economic planning. The budgeting process is a continual tug-of-war with policy or finance committees on the one hand striving to cut down the rate levy and spending committees, on the other, competing between themselves for a greater share of limited resources, not only in money but also for manpower and materials.

The need to establish priorities

In these circumstances, few committees (and that means effectively few councils, since the councils act almost exclusively through or at the recommendation of their committees) have ever been able to plan with confidence beyond the end of the ensuing financial year. Policy, therefore, tends to be built of a series of improvisations and short-term decisions. The cynic has been known to say that no local authority ever had a policy unless it can be called a policy to try to keep the rates down. If that is so it is suggested that even that policy has always been doomed to failure because it is entirely a negative attitude. No one, the argument runs, is in a position to take stock of the available resources and to devise a coherent policy that can be achieved within those resources. Instead policy, if that is what it is, is created like a patchwork quilt by stitching together the ambitions of a multiplicity of committees and then trying to reduce it to size by clipping pieces off the hem, a method that is neither economic nor effective.

The Bains Report[1] dealt with the problem in this way:

> It is impossible to foresee the situation in which a local authority will have sufficient resources, whether of money, land or manpower, to meet all the demands placed upon it by the community and the establishment of priorities and allocation of resources is therefore of critical importance. In many authorities, however, this process is still totally irrational. Committee estimates are cut all round in order to keep within what is regarded as an acceptable level of total expenditure, with no attempt made to evaluate the relative consequences of cuts in the different services which those estimates represent. The establishment of priorities and allocation of resources requires, in our view, an overall plan against which the recommendations of committees can be measured.

The authors of the report also commended evidence put to them that likened the management process to a scale, with the setting of objectives and allocation of resources at one end, moving through the designing of programmes and

[1] Chapter 3.

plans to the execution of those plans at the other end. As one moves through the scale, the emphasis changes from member control with officer advice at the "objective" end to officer control with member advice at the "execution" end.

The need for flexibility

Modern thinking, then, identified and nurtured by Bains, was that policy formulation should be based on corporate planning, the identification of needs, an analysis of objectives and the means of attaining them. The danger in this approach is that plans, once firmly defined, come quickly to be regarded as immutable. But plans are never ideal because they can never be based on complete and accurate data. Forecasts and projections proved to be inaccurate. Unexpected developments cannot be anticipated or provided for. Needs and aspirations vary with the passage of time. Therefore, if planning is to be effective it must be adaptable, with progress kept under continual review in the light of new information and changing needs. When needs vary, so must objectives; when resources change they must be reallocated. The local authority that is not geared to the revision, as necessary, of its policy decisions is going, sooner or later, to meet trouble.

The availability of resources

It is clear that policy decisions must be linked to the availability of resources, particularly the supply of money. It may be a platitude to suggest that it is futile to adopt a policy without the resources to implement it. Yet many local authorities frequently do precisely that. Whether it be from political motives, lack of foresight or plain wishful-thinking, their approach betrays the absence of any coherent planning.

It is suggested by traditionalists that "policy" should be based on idealistic considerations. The availability of money and resources should only be considered as an issue of last resort; even then it should be permitted only to modify and not to exert primary influence on the formulation of policy.

This is the patchwork quilt syndrome once more. Bains firmly rejected it and strenuously argued for the creation of a Policy and Resources Committee having responsibility, subject to the utimate authority of the full council for decision making, for setting objectives and priorities and for the allocation of resources, particularly money, manpower, land and property.

LOCAL GOVERNMENT AND CORPORATE PLANNING

The Policy Planning Process

The recommendation of the Bains Report was widely followed inasmuch as many local authorities established a committee with the title of Policy and Resources Committee but it is doubtful whether many of these committees were given the full range of responsibilities envisaged by Bains. In a political environment there are obvious difficulties in doing so. The adherents of a political party are likely to look upon the implementation of their political beliefs as an end in itself rather than as the means to an end. In the corporate plan it becomes the objective and not the method of attainment. The plan is thus suspect from the beginning and the minority group is immediately committed to opposition and ultimate repeal.

Nevertheless, attempts at corporate planning and better management techniques and processes were made in the authorities that emerged from the 1974 reorganisation, with varying degrees of success.

There are three essentials to sound decision making. First, it is necessary to establish what one is trying to achieve. Second, reliable information is required on the deployment of resources between objectives (which is not the same thing as deployment between committees or departments). Third, it is desirable to measure the effectiveness of current policies, programmes and projects, and, to ensure alternative ways of achieving the objective are fully considered and analysed.

Objectives

The first and basic task is the compilation of a clear and unambiguous statement of objectives. The idea is to express these in such a way that the efficiency and effectiveness of each objective, or activities within it, can be assessed.

An example of such an objective might be "to promote the development of employment policies in co-operation with the private and public sector". Within this objective there might be certain key activities that can be monitored and assessed, eg:

(*a*) maintain existing industrial estates within current limits.

(*b*) identify up to 100 acres of land for development and acquire by means of a three year selling programme.

(*c*) establish two skill centres within the authority.

(*d*) identify and promote sites for office development.

(*e*) establish an Enterprise Agency in partnership with the Local Chamber of Commerce.

There would be similar objectives and activities for other services.

The next task is to allocate limited resources between activities, to come as close to the achievement of objectives or activities as possible.

Unfortunately, the weakness of traditional local authority planning is that finance has often been the only resource seriously considered, and short-term finance at that. There are many other resources that need equal consideration. The availability of skilled manpower is one that ought to be obvious but too often it is not. If scarce professional staff are used on one project they cannot be used on another. It may thus be necessary to make a choice between two desirable projects even though the money may be available for both. Land and premises are other precious commodities that cannot be used for two purposes at the same time. It is as important to consider the commitment of financial resources in the long term as to find the money for immediate needs. The time within which a project can be completed may be as important as the cost.

Performance review

The final feature of a corporate planning system is one of the most important and is one most easily neglected. That is performance review. Planning serves very little purpose unless it is kept up to date continuously or, at least, at regular and frequent intervals. There will, of course, need to be the traditional financial checks to make sure the expenditure on each item is keeping within the financial limitations made. To be meaningful, a parallel check needs to be made to ensure that the objective is being fulfilled. If it is not, the reason needs to be sought. The money provided may prove to be insufficient; if this is so, a decision needs to be made as to the possibility of increasing the sum in future years. But again the reason needs to be sought. Perhaps the needs of the service were underestimated or some essential expenditure was not foreseen. Whatever the explanation, the analysis cannot remain valid in the light of new and better information. It must be corrected and the corporate plan adjusted accordingly.

The Changing World

Much of what has been said above represented the thinking of the early seventies, when the hopes of the reorganised local government was based on expectations of growth.

The statement by Labour Party Secretary of State, that "the Party's over" heralded a new post-oil crisis era of pressures on public spending, reductions in Government Grant, and the collapse of capital spending, particularly on housing. The election of a Conservative Government in 1979, committed to controlling public spending, reinforced these trends.

Other factors too were affecting the local government scene. A period of growth in the fifties gave way to one of standstill or even decline in the 70's and 80's. Population and social changes were affecting local authority services. The post-war baby boom that had led to growth in education provision gave way to declining school population with a consequent need for rationalisation and amalgamation of schools, which has proved difficult to achieve. The provision of council housing was affected by council house sales totalling in excess of 500,000 dwellings in the 1980's, increases in private sector housing completions and home ownership, and a dramatic decline in central government capital allocations for this purpose. An increase in the elderly population required more resources at a time when resources generally were static, leading to pressures for the transfer of funds from education which was in decline, to social services which needed to grow. Most authorities have felt the need to respond to growing unemployment, and many inner city areas face problems of social deprivation of various kinds.

Other changes were also taking place. The Government introduced legislation requiring local authorities to compete with the private sector for construction works and maintenance functions, with a promise to extend this to other areas such as refuse collection, street cleansing, and cleaning. Authorities were required to be more accountable to the general public, while the role of the auditor was extended to cover Value for Money, and to satisfy himself that the authority had arrangements for securing economy, efficiency and effectiveness in its operations.

Finally, politics has become much more of an issue, both within local authorities and between central and local government. Most councils are now organised on political lines, and there is much more confrontation between local government and the respective central government departments. This has taken the form either of more legal challenges to ministerial powers or campaigns against central government spending policies. Within local authorities many members take a much greater control of affairs than before, and there has been a period of adjustment for officers in a situation which for many has changed out of all recognition from the service that they entered, perhaps 20 years previously.

The new emphasis therefore is one of managing change in an era of standstill, but in a much more politicised world. It has changed from one of administering the status quo to one of managing.

THE NEED TO MANAGE

The irrelevance of some of the corporate management systems of the 1970's with their emphasis on needs and growth has not done away with the need to manage. Indeed, the difficulties presented to the present day local authority requires greater management effort, not less. Many of the issues facing local authorities are longer term than the one year rate fixing cycle. Since resources of all kinds are limited, they also need to satisfy themselves that every pound they spend is giving value to that amount, and service delivered. Both of these issues need a management dimension if they are to be achieved, which has not previously been required or seen to be necessary.

Thinking and Planning Longer-Term

Many issues facing local authorities require a longer period than one year to solve. Yet many authorities regard the annual rate-making process as the machinery for addressing some of these issues. Declining school rolls, the increasing number of elderly people, the requirements for care in the community rather than in residential establishments, or the improvement programme for council dwellings, requires at least a three year planning horizon, with a statement of what is to be achieved, and how it is to be done, and the level of finances to be committed to it. Concentrating on key issues such as these will reduce the administrative effort that is required, but also focus attention on those issues that are the most important.

Reviewing Performance

Local government has been and still is very good at recording inputs of resources. The cost of all services is well documented and recorded. Honesty and integrity in public service is maintained, but the outputs from services are not so readily available, and neither is it generally part of the process of government or management. For example, the cost of the refuse collection service is easily established, both in total, and in terms of the cost to the typical ratepayer; the tonnage collected, or the number of bins emptied and the trend of these over the years is less readily available.

Concentrating on where it is going and how it is going to get there and ensuring that it is delivering service efficiently and effectively will be the key task for the local authority of the 1990's. Many of the best managed ones can demonstrate that they are doing this. The task is to get the remainder to be as good as the minority that are.

Important in this too will be to ensure that the administration is efficient in assisting service delivery. In the remainder of this book this concept must always be borne in mind when considering the impact of support and administrative services.

CHAPTER 8

THE ROLE OF THE CHIEF EXECUTIVE

The appointment of a Chief Executive without departmental responsibilities and emerging otherwise than from a clearly defined professional background is a comparatively new departure in local government. Occasional experiments of this kind have been tried in the past by individual authorities. Some of them involved the appointment of managers with a commercial or industrial background. Others were professionals who had previously practised outside the sphere of local government. The results of such experiments were not so spectacular that local authorities at large made any haste to follow suit. However, statutory reorganisation coupled with the demand for a greater degree of corporate planning gave the movement the required impetus. The Maud and Mallaby Reports, which both preceded the major proposals for reorganisation, recommended that the Clerk of the Council should be the official head of its staff and should be chosen solely on grounds of ability irrespective of the professional background. The Clerk of the Council had, of course, important departmental responsibilities and, whereas the Institute of Chartered Secretaries and Administrators welcomed recognition of the fact that the chartered secretary employed in local government was just as likely to merit consideration for the top job as a barrister or solicitor or a member of any other profession, the recommendation brought little comfort to engineers, architects, accountants, town planners and others whose professional duties bore no relationship to the departmental functions of Clerk of the Council. In 1972 the Bains Group, in spite of much criticism of the proposal in evidence submitted to them, went beyond the recommendations of

Maud and Mallaby and firmly recommended[1] that a Chief Executive should be appointed free of administrative or other departmental responsibilities. They recognised a need, even in smaller authorities, "for a detached Chief Executive to secure proper co-ordination and that there is a great scope for him to exercise a wider co-ordinating, public relations and representative role than his counterpart in local government today finds possible". These words found a responsive chord amongst the new local authorities, a large proportion of whom made appointments of Chief Executive according to the Bains model.

Since then, Chief Executives have been appointed from various professional backgrounds but with increasing importance being placed on finance, many have come from the finance profession.

Former Clerk of the Council as Chief Executive

The view that the Clerk of the Council should be the council's principal chief officer was founded on long historical precedent. Evidence was given by the Urban District Councils Association to a former Royal Commission on Local Government as long ago as 1929 in these words:

> The exact duties of a Clerk to a Council cannot be precisely defined, as so much depends on the circumstances of each individual authority, but it cannot be too strongly emphasised that the Clerk should be definitely recognised and appointed as the chief executive and administrative officer of the Council. He should be the mouthpiece of the Council and the natural channel through which the policy of the Council is carried into effect by the various officers concerned. It should be his duty to co-ordinate the various services of the Council so as to avoid overlapping and to prevent any course of action being taken by one department without consideration for its effect on another department. It is recognised that it would be most improper for a Clerk to criticise or interfere with a technical officer in carrying out the technical duties assigned to him. At the same time, it is felt that, unless there is general supervision and control by

[1] Para. 5.28.

one officer, backed by the necessary authority, the standard of administration must inevitably suffer.

This was not an isolated view; on the contrary it seems to have met with widespread acceptance. The Joint Negotiating Committee for Town Clerks and Clerks of Local Authorities eventually wrote into the Standard Conditions of Service for these officers that the Clerk was to be the Chief Executive and Administrative Officer of the Council but, significantly, the committee did not attempt to define the duties that went with the title. It has to be borne in mind that the Committee comprised councillors and town clerks but not officers of other disciplines. There was, however, tacit acceptance by chief officers of local authorities that the Clerk of the Council was *"primus inter pares"* (the leader amongst equals). How effective a leader he was depended upon the force of his own personality and the consequent degree to which his colleagues were prepared to follow his example. Until recent years his pre-eminent position was rarely backed by an express authority.

Job specification for modern Chief Executive

The Bains Group included in their report[1] a job specification for a Chief Executive which will repay careful scrutiny. It is, of course, merely a model and does not necessarily have to be followed by any local authority appointing a Chief Executive but it is of particular interest inasmuch as it reveals the role that Bains expected a Chief Executive to play.

Head of paid services

1. The Chief Executive is the head of the council's paid service and shall have authority over all other officers so far as this is necessary for the efficient management and execution of the council's function.

There is no longer to be any question of the Chief Executive being merely first amongst equals dependent for his

[1] Appendix J.

authority upon the strength of his own personality. He is expressly to be appointed the official head of the council's staff, as foreshadowed by Maud, and all other officers, however senior, are to be subordinate to him.

It must be obvious that no Chief Executive can possibly exercise detailed control over every department. The Bains Report acknowledged that the range of issues and problems facing any local authority are too vast for any Chief Executive to grasp in detail and the responsibility for the effective and efficient running of each department must be left with the chief officer of that department.

In all probability the Chief Executive will be a former head of department and it will be a temptation to concern himself predominantly with the performance of his old department at the expense of those departments where he lacks expertise. The Chief Executive who succumbs to this temptation will be doing another officer's job and neglecting his own. In respect of his relationships with heads of departments the Chief Executive might well adapt to his own circumstances the dictum of Bagehot to the constitutional monarchy: "Question, Encourage, Warn."

Leader of Management Team

2. He is the leader of the officers' management team and through the Policy and Resources Committee, the council's principal adviser on matters of general policy. As such it is his responsibility to secure co-ordination of advice on the forward planning of objectives and services and to lead the management team in securing a corporate approach to the affairs of the authority generally.

There is here recognition of the fact that there cannot be a clean separation of policy from executive action. With political argument, he is not concerned. That is a matter for those who ask for the votes of the electorate and the Chief Executive must remain above the battle. But when the political objectives of the council have been settled it is his duty to take instructions from the political leaders of the council and to brief heads of departments and other key officers as to the general line of policy to be followed. In the reverse direction it is his responsibility, as head of the paid service, to advise his political masters what is and what is not a practicable programme. It is not for him to try to influence their political decisions so that they might match his own ideas but he certainly ought to see that they are properly advised as to the practical results of their policies and the limitation of resources available for the purpose, so that they can adapt their ideas to secure the result most acceptable to them.

Here also is an indication of the purpose of having a detached Chief Executive. He is someone to whom the council will look to secure a co-ordinated approach to the affairs of the authority and to eliminate the competition between departments for the allocation of scarce resources. He may do this by drawing up a corporate plan or programme budget. He may do it by monitoring the reports made to committees by his colleagues and by carefully moderating his own advice. He may do it by means of his influence in the management team. The vital point is that he, and he alone, has no departmental axe to grind and he is thus in a unique position to assist the council in fulfilling their policy ambitions.

Impelementation of programme and policies

3. Through his leadership of the officers' management team he is responsible for the efficient and effective implementation of the council's programmes and policies and for securing that the resources of the authority are most effectively deployed towards those ends.

It has long been the practice in well run local authorities for the chief officers to hold regular meetings at which the Clerk of the Council would normally act as chairman. Sometimes these were formal meetings and sometimes not but either way they served a useful purpose in co-ordinating the approach of different departments to problems of common concern. The Royal Commission on Local Government in England took advantage of this idea to urge the formation in every authority of a Central Management Group of Officers as an essential cog in the management wheel. An independent chairman, in the person of the Chief Executive, is an important ingredient to the success of this venture.

Review of organisation

4. Similarly he shall keep under review the organisation and administration of the authority and shall make recommendations to the council through the Policy and Resources Committee if he considers that major changes are required in the interests of effective management.

The Chief Executive may be a member of any discipline but, whatever other talents he may possess, there is no doubt that he must be a trained, experienced and capable administrator. It may be thought, and indeed it has been so argued, that he is merely duplicating the work of the secretary but that is not what is intended. The Chief Executive is not invited to concern himself with the routine legal work, or licences for lotteries, or control of supplies, or whatever it might be. His administrative contribution is to be pitched at a higher level altogether.

It should be the duty of a Chief Executive to assess the performance of his colleagues and their departments and to advise the council when changes ought to be made in the structure. Sections are set up from time to time to perform a particular activity. Later, circumstances change; perhaps legislation is repealed. The section is no longer serving its original purpose; possibly some of its present duties are being duplicated in another department. The head of the department concerned is not the best person to draw attention to the anomaly. Self-criticism is not everyone's strong suit and habit may be so ingrained that it may not even be noticed that some streamlining is overdue. This is but one possible example; it is at least equally possible that a council committee could become superfluous and go undetected by members. The Chief Executive who is free of departmental responsibility is the person who should have the time, the seniority and the independence to make major reappraisals of this kind.

Development of manpower policies

5. As head of the paid service it is his responsibility to ensure that effective and equitable manpower policies are developed and implemented throughout all departments of the authority in the interests both of the authoity and the staff.

The point has already been established that the Chief Executive must seek to relate his council's policy ambitions to the available resources. One of those resources is manpower and manpower planning may be recognised as a vital part of the general forward planning process for which the Chief Executive is responsible.

There is a great deal more to this than merely assessing and hiring the staff needed to carry out a particular programme. It is necessary to consider the manpower implications of any proposal, naturally, and sadly there is evidence that governments, both national and local, frequently overlook this fundamental requirement. There is a limit to the supply of qualified and experienced staff who can be engaged to help implement a programme and consequently recruitment and training must form an inherent part of any manpower plan.

It may be thought sufficient for the Chief Executive to ensure that each department pursues a sensible and forward-looking manpower policy. On the other hand it may be better to appoint a specialist Personnel Officer responsible for manpower planning and budgeting, wages and salaries, conditions of service, training, recruitment, job evaluation and, possibly, management services.

Internal and external relations

6. He is responsible for the maintenance of good internal and external relations.

As the council's principal officer the Chief Executive

occupies a key position in respect of the authority's relations with other people. He will be the chief contact with the public, the staff, contractors, Government departments, other local authorities and the reputation of the authority will depend very much on his personality and attitudes.

CHAPTER 9

THE ROLE OF THE MANAGEMENT TEAM

It has been a sensible practice of long standing for senior officers of local authorities to meet each other frequently to discuss affairs of common concern and thereby to keep the wheels of administration sufficiently lubricated. Such meetings, however, have usually been of an informal nature and the practice has varied widely in detail between one authority and another.

Informal meetings of chief officers

In relatively small authorities it was sometimes found convenient for the chief officers to meet very briefly each morning. This gave them the opportunity to discuss those items which appeared contentious or which were likely to have repercussions for more than one department. A co-ordinated response could in this way be agreed and all could be kept abreast of important developments. Such a method, however, is impractical for larger authorities, although the idea can be borrowed by any departmental head who wishes, to keep in touch with the work of his subordinates and to insist that they maintain proper liaison with each other.

In larger authorities the chief officers have obviously to be more selective in the matters they discuss among themselves. Some system of co-ordination between departments is clearly necessary. It would be quite indefensible for any department to operate in a water-tight compartment without taking account of the effect of its operations on the work of the whole organisation. But it is not possible to have detailed consultations at chief officer level. Heads of department should certainly liaise at their particular level and their collaboration should be supplemented by similar liaison between their subordinates. It is a matter of local choice whether such meetings take place on a regular and formal basis or whether the appropriate officers are simply brought together for a discussion whenever a particularly thorny problem arises.

Formation of central management group

The practice of holding regular meetings between senior officers has proved its worth over the years and it undoubtedly inspired the recommendation of the Royal Commission on Local Government that the Chief Executive should be the leader of a team of chief officers which would form the central management group. This group was to be the counterpart at official level of the Policy and Resources Committee and it was to be responsible for the preparation of plans and programmes in connection with long term objectives and for general coordination and implementation. Its success, the report commented, would depend on harnessing the enthusiasm of the specialist to the needs of central management.

The Bains Group took up the point, adding the comment that members of the Management Team would not sit as representatives of particular departments, though on occasion it would be necessary for them to speak in that capacity, but would be there as members of a body created to aid the management of the authority as a whole. Suggestions that a professional chief officer would be unable to make any valuable contribution to management affairs except within the confines of a particular discipline were firmly rejected. Indeed, some may consider themselves flattered that so odd an idea was treated seriously at all. The functions of the team are of a planning and co-ordinating nature. It is not for them to discuss technicalities which are properly the concern of one professional officer.

The formal nature of the group

In practice the success of a Management Team depends on many other factors than the enthusiasm and skill of its members. First, it depends upon the recognition by the council of the importance of the corporate approach to management and the vital role which the management team should play as an integral part of the administrative machinery. This means an end to the informality of old. Regular meetings should be held according to an established routine with formal agenda and decisions being fully minuted.

Relationship with Policy and Resources Committee

Second, it depends upon the establishment of a happy and equal working partnership with the Policy and Resources Committee. The committee will need to make clear decisions as to its programme and priorities and to give unequivocal instructions to the Management Team as to the matters upon which they are expected to reflect and report. For their part, the Management Team should see it as their duty to assess the implications of any proposal for the authority as a whole before submitting their recommendations to the Policy and Resources Committee.

Influence of the Chief Executive

Third, much depends upon the personality and ability of the Chief Executive as leader of the team. He will take the chair at meetings of the team and will be expected to guide the discussion and to weld the contributions of officers of differing personalities, trained in contrasting professional schools. The reports of the Management Team will be essentially the reports of the Chief Executive. Bains remarked that reports should generally be unanimous but provision should be made for strong minority views to be presented. That is all very well but the probability is that the council would normally look to the Chief Executive for a firm lead. No matter how talented the members of the Management

Team may be, their corporate effort will be disappointing if their leader is not an officer of the highest calibre.

The role of the individual members of the team

Fourth, the success of the team will depend upon the willingness of every member of it to play a full part. Each member will need to recognise that there are a multiplicity of roles to play, each as important as the others. A professional officer who is expected to give the Management Team the benefit of expert advice. The head of a department, or a group of departments, who will be expected to advise the team both as to the contribution that the department can make to a particular project and as to the effect on existing commitments of undertaking some additional objective. Each member is also, in certain respects, a lay member of a corporate team with a duty to offer an intelligent contribution to the discussion, even though the subject may not be one in which he or she is an acknowledged expert. The failure of any one member to contribute to the fullest extent will seriously reduce the value of much of the team's work.

Delegation to subordinate groups

Inevitably there will be a limit to the quantity of work that the Management Team can do entirely through its own efforts. If the local authority is progressive and enthusiastic and consequently makes heavy demands upon its Management Team, the answer probably lies in delegation to working parties or project teams comprising selected subordinates from the appropriate departments. For example, if the local authority should decide to embark upon a programme of general housing improvement and reclamation, a project team might be set up to work out the details. The Chief Executive's personal assistant or a senior administrator from the Secretary's Department might make a suitable chairman and the membership might comprise a legal officer, a senior officer of the Housing Department, an Environmental Health Officer, a surveyor, a senior accountant and a town planner. The Management Team would draw up their terms of reference and indicate the date by which their report was required. If thought appropriate, an interim report might be asked for. The Management Team would themselves consider the report of the project team, amend it or endorse it as they may decide and submit it in its approved form as their recommendation to the Housing Services Committee and eventually to the Council.

Postscript

Management teams are successful in some authorities but not in others. Much depends on the Chief Executive, the "chemistry" of the chief officers and the relationship with leading members. Much too, depends on the Management Team concentrating on issues that are the strategic and corporate, and not becoming yet another hurdle over which every detailed item must pass before it reaches the members.

CHAPTER 10

CENTRAL ADMINISTRATIVE FUNCTIONS

The administrative support that a local authority needs at the centre depends very much on local circumstances such as the size and character of the authority. What duties any central organisation is expected to carry out, and how these are distributed between service departments and the centre will also affect their size and possibly their organisation.

How central departments are organised also varies from authority to authority. They range from Chief Executives departments embracing the personnel, the Secretary's, computing and information technology functions, to those where each might be a separate department with its own Chief Officer. At many authorities the Chief Executive has no specific departmental responsibilities.

In the Chapters that follow, and in some previous ones specific reference may be made to the Secretary's role, but for reasons given above this may not apply at all authorities.

Perhaps what is most important is not the way these roles are organised but the ability of all central departments to provide an effective and efficient service to members, departments and the general public.

THE ORGANISATION OF DEPARTMENTS

It is impossible to administer any department comprising more than three or four people without giving powers of decision-making to subordinate members of the staff. The number of decisions to be made in a busy office will be considerable but the importance of those decisions will vary widely. To avoid any excessive concentration of routine responsibility on senior members of staff, the objective should be to allocate duties to the most junior member of the staff who is capable of dealing proficiently with them. It is an encouragement to younger administrators to find that their capabilities are recognised and they are permitted to make many of the decisions within their sphere of work without a surfeit of control from higher authority. At the same time, the more senior members of the staff are left free to give the maximum attention to the problems of real moment which only they have the experience and learning to decide.

Giving powers of decision to junior managers, however, does not free their superiors from the ultimate responsibility. There must be adequate supervision of their work so that they are not permitted to fall into serious error. Each must have ready access to an immediate superior to whom reference may be made in moments of difficulty.

Chain of command

What is required is a clear chain of command from the Chief Officer, through the assistant section heads, to chief, senior and junior assistants, as the case may be. It is not a good thing for a senior assistant to be responsible for supervision only. For the sake of personal job satisfaction and in order that employers should enjoy the full benefit of his skill and experience, an officer should have specific duties to discharge. If, in addition, he is expected to supervise too many people, some part of his work will inevitably suffer. It is difficult to be precise on the number of people that an officer should be responsible for. Much will depend of the variation of the work and the inter-relationship of those being supervised.

Division of responsibility

The Chief Officer may be well advised to compile a comprehensive list of duties of the department. This list should be exhaustive, including the most mundane tasks as well as those of great importance. Having done so, there are those duties which will normally require his personal attention. These should be relatively few. Bearing in mind the precept that work should devolve to the lowest acceptable level, it would be foolish to retain too much detail at the top level. The bulk of the work should be divided between the two or three assistant section heads. In what manner the work shall be divided is a matter of local preference and the organisational structure, but one possibility is the separation of legal work from administrative work with committee administration forming the third arm. The work of the Assistant Section heads would then be further subdivided and so on until the work load is equitably distributed.

Job descriptions

By this means a sectional organisation will be built up and the duties of individual members of staff precisely defined. A schedule of job descriptions can then be compiled which should include a clear and complete definition of the duties of every member of staff. This brings several advantages. Every task should be the specific duty of an identifiable officer. Nothing should be left to chance; that which is anyone's responsibility is no one's responsibility. Whenever a new task arises which is not within anyone's job description, it should be allocated to a suitable member of staff. If this is done properly, every officer should know the extent of his duties and cannot plead ignorance if he neglects any part of them. Not only will this allow salary questions to be fairly assessed but it should be possible to recognise which officers are overworked and which have some spare capacity and therefore to make a constructive approach to problems of manpower budgeting.

There is, however, a danger that sections will come to regard themselves as watertight compartments and individuals will come to regard their duties as mutually exclusive. It cannot be over-emphasised that the entire department —

and, for that matter, the entire council staff — is one team. Their duties are interdependent and all must be expected to assist in any way that may be required, particularly in times of stress, sickness and holidays. Job specifications must be drafted in such a way that no doubt is left on this point.

Duties of chief assistants

A vital factor is the relationship between the Chief Officer and chief assistants or section heads. Regular conferences would appear to be essential in order to co-ordinate the work of the different sections and to secure efficiency throughout the department. By these means the Chief Officer can discuss important management problems with principal subordinates and settle a uniform line of action, reviewing personally the progress of work in their sections and issue precise instructions on any matter that might be in doubt.

The duty of attending committee meetings is one to be shared between senior staff. It is best that officers should specialise in the work of particular committees, the Chief Officer taking the most important policy committees with assistants representing him at the remainder. As far as possible the same officer should attend a particular committee on a continuing basis. This gives the opportunity to become thoroughly familiar with all the committee's business and also to develop a relationship with the chairman and members. It is unlikely, however, that all the business will fall within the responsibility of one section. Whoever attends the meeting represents the whole department, including sections of which he is not the head. It is important, therefore, that he should discuss the agenda thoroughly with his colleagues beforehand and also report matters of concern to them afterwards.

A variant of this idea is used in servicing committee meetings when two officers might come from different sections of the department. For example, a solicitor and an administrative assistant might jointly represent the Chief Officer at meetings of a particular committee. The solicitor then handles any legal questions and his colleague does the administrative work. This method has obvious advantages but there is a natural tendency for officers in these circumstances to limit themselves to their own remit and for sections thereby to become watertight compartments.

Delegation

Having taken the essential trouble to make sure that his staff are fully capable of carrying out their responsibilities without detailed supervision, the Chief Officer should be prepared to delegate generously and confidently. The right type of subordinates thrive on responsibility and trust and, provided that they possess the required capacity and knowledge and have the good sense to know when to consult their immediate superiors, sound administration will result from the proper exercise of the power of delegation. It has been said that a chief officer must have time "to muse, to ponder and to plan". They cannot do this if constantly immersed in detail.

Once a decision has been taken to delegate, the Chief Officer must make sure that his subordinates fully understand what is expected of them. To some extent the job description will serve this purpose but it is also necessary to establish the standard of performance that the superior officer will demand. It is also essential that the subordinate should have the resources to do the job effectively. Having made the necessary provision, the superior officer must avoid the temptation to look constantly over the delegate's shoulder and must guard against the danger of over-reacting to his subordinate's occasional errors. That does not mean that a Chief Officer should attempt to shed the responsibility for supervision. Only if a reproof is necessary should one openly interfere but, on the other hand, never overlook the need to praise and to reward particularly good work.

Factors which should never be delegated include overall planning of departmental policies, appointments and promotion to key posts, major disciplinary action and ultimate accountability.

Esprit de corps

Surprisingly, it is not always appreciated that a happy staff is usually an efficient staff. Where a harmonious relationship exists, staff are encouraged to give of their best and good results are thus obtained. Conversely, wherever there is bickering and ill-feeling staff morale becomes low and efficiency suffers.

For these reasons, a good Chief Officer should give high priority to the development of a happy family spirit throughout the department. Ideally, every member of his staff should be pleased and proud to be one of the team. A Chief Officer can set a good example, by taking a personal interest in each Member of staff, whom he should know and address by name, never neglecting to give them a pleasant greeting, whenever appropriate. It may be going too far to suggest that everyone should have unrestricted access to the Chief Officer in person as this might interfere unduly with his professional duties but no one should be discouraged from seeking an interview. Personal problems, even those of a health or matrimonial kind having no direct connexion with the office, can seriously impair performance and it is worth sparing time to assist those seeking advice. It is important, however, that discipline should not be undermined by permitting junior officers to appeal to their departmental chief over the heads of their section leaders. Any grievance of this kind must be dealt with through the formal procedure.

To preserve harmony, there must be an equality of treatment for all staff and it should be made plain to all supervisory staff that either favouritism or victimisation, will not be tolerated.

Value of staff suggestions

A good Chief Officer should try to recognise the particular skill and aptitudes of individual officers. It is his duty to pick the right person for the right job and, having done so, should not hesitate to give him responsibility and encouragement. Many benefits can be achieved by inviting staff to make suggestions at any time relating to the manner of doing their jobs or as to the efficiency of the department at large. Not only may many such suggestions be of value in themselves but staff who are in an enquiring and constructively critical frame of mind are likely to make steady improvement in the standard of performance of their jobs.

THE ROLE OF THE SECRETARY

The Secretary and the decision making process

The precise definition of the Secretary's job, as with any officer who is not limited to a statutory function, will depend upon local circumstances and local decisions. It is probably fair to say, however, that this is the department most closely concerned with the decision making process. In this respect it is to be distinguished from those service departments which exist to perform a particular function or group of functions. Examples of the latter kind are housing, town planning, education or the social and welfare services. A distinction also needs to be drawn between the secretary's department and other centralised departments such as finance, valuation and estate management. The latter have a factor in common with the Secretary to the extent that all exist to provide support to the service departments of the authority. All of them provide expert help of one kind or another but it is the Secretary's particular and distinctive responsibility to manage many functions by which the threads of policy are woven together.

The Secretary and "policy space"

Professor J. D. Stewart has coined a graphic phrase to define the role of the Secretary as the "geographer of the policy space of the authority". How successful he may be will largely depend upon the personality of the individual. He can, if inclined, take a purely negative attitude, merely advising the council when a proposal is *ultra vires* or is otherwise subject to legalistic objection and, in every other respect, leaving them to work out their own salvation. On the other hand he can take a positive view of his duties, not only warning of difficulties but pointing out, whenever possible, alternative ways by which the desired objectives can be achieved. To make further use of Professor Stewart's expression, the Secretary can seek to extend the boundaries of policy space by explaining and interpreting legislation as enabling the local authorities to exercise a greater freedom of choice rather than by concentrating on the limitations that legislation imposes upon them.

The Secretary and co-ordination

The Bains Report defined the "prime roles" of the Secretary's Department as the provision of a secretariat for the council, for all committees and for the Management Team and to assist the Chief Executive's co-ordinative capacity. In this respect the reasoning appears to be somewhat weaker than in other parts of the report. The authors of the report had already said in an earlier chapter that they failed to see much merit in the appointment of a Deputy Chief Executive to match the former post of Deputy Clerk of the Council. They commented that it would be difficult for other chief officers to accept a someone who, whilst not senior to them in grade, would inevitably sit closer to the centre of affairs.

The Secretary is not *primus inter pares* the other principal chief officers as the former Clerk of the Council was. He is their equal and each, according to Bains, may be considered deputy to the Chief Executive within his own particular sphere. It may reasonably be said that it is the duty of every departmental head to assist the Chief Executive's co-ordinative capacity. To single out the Secretary for special mention is to appear to put him into a particularly close relationship with the Chief Executive which might well be resented by other principal chief officers. This could especially be so if the object is to provide within the

Secretary's Department a team of specialist co-ordinators for the benefit of the Chief Executive. The argument for appointing a Chief Executive without a department rests largely on the fact that the Chief Executive can call upon help whenever required from any and every department. If specialist co-ordinators are needed, it is submitted that it is better to appoint them directly to the Chief Executive's personal staff than to hide them under the umbrella of one department.

The Secretary's departmental functions

In addition to the council secretariat, there are several functions which fall naturally under the general heading of central administration some of which come clearly within the normal ambit of the Secretary. These functions include the full range of legal services, local land charges, elections and electoral registration and a variety of licensing and registration responsibilities. At the smaller authorities they may also include personnel management, public relations, archives, management services, district officers and common office services like printing and central control of supplies. These functions will be considered in their due turn.

The Bains Report also referred to certain specialist services used in the management process which do not justify separate departmental status. The examples quoted are Research and Intelligence, Organisation and Methods, Work Study, and Project Control. The authors recommend that "in the interests of administrative efficiency" these services should be located as sections within the Secretary's Department for day-to-day control "and to provide the necessary internal supervision" but should nevertheless be accountable to the Management Team.

Again, this recommendation appears most odd. There appear to be no pressing reasons why these services should necessarily lie within the Secretary's Department at all. Certainly the first and the last are matters that might best be under the personal control of the Chief Executive, assuming him to be the local authority's corporate planner.

It is hard to see what administrative efficiency can be hoped for from the proposed division of responsibility.

The Secretary and communication

As the principal chief officer most closely identified with the decision making process, the Secretary also has a number of intangible but vital parts to play. Some of these may be grouped under the general heading of communication. The exchange of relevant information is an essential part of decision making and the Secretary occupies a key position both for gleaning and disseminating information. There is, of course, a steady supply of official information — Government circulars, statistics, official correspondence of one kind or another — which the Secretary ought to bring to the notice of committees, the Management Team or individual officers who are handling the subject matter. But, less obviously, there is an unlimited quantity of unofficial information — straws in the wind, expressions of opinion, indication of trends — which should be recognised and acted upon. Thus a remark made *sotto voce* by a member of a committee, although not vitally relevant to the matter immediately under discussion, may be an important clue to the way in which members' minds are working, and, if conveyed to the proper quarter, may enable an officer to allay a lot of misgivings in a subsequent report to another committee.

The flow of information

There are four sources from which the Secretary and his staff can glean such information, that is from members of the council, from members of the council staff including his fellow chief officers, from colleagues in his professional society or association, and from the public. He will not merely use this knowledge to qualify advice to the council and committees but will pass on information, as may be appropriate, to members, to the Chief Executive and the Management Team and to other departments. He may also draw on this knowledge when giving instructions to staff, when answering enquiries from the public and when speaking at professional meetings. Thus the flow of information may be seen as a complete two-way process in which an alert and intelligent Secretary has a very important role to play.

The maintenance of administrative machinery

Another intangible part of the Secretary's role is that of keeping the decision making machinery in working order. He must, for example, make sure that the terms of reference to committees are kept up to date, taking into account changes in legislation and variations in working practices. It is usually an illustration of the Secretary's failure if there is duplication between two committees or between two departments. Other examples are the revision of standing orders and the overhaul of internal organisational structures. If possible, the Secretary should try to make sure that a vacuum does not exist. The range of services provided by a local authority is constantly changing. It is very easy for a problem to arise that does not appear to come within the province of any department. Often it will seem simple for the Secretary, as the recognised (if unofficial) custodian of the bits and pieces of administration to take the responsibility upon himself. Generally, however, it is better that he should arrange for the organisational structure to be changed so that the matter comes within the ambit of the most appropriate department.

Relationship of the Secretary with the Chief Executive

It has been suggested in this chapter that the Bains Working Group really did not do very well when they attempted to define the division of responsibility between the Chief Executive and the Secretary. It cannot be said overemphatically that a harmonious relationship between the two is essential to the efficient working of the authority and this will only be achieved if both clearly understand their respective roles.

The Chief Executive's role may be likened to that of an

architect. He is concerned with wide policy implications, with corporate planning and project control as well as being the co-ordinator and the leader of the Management Team. He is closely concerned with the realisation (but not the formulation) of political objectives. The Secretary's task is to keep in first class working order the administrative machinery whereby policy is determined and to provide efficient common administrative functions.

CHAPTER 11

PERSONNEL MANAGEMENT AND MANAGEMENT SERVICES

Personnel management is certain to form an important part of any local authority. Notwithstanding the recommendation of the Bains Report that the head of the personnel department should have direct access to the Chief Executive and should not be a subordinate of the Director of Administration, some will have the personnel function under the umbrella of this department. Even if that is not so, any Chief Officer will still have to give a large slice of time to problems of manpower affecting the members of their departments.

MANPOWER PLANNING

A consistent weakness of local government and the way it is administered is that local authorities have always tended to react to circumstances after they have developed instead of thinking ahead and trying to influence the course of events. In no field is this truer than in that of manpower planning. Manpower planning may be defined as the integration of manpower policies, practices and procedures so as to achieve the right number of the right people in the right jobs at the right time. In local government this is something that traditionally has been left almost entirely to chance. School leavers may have been recruited solely because there happened to be a vacancy for a junior clerk at a given moment and their subsequent training is carried out in a haphazard fashion, largely according to the inclinations of the recruit. Policies are determined with real regard to money being available but usually without any regard for the availability of the necessary manpower to carry the policy into effect. Any difficulties in this respect, if tackled at all, are normally dealt with by advertising a vacancy in the hope of attracting applicants from the service of other local authorities.

Fortunately there is evidence that some local authorities are beginning to recognise the need for coherent manpower planning policies. We have observed, in an earlier chapter, that policy decisions must be linked to the availability of resources. Manpower differs from other forms of resource in the fact that the local authority can never acquire it outright. If specialist staff are unwilling to work for a particular local authority, that local authority will have no means of translating its policies into effect. It is therefore of paramount importance to plan the deployment of manpower in such a way as will secure both effectiveness and employee satisfaction.

Benefits of manpower planning

The reasons for manpower planning are that the local authority should:

(*a*) be persuaded to formulate its political objectives in terms that can be translated into effect by the staff available for the purpose.

(*b*) be persuaded to tailor its staff structure to fit the tasks that it will be given to do.

(*c*) be persuaded to examine the skills and aptitudes of the people it employs in order to establish whether these talents are being effectively utilised.

(*d*) be persuaded to consider its recruitment and training policies in the light of their true cost-effectiveness and usefulness in the long term.

(*e*) be persuaded of the importance of anticipating their future staffing needs and the necessity of providing for them in good time.

(*f*) be able to meet its objectives as quickly and effectively as possible, at the least cost and to the maximum satisfaction of everyone concerned, not least the employees involved.

Analysis of demand for staff

Any manpower plan must depend upon the interrelationship of two factors, the expected demand for staff and the likely supply of staff to meet the demand.

Forecasting demand is particularly difficult in the public service where policies are liable to change from year to year with shifts of the political climate. Nevertheless there is a broad base of demand which is virtually permanent. The number of maintenance staff, for example, is dictated by the number of houses to be maintained. The effect of council house sales could effect the number required. Equally, falling school rolls will affect the demand for teachers while other departments may need to expand.

A decision, therefore, needs to be made as to the period for which a forecast can reasonably be attempted. An attempt might be made to predict up for four years ahead (a period that coincides with the life of a council) but room must be left for annual adjustment. As with other plans, manpower plans cannot be considered immutable.

The prediction must take into account a large number of factors, national and local policies so far as they are known or can be reasonably anticipated, movements of population, natural developments or contractions of the existing work load, purchases of labour-saving equipment, development of new methods of working (for instance, computerisation of clerical tasks) and improvements in organisational efficiency.

Analysis of supply of staff

A sound personnel records system is a prerequisite of any attempt to analyse the probable availability of staff in the future. Such records must include details of each employee's education, qualifications and training records, age, length of service with the authority and standard of performance.

An assessment will need to be made of likely staff movements in the period under review. Given complete and accurate records, it should be possible to identify within tolerable limits the officers of whom most are likely to remain with the authority for an indefinite period, those on the promotion ladder who are likely to be on the move before long, and those who are not committed to a local government career but who may be easy to replace anyhow.

It may be assumed that the wastage in each category may be the same as the average for previous years or it may be necessary to make adjustments to allow for external factors, such as changes in community groups eg numbers of school children or elderly population or a demand for qualified staff stimulated by new legislation.

Matching supply to demand

The assessment of probable supply and demand will indicate whether there is likely to be a shortage or surplus of manpower, both generally and in specified areas, and will enable a constructive attitude to be taken in recruitment and training attitudes. If investigation reveals that there is likely to be a severe shortage of qualified and experienced staff in any particular category, this fact should be pointed out at an early stage as policies will need to be modified accordingly. It is pointless to adopt policies, however desirable, unless the means are available of carrying them out.

SELECTION OF STAFF

One of the most important ingredients of good administration is the selection of the right people for the right jobs. It is surprising, therefore, how little attention is often given to the choice of staff. Frequently it seems that a short list is prepared on arbitrary and irrelevant criteria and the final choice is made purely on the basis of hunch.

Attracting the right applicants

The first truism is that the right person cannot possibly be chosen if that person is not an applicant for the post. Yet the local government press regularly carries advertisements of situations vacant that give no details of the job beyond its title and salary. If the employing authority have any idea of the type of person they are looking for, they appear to be at pains to conceal the fact from prospective applicants. Considerable care should be taken in drafting advertisements. It is very much to the benefit of the local authority as well as the candidates for appointment that prospective applicants should be able to tell whether they have the qualifications and experience which will be required.

If the office is well administered, a job description will already exist giving the basic information of duties, salary grading and the professional qualifications and experience required. The occurrence of a vacancy is an opportune time to do a thorough job analysis examining in depth the qualities required and their relative importance. For example, the job description of a private secretary may call for both shorthand and typing but, if dictation is only a minor part of the job, fast shorthand may be less important than a high standard of typewriting, whilst initiative, discretion and elocution may be more important than either. If these points are established from the beginning, the likelihood of picking out the right person is much improved.

Care should also be taken to place the advertisement in the journals where it is most likely to be seen by the type of people it is aimed at, and also to monitor the success rate of different advertising media.

Selecting the right short list

Having taken the trouble to ensure, as far as possible, that the most suitable people apply for the job, it is necessary to make certain that the best of them are invited for interview. The system of selection by interview has been criticised as

an imperfect method of assessing the merits of different candidates. Whilst this is undoubtedly true, no one has thought of a satisfactory alternative; the only safeguard against error is to conduct the interviews with skill and judgment. The persons charged with the duty of selecting the short list will need to have certain basic information about the applicants, their age, education, professional qualifications and previous experience being among the data normally required. Many local authorities also arrange training for those who interview staff, since it is a most important task.

It will usually be a good thing to supply a standard application form calling for the essential information to be stated. A relative novice often lacks skill in compiling a job application; it would be a pity to lose the right applicant because of inexperience in advancing his or her cause. It is a different matter with senior staff. No one seeking a senior post should be fundamentally incompetent but the manner in which an application is presented may provide valuable clues as to initiative, literacy and intellect. Indeed it should form part of the interview process. In every case, however, an opportunity might be created to send to every potential applicant a full job description and greater details than can be included in a Press advertisement. It pays to make sure that applicants know precisely what the job is that they are seeking.

In weighing the claims of one candidate against another, those choosing the short list should try to assess those factors which have an effect on his ability to do the job. Such arbitrary devices as eliminating all applicants under thirty or over fifty, should not be used unless there are genuine reasons why such persons might be at a disadvantage. A random purge of this kind is unfair to applicants and might result in the elimination of an outstanding candidate.

The interviews

As a general principle, it seems fair that those who know what is required and have the responsibility for getting the job done, should have the right and duty to pick the staff to do it. There can be no hard and fast rule but councillors might well be expected to leave all but the most senior appointments to their chief officers and appropriate section heads. If members are to be concerned in the selection process, they will need to be very fully briefed on the requirements of the job in addition to having all the available information about the candidates, such as their application forms and references. Without this information, the most conscientious member cannot rise above a superficial level of questioning and the inevitability of selection by hunch. Training of members in interviewing techniques might be considered or be regarded as essential.

Some people pay no attention to references, which they always regard as suspect. However, not many people supply references that are patently false and the opinion of someone who has known the candidate for years must have some value in augmenting the impression given by the applicant in a short interview. It should be remembered, though, that the referee has been nominated by the candidate and is someone whom the candidate expects to write in his favour. The most revealing part of a reference is often the things that the referee leaves out. A telephone call to the referee, particularly the present employer is an essential part of the appointment process which may prove to be very enlightening. Wherever possible, it is a good plan to put one or two questions to the candidate for the deliberate purpose of verifying the accuracy of references.

The art of questioning

The pattern of questioning needs to be properly planned beforehand. The object of the exercise is to find as much about the candidate as possible in a very short space of time. Thus splitting the interview panel into small groups, each concentrating on a specific aspect, ending with a more general forum, ensures that the candidates suitability is adequately probed. Candidates should always be put at ease right away and given a comfortable chair where they can see and hear distinctly. The aggressive questioning favoured by some interviewers is without merit. A candidate's ability to stand up to cross-examination is no test of ability to do a normal job of work, under stress or otherwise, and is unlikely to do justice to the process if he is driven on to the defensive by the questioner. However, for some posts coping with pressure or aggressive behaviour may be a requirement that needs to be assessed.

Questions should all be short and open-ended. Whilst the interviewer is talking, nothing is being learned about the candidate. Questions that indicate an obvious answer or which call solely for a Yes or No get the interview nowhere either. Interviewers should guard against the temptation to show off and, should suppress any line of questioning which is apparently designed to demonstrate the superiority of the questioner. The art of good interviewing is to keep the spotlight continuously on the candidate.

The final selection

The job analysis will have indicated the qualities required to do the job and their relative importance. These may be categorised in the manner of the following example.

(*a*) Impact, e.g. Appearance, Speech, Conduct etc.

(*b*) Qualifications, e.g. Education, Training, Experience etc.

(*c*) Skill, e.g. Intellect, Aptitude, Dexterity etc.

(*d*) Motivation, e.g. Ambition, Enthusiasm etc.

(*c*) Adjustment, e.g. Versatility, Adaptability etc.

Agreement may be reached beforehand of a standard of marking in each category, calling for a higher mark in the more important categories. To procure independent assessments and reduce the possibility of prejudice, interviewers may be required to mark their papers at the end of each interview independently and defer any comparison until all interviews are complete.

A candidate who fails to reach an agreed minimum standard in any one category would naturally be eliminated as unsuitable. Those who score most heavily, particularly in the key categories, are likely to be the ones seriously considered. But interviewing is not a game and the highest scorer need not be the winner. If two or more candidates reach the desired standard there is no reason why the Chief Officer should not exercise a personal preference, perhaps for the person who would get on best with existing staff.

CONTRACTS OF EMPLOYMENT

An employment contract may take any form, be it written, oral, by conduct, or by a combination of any of them. The normal rule of offer and acceptance applies and the simple act of turning up for work may be sufficient acceptance of a previous offer. However, the Contracts of Employment Act 1972, requires an employer to give, within thirteen weeks of appointment, a written note of the major terms of the contract, such as pay, holidays, period of notice and sickness benefits. A reference to a national scheme of conditions of service, such as the "purple book" for administrative, professional, technical and clerical staffs, is sufficient. The note is only a reminder of the main items in the contract and is not the contract itself. The law will therefore enforce oral terms, even if they are not confirmed in writing, and will imply others from normal usage. All the provisions of the purple book will probably be presumed to apply to a relevant appointment unless they are expressly varied. On appointment, information should be given to the employee on such matters as job content, training, promotion, discipline and grievance procedure.

The statutory period of notice to terminate an officer's appointment is based upon length of service. The employing authority's power to dismiss, however, is now severely restricted as the employer must either be able to rebut claims for redundancy and unfair dismissal or pay the appropriate compensation. In order to rebut a claim for unfair dismissal, the employer is required to prove a valid ground for discharge, such as incompetence, incapacity or misconduct, and must also show that the industrial code of practice has been followed in the matter of previous warnings and consideration of explanations. This makes it necessary for the personnel manager to keep detailed records since the burden of proof is on the employing authority. Claims for unfair dismissal are considered in the first instance by conciliation officers and then, in the same manner as redundancy claims, by an industrial tribunal.

TRAINING

A relatively small number of local government officers enters the service already trained and qualified for the duties they will have to perform. The bulk of career officers, however, begin as school leavers or graduate entrants with the intention of undertaking part-time study for the professional examinations which they hope will lead to promotion. Local authorities, should advise and encourage their staff to undertake approved courses of study and training. It should be the duty of a responsible officer to interview entrants shortly after their appointment in order to provide them with initial guidance. This officer should be familiar with the training facilities available for the various professional examinations appropriate to the local government service, either locally or by correspondence course, not overlooking skills such as word processing and computer operating. If the authority has done its manpower planning adequately, it should be able to advise recruits of the avenues in which future advancement seems most probable. Further advice can be sought from education officers of the provincial councils.

Wherever possible, young officers of outstanding talent should be considered for secondment to attend full-time university or sandwich courses. The future of the local government service depends upon the encouragement of this type of officer. If officers cannot be spared full time, they should be encouraged to take up part-time study, including day release if appropriate.

Officers who enrol for courses of study approved by their employing authorities should receive their full salaries and their educational and other approved expenses. The facilities would be withdrawn if an officer fails to make satisfactory progress or to sit for the examination at the due time.

Some authorities make it a condition of their assistance that an officer shall remain in their service for two years after qualifying. This practice is often of doubtful merit. Officers cannot, in fact, be compelled to remain in their posts against their will although they may be called upon to repay the whole of their financial assistance (other than salary) if they take posts outside the local government service. It may be borne in mind that the officer has been of progressively greater value to the employing authority during the period of training and, in moving on to higher things with another local authority, this may be classed as a contribution to a qualified service from which the employing authority will no doubt gain in its turn.

Apart from formal training for examinations, local authorities can assist their staffs in a variety of ways. Seconding officers to another authority or another department for a spell is one way, attendance at summer schools, seminars and refreshers is another. Junior staff may be given the chance to sit in committee meetings; arrangements may be made for more experienced officers to visit new works, institutions and exhibitions. However senior and well qualified an officer may be, the possibility of acquiring valuable new knowledge is never exhausted. Developing senior management is indeed a major task for local authorities who now face problems which are as much managerial as professional.

Local government training board

The Local Government Training Board was established in 1968 to ensure that the total training effort of local authorities was adequate to meet the present and future needs of the service. The Board is financed by a direct allocation from the Rate Support Grant.

The objectives of the Board may now be stated as follows:

(*a*) To establish patterns of training for various occupations employed in local government and to ensure that necessary resources are available;

(*b*) To encourage the provision of "on-the-job" training;

(*c*) To provide advice and support services, usually in the form of training recommendations and the publication of a regular "newsletter";

(*d*) To carry out research and development of training on behalf of local authorities collectively.

PROMOTION AND GRADING

The grading structure of every local authority department (which, in the accepted jargon, is called the "establishment") is determined by allocating a number of posts sufficient to cover the duties to be performed and by choosing a suitable salary grade for each post by reference to the responsibilities attaching to it. The salary grades are contained in the National Scheme of Conditions of Service ("the purple book") agreed between representatives of the local authorities and their staffs.

Annual review for salary grading purposes

The purple book requires that an establishment shall be reviewed at regular intervals and it is generally found advisable to do this annually around the end of the calendar year at the smaller authorities, but is part of the regular process at the larger ones. Duties and responsibilities do change with the passage of time and staff who find their work enriched naturally look for additional pay.

Whilst any officer who so wishes must be permitted to make a submission to the Establishment Review Sub-Committee personally, the review should cover all members of staff both in fairness to the staff as a whole and in order that the reviewing panel shall have a complete picture of the department and its activities. For this purpose a comprehensive report is needed from the Head of the Department.

To be of real value, such a report must make an appraisal and evaluation of the tasks performed by each officer. The purple book requires a report, prepared according to a common standard, to be submitted in respect of an officer who has completed one year's service, conveying the views of the Head of Department on the officer's character and personality, capacity, performance and fitness for promotion. Similar reports may be submitted annually but few authorities seem to do this.

Promotion to a higher grade is dependent upon the existence of a vacancy in that grade and upgrading depends upon the recognition of additional duties and responsibilities. Selection of staff for appointment or promotion is on merit and the possession of the necessary qualifications. It is essential that the personnel manager should keep detailed records of the performance and potential of every member of staff so that, when a vacancy arises, the claims of every officer having the right qualifications and experience might be fairly assessed. The doubt is whether any purpose is served by submitting such reports of the annual review when no vacancies are due to be filled.

Staff Appraisal

This is not to say that no review of an officer's performance is required. On the contrary such reviews need to be carried out on a systematic basis and, if officers fail to reach the standard expected, the matter should be discussed with them in order that a determined effort is made to overcome their shortcomings. Some authorities relate such a staff appraisal system to their staff training programmes, while a few relate it also to merit payments.

STAFF WELFARE AND CONDITIONS OF SERVICE

Reference has already been made to the "purple book" — the National Scheme of Conditions of Service for Administrative, Professional, Technical and Clerical Staffs. This is an agreement made at national level by the accredited representatives of the employing councils and the staffs in question and is continually reviewed and kept up to date by them. It is invariably adopted as part of the contracts of employment of the individual members of staff to whom it relates and, in this way, changes in salary grades, holiday entitlement, or other conditions of service are applied automatically without the need for local negotiations. Similar agreements exist for other local authority staffs, such as police, fire and probation officers, and manual workers.

Consultation is nevertheless often necessary at local level and local authorities have been recommended to set up Local Joint Consultative Committees for both their salaried staffs and manual operatives. Such committees should properly consist of an equal number of councillors and employees, with the chairmanship going to both groups in turn.

The welfare of the staff will engage much of the attention of the appropriate local joint committee but, a Head of Department will surely wish to create conditions in which his staff will do their best work without having to be prompted to do so. The Offices, Shops and Railway Premises Act lays down minimum standards in such matters as lighting and ventilation and a considerate Chief Officer will hope to persuade the council to provide working conditions somewhat higher than the minimum. If staff have to stay for meals, either at midday or in the evening, suitable dining facilities or, at least, an adequate mess room ought to be provided. It is a good thing for staff to be encouraged to provide for their own material comfort instead of relying wholly on their employer. A happy family spirit can be engendered in this way and facilities can be provided by private effort which it would not be appropriate to charge to public funds. The Head of Department can play a part by participating to a reasonable extent in the activities organised by the staff welfare committee and by giving permission for the committee's officials to perform their honorary duties in office hours whenever these will not interfere with their official tasks. One can justify this small privilege by the argument that a contented staff will produce more and better work than one that is dissatisfied.

Local authorities conditions of service advisory board

In order to carry out collective negotiations at national level with the representatives of the relevant trades unions and professional staff associations, the local authorities need machinery backed by an expert advisory service on manpower questions. For these reasons the Local Authorities Conditions of Service Advisory Board was set up in 1948. The name, commonly shortened to LACSAB, is now rather out of date. The name "Local Government Manpower Advisory Board" would better represent the range of the Board's functions, since it not only provides the secretariat for the Employers' Sides in national negotiations but it also provides a manpower advisory service to all local authorities.

To do its work effectively, the Board needs to be sensitive to the local situation in every part of the country. They are assisted in this task by a network of provincial councils, each with a full-time staff, to which each local authority is able to appoint at least one member. These provincial councils interpret national agreements at regional level and endeavour to resolve disputes. They are also frequently asked for their views on salary claims and other national manpower questions. This is known as "the Sounding Board Procedure".

LACSAB maintains close contact with other bodies in the manpower field, such as the Local Government Training Board (LGTB) and the Local Authorities Management Services and Computer Committee (LAMSAC).

DISCIPLINE AND GRIEVANCE PROCEDURE

The chief officer of any department is responsible for the discipline of staff. It is most important that he should at all times exercise authority justly and judicially and strictly in compliance with agreed procedures. Having regard to the possibility of his actions being examined by an appeals tribunal, a complete written record needs to be kept of everything done, including any verbal rebuke administered to a member of staff.

Where an officer's work or conduct calls for disciplinary action, a warning should be administered. If the officer is interviewed it is preferable that the warning be confirmed by letter. In a case of gross misconduct the officer may be suspended from duty forthwith and the matter reported to the appropriate committee. If an officer is proposed to be dismissed, a letter must be sent to the officer concerned, signed by the chief officer, stating the reasons for the proposed disciplinary action. The officer is permitted to appeal within seven days and has the right to appear before the appeals committee of the council, either personally or through his trade union representative. An agreed procedure for hearing such appeals is contained in the purple book.

Apart from disciplinary matters, officers are entitled to appeal to their employing authority in the first instance and subsequently, if still aggrieved, to the Provincial Council on any question relating to conditions of service, including salary. The Appeals Committee of the Provincial Council invariably consists of an equal number of councillors and staff representatives. The procedure is comparatively informal but is judicial and thorough.

The Code of Industrial Relations Practice contains outline suggestions for grievance procedures. Such procedures are established by collective agreement and local authorities have been advised to negotiate them, and any variations in them, with the representatives of their employees. LACSAB is available to provide advice to any local authority that asks for it.

On the basis that any grievance is best settled as near as possible to its point of origin, a model procedure could suitably provide for a complainant to discuss a grievance in the first instance with his immediate supervisor. If this does not resolve the matter, the question may then be referred to the departmental head (who might appropriately ask the complainant's trade union representative to discuss the matter). Provision might be made for further reference, if necessary, to the employing authority and to the Provincial Council.

Whatever procedure is adopted, all staff should be supplied with a copy and the complainant should be kept fully informed at all times of the steps that are being taken to resolve the issue.

HEALTH AND SAFETY AT WORK

The Health and Safety at Work Act 1974, augmented the health and safety provisions of earlier legislation, notably the Factories Act 1961, and the Offices, Shops and Railway Premises Act 1967. It placed a duty upon every employer to ensure, so far as reasonably practicable, the health, safety and welfare at work of all employees. It also imposed a corresponding duty in relation to the health and safety of persons not in employment but who might nevertheless be affected by the employer's activity. A duty is therefore owed by local authorities to any member of the public visiting local authority premises or otherwise coming into contact with local authority activities, a category that appears to include children attending local authority schools.

It is essential to ensure that members and officers, particularly those with managerial or supervisory responsibilities, are conversant with the obligations of local authorities towards their own employees or the general public and are kept informed of regulations and codes of practice issued under the Act. Employees should also be made aware of their own responsibilities in the matter.

The Act provides machinery for the service of Prohibition Notices and Improvement Notices. Responsible officers should be familiar with the procedure and must be required to report to their superiors any discussions with enforcement inspectors on such notices. Upon receipt of a notice, the possibility of an appeal to an Industrial Tribunal will need to be considered.

A Chief Officer should be made responsible for implementation of that part of the Act which requires the local authority, as an employer, to prepare and revise from time to time a written statement of the authority's safety policy and the organisation and arrangements currently in force for carrying it out. This statement has to be brought to the notice of all employees.

MANAGEMENT SERVICES

The practices of local authority administration have changed considerably in recent years with the development of advanced modern management techniques. Local government reorganisation acted as a catalyst to this movement, particularly in those authorities that are strongly led by their Policy and Resources Committee and their Chief Executive. The study of the whole range of management activities is virtually a profession in itself and here we shall not attempt to do more than indicate some of the uses to which management techniques can be put by the local government administrator.

Computers and Information Technology

Because of the departmentalism prevalent in many of the former authorities, Chief Officers tended to recognise the value of computers only in their own restricted sphere and, because its application to financial procedures was most obvious, the computer was thought of by many people solely as a tool of financial management. This came about also because financial work was large in volume terms (e.g. the number of ratepayers), many aspects were repetitive (e.g. weekly payroll) and computerisation could therefore be costs justified.

The financial applications of the computer are, of course, considerable. In one local authority much computer time is absorbed in payments to staff, grants to students, costing of items such as school meals and office supplies and calculating and allocating various management expenses.

But there are important non-financial uses as well. Records are maintained of all children receiving education, parents and doctors are notified of appointments and the content of school meals is analysed. Information is provided to highways engineers about road accidents and contour measurements. The needs of handicapped people are registered. Crime statistics are stored for speedy reference by the police. Library books are catalogued so that special requests from borrowers can quickly be met. In addition electronic equipment has been revolutionary in the development. It is significantly cheaper, faster and easier to programme and use. As a result many applications for computers and word processors are being introduced. Computer terminals are now part of the everyday processes of many authorities. The electronic office is no longer a thought, it is possible, with wide ranging implications for the way in which organisations are structured, for the development of new skills, and the ability to bring more relevant information to managers and the general public.

Organisation and methods

Organisation and Methods (commonly referred to simply as O & M) is the name commonly given to techniques which examine the value of non-manual work. The use of such techniques may greatly assist the development of administrative procedures. The fields in which O & M may be suitably applied include the planning of duties and deployment of staff, the arrangement of available accommodation and use of equipment.

The aim of O & M is to secure maximum efficiency in the Council's organisation and, in examining any particular branch of the work, the questions to be asked are: What is the object to be achieved? Are the best possible results obtained? Is it done by the most efficient and economic method? It is therefore necessary to discover and carefully scrutinise the facts about the job, the people who do it, the way they do it and the cost of the operation.

A trained investigator will find it easier to detect flaws in the method of operation and unnecessary or duplicated work. But if specialist staff are not available, there is no reason why capable administrators should not achieve worthwhile results if they make systematic use of their critical faculties.

Indeed, there is a danger that managers will leave these questions to experts rather than seeing themselves as being predominantly responsible for the efficiency and effectiveness of their organisations. However, Managers need to recognise when they need outside help from management experts.

Work study and productivity schemes

Work study commonly relates to the examination of manual working methods and the measurement of output. It is often linked with bonus incentive and productivity schemes, the determination of manning levels and the provision of relevant information relating to the control of manual workers.

The technique has been used in local government for many years and has been responsible for many worthwhile improvements in operating methods. The movement received a fillip that was wholly artificial a few years ago because of the insistence of the Government of the day that all pay increases to public service workers must be linked to increased productivity. Under pressure from trades unions, local authorities engaged additional work study staff for the purpose of introducing bonus incentive schemes as the only acceptable means of paying their work force at competitive rates.

Bains commented that a large central work study unit was unnecessary but suggested a relatively small unit to control the overall deployment of work study staff in the interests of the authority as a whole. Individual departments would obtain the services of work study staff from the central unit to operate under the day to day control of line managers.

Upon reorganisation in 1974 there was also a substantial amount of administrative work to be done in rationalising and combining services. There were many instances of new authorities being faced with the problem of merging different bonus schemes for particular categories of worker. Many such schemes were an excuse just to pay more money rather than an attempt to obtain increased productivity. However since then many improvements in manual workers' productivity eg refuse collection, have been achieved and the emphasis in the future will be towards obtaining similar productivity improvements from non-manual staff. The efficient employment of manpower represents a continuing challenge to the administrator engaged in the field of work study.

CHAPTER 12

LEGAL FUNCTIONS

The link between the administrative and legal work of a local authority is a strong one and there are powerful precedents for concentrating the responsibility for both in the hands of the same officer. In the years immediately preceding the reorganisation of 1974, the appointment of anyone other than a lawyer as Town Clerk of a major county borough or as Clerk of a county council was so rare as to make national headline news whenever it occurred. Among the smaller urban and rural district councils the appointment of a lawyer-clerk was less customary but it was not by any means exceptional.

The Royal Commission on Local Government in England (1966–1969) recommended that the Clerk or Chief Executive should be chosen solely on the grounds of ability and the post should be open to members of all professions, including the lay administrator. The Bains Report took up the point when it said that

> the field of selection should not be restricted to those holding particular professional qualifications, nor indeed to those holding any. The important thing is to get the best man for the job.

The first Chief Executives of the new authorities appeared to be predominantly former lawyer-clerks. This was hardly surprising. Their training and broad experience with the former authorities gave them an advantage over others of equivalent ability who had pursued their careers up to that point in a narrower technical discipline. However the predominance has now changed with other professions particularly Treasurers, filling many Chief Executive positions.

Whether the local authority Secretary is or is not a lawyer by profession, many of the instincts of the lawyer will be necessary for such a post. "The Profile of a Chartered Secretary", published by the Institute of Chartered Secretaries and Administrators, defines the functions of the top administrator as including "Advice to the board of directors, or their equivalent, involving prior consultations and drawing attention to legal obligations" and "Maintenance of statutory and other records and, in many organisations, responsibility for certain legal work or for obtaining professional legal advice when needed".

In this chapter we shall examine the role of the council's chief legal adviser. In doing so, we shall be concerned only with the organisation of the legal section and not with the technical execution of its work, still less with the ability of any officer to fulfil it.

SOLICITORS ACT 1974

Reference must, however, be made to the statutory limitations imposed by the Solicitors Act 1974, which prohibits an unqualified person from acting as a solicitor. Expressly, such a person must not prepare any instrument relating to real or personal property or to any legal proceeding unless he can prove that he did not do so "for or in expectation of any fee, gain or reward". A person is not considered to be unqualified for this purpose if he is a barrister, a notary public or a public officer doing such work in the course of his duty.

To the words "public officer" different meanings can be given according to the statute in which the words occur. In 1949 the Lord Chief Justice, Lord Goddard, said in a judgment: "We have to consider whether in this Act the expression 'public officer' refers to any clerk of a local authority or whether it must not be given a stricter interpretation, that is to say, a public officer who is an officer of a public department . . . The words . . . should be limited to a public officer in the strict sense, that is to say, to an officer of a public department, whose salary is charged on national and not local funds". (*Beeston and Stapleford U.D.C. v. Smith* [1949] 1 K. B. 656.)

The Act to which Lord Goddard was referring was the Solicitors Act 1932, which has since been repealed but there is no reason to doubt that the same judicial interpretation applies to the identical words used in the current Solicitors. Act. A local government officer must not, therefore, undertake in his own name the professional work of conveyancing or litigation in the High Court and County Court unless he is a barrister or a solicitor in possession of a current practising certificate, but it is well established that a lawyer may be assisted by an unqualified person.

There is, however, other work, often conveniently classified as legal work, which may legitimately be undertaken by persons other than lawyers and it is a matter of discretion whether such work is performed in the legal section or otherwise.

THE LEGAL SECTION

If the Secretary happens to be a solicitor, whether or not there is any legally qualified assistance, no problem arises. He can properly undertake responsibility for all the council's legal work even though the bulk of it may be performed on his behalf by his lay staff.

In other cases, the legal section may be headed by a solicitor but may be placed, in parity with other sections, under the general umbrella of the Secretary's Department. The Secretary, though he may not be a lawyer, will take general responsibility in the Management Team for the routine operation of the legal section. This is in order so long as the solicitor retains personal responsibility for conveyancing and litigation. However, the legal officer will certainly expect, and should be granted, direct access to the council and the Management Team when it comes to advising them on delicate points of law.

A third possibility exists and that is that no member of the staff will be legally qualified. The Secretary will then be responsible for obtaining professional legal advice when needed and for giving instructions for the performance of legal work, such as conveyancing and litigation, by solicitors in private practice. So long as he obtains professional assistance when he should do so, there is no reason why the Secretary should not organise his department in such a way that all the work of a legal flavour is handled by a section staffed entirely by unadmitted legal executives.

Subdivision of Legal Work

The way in which the work of the legal section is apportioned will depend upon the quantity and nature of the tasks to be performed and upon the qualifications and skills of the available staff but the following model, adapted to suit local circumstances, might provide a useful pattern.

(1) Advocacy; Appearances in Court and before other tribunals, local inquiries and hearings; Drafting of preliminary written statements and submission of written representations under alternative procedures; Preparation of cases for Opinion of Counsel.

(2) Common Law Actions; Insurance claims by or against the council, including correspondence with insurance companies and, in appropriate circumstances, with potential claimants; Initial defence of legal proceedings against the council.

(3) Contracts and Agreements; Building Contracts; Agreements for Supply of Goods and Materials or for the Execution of Works; Licences; Tenancy Agreements.

(4) Conveyancing and Legal Drafting; Acquisition and Disposal of Freehold Property; Compulsory Purchase Orders; Oversight of terms of purchase by agreement.

(5) Debt Recovery; Rent and Rate Arrears and Overdue Accounts; Distraint; Notices to Quit and Recovery of Possession; exercise of Powers of Sale.

(6) Housing Advances and Mortgages; Applications for Loan Sanction; Completion and Custody of Mortgage Register, Deeds Register and Terrier of Property; Custody of Title Deeds and other Muniments.

(7) Promotion of Legislation; Opposition to Parliamentary Bills; Drafting and Promulgation of Local Byelaws and Regulations; Revision of Standing Orders and Terms of Reference; Review of new legislation and law reports and presentation to council of reports thereon and on legal matters generally.

(8) Prosecutions and proceedings under the Housing, Highways, Public Health and Town and Country Planning Acts etc. (such as the service of Demolition or Diversion Orders). Enforcement of Planning Control.

Unless the legal section is very large, several of these groups are likely to be placed in the hands of the same officer. In any event, they must not be looked upon as watertight compartments. The same matter may touch upon more than one aspect of the legal section's work. Another matter may primarily concern an officer of another department or section — a committee clerk, for example — and all may need advice on the law or the preparation of a suitable form or precedent.

The legal section exists to ensure that the law is complied with. To the good lawyer this means that his object in life is to help his colleagues to find the right way of carrying policy into effect and it is not enough to point out the legal objections to the course of action originally proposed.

THE LAW LIBRARY

Books are the tools of a lawyer's trade and no legal officer can be expected to do a worthwhile job unless there is access to an adequate and well-balanced library. For this purpose reasonable annual expenditure on new purchases is indispensable. Law books that are out of date are worse than useless. They are dangerous. Any local authority that tries to administer an Act that has been repealed will certainly make itself look foolish. It might also render itself liable to heavy abortive expenditure. Assuming that an adequate law library already exists, a relatively small expenditure each year will enable it to be kept up to date. The latest edition of every standard work should be purchased as also should the first edition of any new work that fulfils a basic need. A good example is a book that deals with some new and important item of legislation.

More difficulty might be experienced in purchasing a particularly large work. Some of the major encyclopaedias are published in 40 or more volumes and a new edition of such a work (which must be undertaken from time to time) represents a very considerable expense. Generally, however, such revisions are spread over several years and the publishers offer facilities for purchase by instalments.

Service Supplements and Periodicals

In an age when legislation changes rapidly, particularly in the local government field, or is augmented by voluminous statutory instruments, publishers have hit upon the useful idea of issuing many of their reference works in loose leaf form. These are subsequently kept up to date by supplements which can be inserted at the appropriate place in the binder and the obsolete pages thrown away. Care should be taken to budget for the purchase of all service supplements otherwise a useful, and probably expensive, encyclopaedia will become out of date and unreliable.

It is also the general practice for local authorities to take out a subscription to the principal municipal periodicals. If full value is to be taken of this, articles and news items must be brought to the attention of the officers affected as quickly as possible. It should be the duty of a reliable officer to pick out items of special interest and bring them promptly to the attention of the officers concerned.

Books are valuable property and a good library represents a considerable investment. They should be carefully kept in suitable glass fronted bookcases and such reprehensible practices as defacing books, spraining the spine or leaving them on floors or window sills to gather dust or damp should be absolutely prohibited.

It is a good practice to appoint a senior member of the staff to take charge of the library, to see that books are well cared for, do not get lost or stolen, are kept up to date (by the insertion of loose-leaf, supplements) and are replaced by new editions at the proper time.

Dissemination of Government Circulars

The regulations, orders and circulars issued by government departments of state have an importance comparable with Acts of Parliament. In fact, the statutory instruments, as distinct from circulars, have the force of law. Very many of them have a significant bearing on the activities of local authorities and it is essential to have an efficient system for handling them.

Every instrument relating in any way to the responsibilities of the local authority should be available for reference. The best place to keep them is in the law library and the officer in charge of the library should be required to maintain at least one complete file of relevant circulars from each government department which can be consulted in the same manner as any law book.

Government circulars are not only works of reference. Often they do require some immediate action and this is not likely to be forthcoming if the only copy is filed on the library shelves. It must, therefore, be the duty of a senior officer to read every new circular sufficiently throughly to ascertain which committee or officers will need to take the required action. An agenda item should then be raised and a report prepared for the committee. Sufficient copies of the circular, or extracts therefrom, should be supplied to the officers concerned.

THE COUNCIL'S SEAL

Every principal council (but not a parish or community council) must have an official, or common, seal for the authentication of formal documents. There is no need to have any special design. If the council has its own armorial bearings it is usual to incorporate the arms into the design but otherwise the name of the authority, possibly in ornamental lettering, is sufficient. The use of sealing wax is nowadays obsolete. The modern practice is to use a die-stamping machine to emboss the impression of the seal on to the document. Quite often a red wafer is stuck on the document and the impression is made upon that. This is done purely for effect, there being no legal significance in the use of the wafer.

As a safeguard against unauthorised use, the sealing instrument should be kept under lock and key in the custody of a senior officer. It is customary also for the instrument itself to be secured by two separate locks. The keys should be retained by two different and responsible people so that the instrument can be used only with the consent of both persons.

The seal is the official signature of the council and its improper use can have serious consequences. It is desirable, therefore, that standing orders should lay down strict rules to control the use of the seal. It should never be affixed to any document unless authorised by the council or a committee acting under delegated powers.

A proper register should be accurately kept containing a precise, consecutively numbered record of documents sealed. Some sealing instruments are fitted with a numbering device which operates whenever the machine is used and provides an additional check against its unauthorised use. The number of the entry in the register is customarily marked, in addition, on the sealed document itself.

A suitable form of a register can be purchased from leading local government stationers. Apart from the consecutive sealing number, the entry should show the title or description of the document, the date and minute reference of the decision authorising the sealing, the date when the sealing takes place and, preferably, the ultimate destination of the document. This last entry may enable the document to be recovered and examined if any questions are subsequently raised about it. Every entry in the seal register should be signed by the two persons attesting the sealing.

CUSTODY OF DOCUMENTS

It is the statutory duty of a principal council to make proper arrangements with respect to the custody of documents. Certain public documents are required to be received and retained by the "proper officer" of the local authority. A local government elector has the right to inspect other documents, such as the minutes or accounts of the local authority.

Suitable steps must, therefore, be taken to ensure that all deeds and other documents of importance are maintained in a strong room under adequate supervision and security arrangements. Generally speaking, it is a convenient rule to place the immediate rsponsibility for this task upon the shoulders of the chief officer of the legal section.

The selection of documents to be kept in the strong room is a matter of judgement. It is clear that records that must be maintained and kept available for inspection by law, such as minute books and rate books, come into this category. It is also obvious that title deeds, contracts, insurance policies and any other documents that may constitute essential evidence in any legal proceedings should be kept in safe custody. There will be many other examples where administrative prudence will suggest that papers should be kept in a strong room rather than an ordinary filing cabinet.

Maintenance of documents register

To facilitate the recovery of documents when they are required, it will be found highly desirable to maintain up-to-date registers of all documents kept in the strong room. According to preference, separate registers may be kept for the different categories of document or one register may be kept in specialised sections. Because new documents will continually be taken into custody and old ones released or destroyed, there is much to be said for a loose-leaf register or card index.

Every entry in the register must give a description of the item to which it refers, including its nature and the parties or issuing authority, and the reference number by which it will be identified. If the item is a wallet or envelope, a list of the contents will be necessary to safeguard against partial loss. A note of the relevant date might also help in its identification. Most important is a correct record of the shelf and bin number in which the document is kept. It is, of course, of the utmost importance that every document should be systematically stored in its allocated place at all times.

At discretion, the documents register may be used as a check on the completion of the administrative process. It is not strictly necessary to record the date on which a document is sealed or stamped but if the registration clerk is required to do this it will be a safeguard against the document being put away before some essential step has been taken.

Destruction of documents

Since no strong room is ever built with elastic walls, the time must come when unwanted documents have to be destroyed to make room for those of current importance. Undoubtedly, the officer charged with this task will err on the side of caution. First, those documents required to be retained by law will never be destroyed. Second, documents will be retained so long as there is a possibility that they will be needed in legal proceedings or if they establish the council's title to property. Third, documents should be kept if they are of practical administrative value as office records. Fourth, documents may be worth retaining for their historical importance. In this respect, the advice of the archivist or museum curator may be invaluable.

There will probably remain a residue of documents that have served their purpose. These will need to be kept, as a precaution, until the Statutes of Limitation have rendered them completely obsolete. A note may be made of the date when the life of such documents will expire at which time they may be withdrawn and destroyed on the instructions of the senior officer in charge.

Terrier of property

The maintenance of a simple index of all land and property owned by the council will certainly repay the time spent on it. If, as is usually the case, the council owns a good deal of real estate, there will be many occasions when it will be vital to establish the limits of the council's ownership. The question may be nothing more than a dispute as to who should trim a hedge or it may be queried whether the council own all the land proposed to be used for a block of multi-storey flats. Whatever the issue, it is a time-wasting and frustrating process to have to examine many deeds to discover the answer.

If practicable, a map index is ideal. The maps must, of course, be kept on a suitably large scale. The boundaries of all the council's properties should be plotted from the deeds and distinctly colour-washed. When property is disposed of, that also will be plotted and the colour-washing obliterated either by cross-hatching or by the use of a stronger colour. Once ownership has been established by reference to the map, recourse will be necessary to the deeds for details of covenants and other matters. A cross-reference will therefore be necessary to the deeds register. If feasible this can be endorsed on the map but, if that practice would be likely to cause confusion, a simple written index will suffice.

CONTRACTS AND TENDERS

Contracts made by local authorities are subject to the same legal principles as those of private persons but they are also subject to special rules and practices because the activities of local authorities are open to public scrutiny and potential criticism. Public expenditure is involved and it is important that the method of contracting should be unimpeachable.

The Local Government Act 1972, at section 135, therefore provides that standing orders may be made with respect to the making of contracts by local authorities. It is obligatory to make such standing orders for contracts for the supply of goods or materials and for the execution of works. It is required that standing orders shall make provision for competitive tendering and regulating the manner in which tenders are to be invited but it is permitted to exempt small contracts or others to which special circumstances apply.

Invitations to tender

The manner by which contractors may be invited to submit tenders will normally be prescribed by the standing orders. Two methods are in common use. The first is by public advertisement in local newspapers, trade journals or other periodicals. The announcement does not have to be in any prescribed form. It is usually necessary to give the name and address of the person from whom the specification, plans and other particulars, and a blank form of tender, can be obtained and the date by which the completed tender is to be returned. If, however, the proposed contract is a simple one, it may be sufficient to give an address to which offers should be sent by letter before a certain date.

The alternative method is to invite tenders from nominated contractors. Local authorities using this method maintain lists of approved contractors who are known to be able to supply particular goods or execute works at competitive prices and they write direct to selected firms inviting them to tender for suitable contracts. This relieves many contractors from the trouble and expense of submitting tenders for contracts they may have little chance of obtaining and enables them to concentrate on contracts they are well equipped to perform. It also protects the council from the risk of appointing an incompetent contractor, but it is important to keep the approved lists under continual review so that new and capable contractors have a fair chance of obtaining a share of public works.

Form of tender

Unless the contract is a very simple one, a carefully drafted form of tender will be issued for signature by intending contractors who will be required to state not only the tendered sum but also the time within which the contract is offered to be completed. They will also have to undertake to comply with detailed conditions of contract and may have to offer a bond or other surety for due performance of the contract.

Standing forms and conditions for contracts of various kinds are issued by professional and trade organisations and, where one of these is to be used, the fact can be stated in the invitation. This will save the council the trouble of issuing its own forms. If the council devises its own forms and conditions, it may be economic to have a quantity printed if it seems likely that similar contracts will be of frequent occurrence.

Receipt of tenders

All tenders should be required to be submitted in suitably marked envelopes so that they might be readily identified. They must be put aside, unopened, in a safe place; a locked ballot box is sometimes used. It is a good plan to stamp the envelope with the date and time of receipt as a precaution against subsequent dispute; a note should also be kept of the number received.

The latest date and time for the receipt of tenders will have been notified to contractors, either in the advertisement or in the documents sent to them, and must be strictly adhered to. No tender must be scrutinised whilst there is yet time for a rival to submit a competitive tender nor must one received late be considered. Even if no improper motive is intended, both practices are open to abuse and any objection to them would be fully justified.

Opening tenders

The opening of tenders is an important and responsible job which should only be entrusted to persons of proven integrity. Where practicable the box should be unsealed and the envelopes opened by or in the presence of a committee. At the very least they should be opened in the presence of two senior officers. Generally, standing orders will make suitable provision but, if not, the council should be invited to give clear instructions and authority.

As the tenders are opened, details of them should be entered in a book or other form of record. The tender forms themselves should be consecutively numbered to coincide with the entry in the record and initialled by the person in charge. A check should be made on the number of envelopes to make sure that none is missed.

Although the council should have taken the precaution not to bind itself to accept the most favourable or any tender, the principle of tendering is that the best tender should be accepted unless there are strong reasons for doing otherwise. The successful tender will have to be scrutinised by a technical officer to ensure that the details are correct and acceptance is usually conditional upon its being found to be so. If, after correction, it is no longer the best tender, the next most favourable will be accepted in its stead. In committee it is sometimes found advisable not to give the name of the successful contractor until the tender has been verified. This discourages the rejection of tenders for reasons that are purely personal or lacking in impartiality. If the most favourable tender is not accepted, the reason for the decision should be published in the minutes or report.

All tenderers, including those whose bids arrived too late for consideration, should be promptly notified of the result and, if unsuccessful, the reason. The detailed record should be retained for a reasonable period as a precaution against dispute. Sometimes contractors complain because the contract sum published in the Press is higher than their own bid. This may be because the published figure includes extra items, such as the cost of buying the land. For this reason it is often as well to publish the tender figure of the successful contractor.

CHAPTER 13

ADMINISTRATIVE FUNCTIONS

The detailed responsibilities of a local authority Secretary vary as between one authority and another according to local circumstances. He may or may not be the council's solicitor. Likewise he may be their personnel manager or their public relations officer. One thing is virtually certain. He will be their chief administrative officer.

Bains defined the prime roles of the department as the provision of secretariat for the council, committees and Management Team, and assistance to the Chief Executive's co-ordinative capacity. Furthermore, the report suggested, certain management services which cannot justify separate departmental status should be placed under the wing of the Secretary.

PROFILE OF A CHARTERED SECRETARY

Brief reference has been made earlier to the definition of a senior administrator produced by the Institute of Chartered Secretaries and Administrators under the title "Profile of a Chartered Secretary". It is worth giving here in full with a word changed here and there to match the normal language of local government because, when so adapted, it becomes a model definition of the duties of a local authority Secretary.

The functions of a chief administrative officer in local government normally include:

(a) Responsibility for general administration, including planning and control through the formulation and maintenance of systems, procedures and practices, promoting the smooth working of the organisation through a co-ordinating and consultative role and encouraging management and employee participation in measures to promote administrative efficiency.

(*b*) The establishment and co-ordination of the main channels of communication of the authority, both internal and external.

(*c*) The provision of services to management, including information and advisory services, the preparation of memoranda and reports, the briefing of senior officers, the preparation of speeches for leading members, and the drafting of evidence to government and parliamentary bodies.

(*d*) Advice to the council, involving prior consultations and drawing attention to legal obligations. The collection, collation and presentation of information on which council decisions are based. The recording of the council's discussions and decisions, including those of their committees, and ensuring that the communication of management policies and instructions reaches all those concerned in a clear and unambiguous form.

(*e*) Responsibility for the arrangements of the meetings of the council and committees, and for the arrangement of conferences, including press conferences.

(*f*) Maintenance of statutory and other records and responsibility for legal work that the person is qualified to perform and for obtaining professional legal advice when needed.

(*g*) At least some financial responsibilities through familiarity with accounting procedures, including legal requirements, the interpretation of the accounts and the implications for the authority.

(*h*) Other important areas of work may include the administration of property, including the provision and maintenance of office and other accommodation, the arranging and periodic review of insurance cover, purchasing policy, the handling of contracts, elections, electoral registration, local land charges, public relations, licensing, burials administration, archives and the provision of common office services for all departments.

THE GENERAL ADMINISTRATION SECTION

The main division of the Secretary's responsibility will probably be between the legal and administrative aspects, although there may be other sections of the department with specialist functions. It was stated in the previous chapter that there are duties which are required by statute to be performed by a solicitor. Apart from these, there is no clear distinction between legal and administrative work. Some tasks may fall into either category. Some may fall, in part, into both and will require close liaison between the two sections. Some administrative staff, such as committee clerks, may be considered specialists spending their whole time on one particular facet of administration. These specialist duties will receive separate attention in a later chapter. In this chapter we shall examine some of the tasks which cannot be classified as legal or personnel but equally do not fall into the category of routine office services.

PARLIAMENTARY BILLS

By section 239 of the Local Government Act 1972, all local authorities, except parish or community councils, are authorised to promote or oppose any local or personal Bill in Parliament, if they think it expedient to do so, and they may incur expenses for that purpose. These powers are not exercised very widely. Parish and community councils are empowered to oppose such Bills but not to promote them.

A local or personal Bill is commonly referred to as a 'private' Bill to distinguish it from public Bills of the kind usually sponsored by the Government and applicable to the country as a whole. A private Bill should never be confused with a Private Member's Bill, which is a form of public Bill but one which is not necessarily supported by the Government.

Statutory procedure for promotion of a private Bill

The initial procedure prior to the promotion by a local authority of a private Bill is laid down in section 239, previously mentioned, and must be strictly followed.

A resolution to promote the Bill must be passed at a meeting of the local authority by a majority of the whole number of members, not merely a majority of those present. The resolution may be passed at an ordinary meeting of the authority, or at a special meeting if thought fit, but in either case 30 clear days' notice must be given of the meeting, and of its purpose, by advertisement in one or more local newspapers circulating in the local authority's area. This notice must be given in addition to the ordinary notice required for convening a meeting of the local authority.

The former requirement to obtain the consent of the Secretary of State has been repealed. So has legislation requiring the approval of a town meeting.

When the Bill has been drafted and has been deposited in Parliament for 14 days, a further meeting of the local authority must be held as soon as possible for the purpose of passing a confirming resolution. This meeting must be convened in the same manner as the previous one, except that ten clear days' notice is sufficient, and a majority of the whole council is again required. If the resolution is not confirmed the Bill must be withdrawn.

Statutory procedure for opposition to a private Bill

The procedure which must precede opposition to a private Bill is now identical to the initiating procedure relating to the promotion of such a Bill but a confirming resolution at a subsequent meeting is not required.

Parliamentary procedures

Each House of Parliament has made standing orders which lay down the procedure to be followed and the formalities to be complied with in promoting or opposing a Bill before each House. These standing orders are detailed and complex. The procedure for publication of a Bill, for example, requires that copies of the Bill must be submitted to the Government departments concerned and must be made available for sale to the general public. A concise summary must be published in two successive weeks in a local newspaper and an announcement must appear in the London Gazette giving the title of the Bill, the local newspaper in which the summary has appeared and the address from which copies may be obtained. According to the nature of the Bill, plans, estimates and other particulars must be deposited.

The officers of a local authority will ensure that the requisite statutory steps are taken outside Parliament but they are rarely familiar with the internal procedures of Parliament and promoting authorities invariably find it necessary to employ parliamentary agents, lawyers who specialise in this kind of work. Their experience enables them to advise promoters on the rules to be followed and to steer the Bill through its various parliamentary stages. Failure to comply with the necessary formalities would put a Bill in serious jeopardy. Parliamentary agents are also competent to draft Bills. By their experience they are able to judge a Bill's chances of success and to draft it in the form that is most likely to be approved by Parliament. They will also brief counsel to appear before committees of Parliament and prepare the statements of evidence to be given by witnesses.

Parliamentary timetable

For purposes of private legislation, the parliamentary year begins and ends in the autumn. Private Bills must be deposited by November 27th each year. Various formalities have to be complied with before a private Bill can start its progress early in the New Year and, if all goes well, the Bill will receive the Royal Assent in July before the summer adjournment. In order to meet the time table, the promoting authority must pass its initial resolution not later than June or July of the preceding year and parliamentary agents must be instructed immediately in order to allow sufficient time for all the preparatory work to be done.

Local interests have until January 30th to register their objection to a private Bill. They do so by petition to Parliament whereupon the Bill is referred to a committee on opposed Bills. Often a compromise is reached by negotiation, the petition is withdrawn and the unopposed Bill is usually assured of an easier passage.

THE REVIEW OF LOCAL GOVERNMENT AREAS

Areas change over a period of time, some quite considerably, new development brings about population growth, while many of the large cities are losing population. As a result it is necessary to review periodically areas and arrangements for elections.

A weakness of the local government system prior to 1972 was that there was no provision for the regular review of areas and boundaries. Under Part IV of the Local Government Act 1972, the Local Government Boundary Commission for England is under a duty to review the areas of principal councils, other than non-metropolitan districts, at intervals of not less than ten years and not more than 15 years unless otherwise directed by the Secretary of State. Non-metropolitan districts are also to be kept under review but no time limit is specified. The Welsh Commission is expected to maintain a continuous review.

It is the duty of the district council to review their district and to bring forward proposals to the Boundary Commission for the constitution of new parishes or the abolition or alteration of existing parishes (or communities in Wales). Unless they consider that it would impede the proper discharge of their functions, the district council must consider any request by a parish council or parish meeting.

If the district council does not make proposals that are considered satisfactory, the commission may themselves undertake a review.

The recommendations of the commissions require the confirmation of the responsible Secretary of State who also has power to direct that a review be conducted or, in England, that a review be delayed. The latter power does not apply to Wales.

The review of electoral arrangements

Somewhat similar provisions are made for the periodic review of electoral arrangements but it is specifically enacted that such a review must be conducted separately and not as part of a review of the local government areas. The same time limit of ten to 15 years is laid down but, in this case, it applies to all principal councils, including those in Wales.

It is the duty of a district council to review the electoral arrangements in respect of the parishes or communities in their area and they must consider a request for such a review from a parish council or from at least 30 electors in the parish. They may then make the appropriate orders.

Upon receiving a similar request, the commission may themselves undertake a review and submit their proposals to the district council. The district council may then make an order, possibly incorporating amendments agreed with the commission, but if they do not do so the commission may make proposals direct to the Secretary of State.

The consideration of electoral arrangements

The administrator who is called upon to draft a revised scheme of electoral arrangements is going to meet certain practical difficulties. The statutory rules, which are contained in Schedule 11 of the 1972 Act, require that every electoral division of a county shall lie wholly within a single district. They also require that the number of local government electors shall be, as nearly as possible, the same in every electoral division. Furthermore, every parish or community must lie wholly within a single electoral division or, if it is divided into wards, every ward must be contained in that way. Similar rules apply to district electoral arrangements.

Although the Act provides that areas and electoral arrangements are to be reviewed separately, it may be impossible to comply with the Rules of Schedule 11 unless the boundaries of districts and parishes are first rationalised. It will also be necessary to maintain the closest co-operation between counties, districts and parishes or communities.

Assuming that there is a convenient practical size for the county council, which the Boundary Commission would be prepared to approve, it is a straightforward matter to calculate the number of electors to be included in each electoral division. As districts will normally vary in size of electorate, it may be more difficult to devise electoral divisions of equivalent size in each district and some adjustment may be necessary. The district then has the problem of drafting its own electoral arrangements to comply with the rules and, at the same time, to make satisfactory arrangements for parish or community representation.

It may, in fact, be necessary to create new district or parish wards in an attempt to meet the Rules of Schedule 11 but any proposal to ask some villagers to vote in an adjoining parish is not likely to be popular. What is more, it is likely to be attacked by the parish councils concerned as a potential threat to their area and status. A proposal to require rural dwellers to vote in a nearby town ward is especially likely to cause suspicion and annoyance.

There is no simple solution. The administrator must be aware of the pitfalls and must seek the fullest consultation and exposition before any firm decisions are taken as to either areas or electoral arrangements. Furthermore, it is not alwayss possible to carry out county and district reviews at the same time, so that the boundaries for each one may be slightly different at any particular point in time.

CO-ORDINATION

Committees, departments and individual officers of a local authority cannot act in isolation. Their activities must be harmonised so that their actions and their expenditure accord with the council's policy and so that their operations do not overlap or conflict and so cause waste and confusion.

The primary responsibility for co-ordination must rest on the shoulders of the Chief Executive supported by the Management Team. As envisaged by Bains, however, there are many ways in which assistance will be expected in particular from the Secretary's department.

The first is to arrange that clear and unambiguous terms of reference are provided for each committee and to make sure, particularly when compiling agenda papers, that each committee deals with its own brief and does not overlap on to those of others.

The second check is by budgetary control. The council's estimates will provide for sums of money to be spent by nominated committees on certain items. In some cases the committee may have power to spend the money on its own authority; in other cases ratification by a Finance Committee will be required. In no case will a committee be permitted to spend money without complying with budgetary control, either through its annual provision or by way of supplementary estimate. Normally the council's treasurer will keep a tight rein on the budget but the legal officer should also look upon it as his duty to ensure that financial regulations are observed. This latter role has become important too, where authorities embark on various forms of what have been called "creative accounting", some of which come close to the boundaries of the law.

Whether or not the council has granted them delegated powers, all committees should be required to submit a full report of their proceedings to the council at frequent and regular intervals. It is incumbent upon senior officers of the department to read committee reports thoroughly in order that they may be acquainted with everything that is happening and not merely with the decisions taken at meetings at which they happen to be present. It is good practice to have regular meetings of senior officers at which committee proceedings and departmental developments can be discussed. If this is done, potential misunderstandings can often be stifled at birth.

Just as committees should have terms of reference, executive action on particular sections of the work should be the clear responsibility of particular officers. If the work is of an administrative nature, the responsible officer will probably be a member of the Secretary's Department; if it is not, it will probably be an officer of another department. It should be the regular duty of the administrative assistant for a committee to go through committee reports, picking out all items requiring attention of any sort and drawing them formally to the attention of the officer who is due to deal with them. Confusion can arise if officers are permitted to deal with items at their own discretion particularly if more than one department is involved on a particular issue. Individual and departmental responsibility needs to be made clear.

INSURANCE AND RISK MANAGEMENT

Local authorities, their officers and workpeople and, to some extent, their members are subject to a wide variety of risks. It is important that such risks should be regularly reappraised and the insurance cover kept continuously up to the mark. An officer, should be deputed to do this as one of his principal tasks.

Many precautions need to be taken to minimise risk. Measures necessary under the Health and Safety at Work Act 1974, have been mentioned earlier. Vehicles and plant must be regularly inspected and serviced. As far as possible, buildings must be made secure against burglary and arson. Special precautions should be worked out to safeguard cash in transit. Crime prevention officers of the police force will gladly advise councils how to protect themselves from this kind of risk.

When an incident does occur, all employees must be aware of the procedure to be followed and those affected must be required to carry it out. A standard procedure must therefore be worked out and checks made from time to time to ensure that employees — bearing particularly in mind new employees — are familiar with it. A copy of the incident report procedure should therefore be prominently displayed at all offices and depots.

Employees should be required to report any accident or other incident that comes to their attention within twenty-four hours. To ensure that such reports give all the detail required, they should be submitted on a standardised form of which sufficient copies should be readily available. Copies of the report must be promptly submitted to the officer's immediate superior, to the officer responsible for insurance claims. Other officers may also be entitled to receive a copy in certain circumstances. If a council house is affected, the Chief Housing Officer or Housing Maintenance Manager should be notified. In other cases, perhaps the Properties Manager or Works Manager should be told. The Secretary, as Chief Administrative Officer, should institute a procedure for making sure that this is done. Possibly an incident register may be kept, including details from the report, the names of the persons notified and any further action taken.

A decision will need to be taken as to whether immediate repairs are necessary on grounds of safety. If not, work should not be started until clearance is received from the insurance assessor. It should be clearly established who has the authority to order repairs to be commenced.

No employee should admit liability or blame, either verbally or in writing. Although this may at times conflict with good public relations it may subsequently embarrass the council's legal advisers and insurers if it transpires that the council have a good defence against a claim. Furthermore, the injured party cannot be prejudiced by the fact that blame is not immediately admitted. The importance of this instruction should be firmly impressed on all employees.

MANAGEMENT OF PUBLIC BUILDINGS

A local authority will certainly be the owner of many premises, to several of which the public will have access. Several departments will have some responsibility for their management. The Technical Services Department, for example, may be responsible for maintenance and possibly for cleaning; the Financial Services Department for collection of rents and hire charges. The Secretary may be directly responsible for administration and supervision. Even if that job is done by the administration section of a separate Properties Department, the Secretary may be responsible for co-ordinating the contributions of several departments.

A building is required to be specifically licensed for music and dancing, for stage plays, or for cinema performances, before it can be used for any of those purposes. The appropriate licence must therefore be obtained before any application to hire a building for such a purpose can be entertained.

A policy will need to be established in relation to the letting of public premises. Resentment might occur if one hirer is permitted to establish a predominant use.

All applications for hire of council premises should be made on a standard form on which hirers must be required to indicate clearly what facilities are required.

If the application is accepted, immediate confirmation must be sent and any conditions or regulations to be observed must be clearly stated on the face of the letter of acceptance. If these are too lengthy to be incorporated in the letter, they may be set out on a separate form but attention needs specifically to be brought to them. They form part of the contract between the council and the hirer but if the hirer is not made aware of them they may prove impossible to enforce. The hirer should also be told the balance of fee due from him and the last day for payment.

CHAPTER 14

OFFICE SERVICES

COMMON OFFICE SERVICES

All sections of a local government office make use of certain basic services. These services are so commonplace that it is easy to take them for granted and to give very little thought to their organisation. Yet they are so fundamental to the success of the authority's work that they need to be planned and controlled with the utmost forethought and care. The position of office manager ought not to be considered suitable for an employee of limited imagination. The authority will benefit if the post can be used as a proving ground for a young professional officer seeking the opportunity to demonstrate organising ability.

ORGANISATION OF POSTAL SERVICES

The efficient and speedy receipt, distribution and despatch of mail is one of the main essentials of a competent office organisation and the staff of the post room, particularly the supervisor, should be carefully chosen for their reliability, industry and trustworthiness. The routine of the section should be carefully worked out and must be known and observed by everyone, including messengers from other departments, otherwise chaos and ineffciency is likely to result.

The first task every day must be to deal with incoming correspondence. Here the key is the time at which the mail is delivered or can be collected from the Post Office. The task of opening and sorting the post needs to be completed at the earliest hour possible. If this is not done, avoidable delay and loss of productivity will occur throughout the authority's offices. If practicable, therefore, arrangements should be made for postal staff to begin their work earlier than the remainder of the staff.

The second key is the time by which the outgoing mail must be in the hands of the Post Office if it is to receive the required attention on the same day. The routine of the post room must be geared to meeting that deadline and because the postal staff must have sufficient time to do their own work of making up and weighing packages, sealing and stamping envelopes and so on, originating departments must be called upon to comply with an earlier deadline. On occasions some may default. The Office Manager should not be needlessly officious in a case of genuine urgency but, as a general rule, should firmly insist on compliance with the rules. If not, he will soon find that the council's mail, including matters of urgency, is regularly missing the evening collection and serious problems may ensue. Often the real culprit may be a senior officer who has neglected to sign his letters at the proper time. If any officer is so busy that he cannot spare a moment to sign his letters, he should either delegate the task to a subordinate or accept the inevitability of his letters being held over to the following day.

Incoming Correspondence

The incoming correspondence of a local authority frequently contains documents of importance, the loss or mishandling of which can cause serious trouble. Some letters are confidential, some of special legal significance. Some envelopes may well contain remittances in cash.

Many authorities keep a register of all incoming documents with a record of the officer to whom each has been sent. If the correspondence is at all weighty, this is likely to be a major task and it must be carefully considered whether the trouble and expense is justified. Certainly a record must be kept of all cash received as an elementary precaution. From time to time debtors will claim that they have sent money through the post and the post must be protected as far as possible against the suspicion of peculation.

Otherwise there can be no hard and fast rule. If the division of responsibility within the organisation is such that it is self-evident from the subject matter which officer or section should be dealing with the matter, a register is unnecessary. But if many letters do go astray, some central record will have to be introduced.

Every letter should be date stamped on receipt and it may be convenient to include boxes to indicate that the letter has been acknowledged or copied, by whom it is to be answered and eventually where it is to be filed. If it is to be referred to a committee, that fact might also be indicated.

If a letter is likely to be answered within two or three days, no prior acknowledgement is really needed but, if it has to await the attention of a committee or much research is needed before a full reply can be sent, an interim acknowledgement that the letter is being dealt with is a necessary courtesy. Generally a printed card will suffice but, if the subject is of a confidential nature, a short letter of acknowledgement is called for.

The subject matter of a letter may fall wholly within the province of a particular officer, in which case the original letter may be referred to him for reply. If more than one officer is involved, copies should be provided so that the officers can be dealing with their separate responsibilities simultaneously. Normally a co-ordinated reply should be sent on behalf of the authority and the officer who is to be responsible for this should retain the original letter. It must be made apparent to the other officers who is to co-ordinate their efforts.

The designation of incoming correspondence is a job for an experienced and competent officer and, if possible, it should be checked by a senior officer before being distributed. It is particularly important that letters intended for a committee agenda are not lost sight of and, if there is the slightest doubt, the advice of the chief committee clerk should be sought.

it is a good practice for the Secretary to thumb through the incoming mail whenever possible. This may not be possible as a regular practice but there is no more effective way of keeping abreast of activity in the department.

Outgoing correspondence

The contents of outgoing correspondence will be a matter for the responsible departmental and section heads. Such letters, however, are written by the authority and not by any individual in a private capacity. A recognised form and style should therefore be used by everyone.

The rather flamboyant form of address used in official correspondence at one time has gone completely out of fashion. Nowadays a letter beginning "Dear Sir" and signed "Yours Faithfully" would be considered normal. If the addressee is a close personal acquaintance of the council, such as the local member of parliament, his name might be used, in which case the letter would end "Yours Sincerely". Many authorities encourage staff to deal with correspondence in a non-bureaucratic way, addressing letters as "Dear Mr   " or "Dear Mrs   " rather than "Dear Sir" or "Dear Madam".

The practice whereby every letter used to be signed by or in the name of the Town Clerk or other chief officer is still in widespread use but it is no longer, as formerly, the invariable practice. The practice grew up at a time when local authorities had to appoint certain statutory chief officers and it was felt that their assistants enjoyed no real standing for signing correspondence. This line of reasoning has little merit at the present time when local authorities are free to appoint any officers they wish. Nowadays there is no reason why any officer who is empowered to sign letters should not be allowed to do so personally.

It is important that every outgoing letter should contain a reference which correspondents should be asked to quote.

This is of great assistance to the postal staff when the reply arrives and is a useful precaution against the possibility of the reply being misdirected. The reference should contain the code letter (if any) of the department or section concerned, the initials of the originating officer and the file number. The name of the person dealing with the matter is also very helpful on correspondence, particularly in connection with telephone calls. Commonly the initials of the typist are also given but this is mainly of internal benefit to allocate work or to refer back alterations. References should be kept as short as possible. Long references are an imposition on the correspondent who is asked to quote them and are less likely to be repeated accurately.

The post room will be concerned only to ensure that the proper rate of postage is paid on all envelopes and parcels, that packages are properly secured and are promptly despatched. Probably arrangements will have been made with the Post Office for all envelopes to be passed through a franking machine which will endorse the appropriate rate of postage on the envelope and record the fact on its own meter. A remittance is made to the Post Office from time to time and the metering mechanism returned to zero. A recognised system must be instituted whereby departments clearly indicate those letters which are required to go by first class mail. Separate reception trays may be used but, as an added precaution, a mark should be placed on the envelope itself. The use of postage stamps will be largely eliminated but a small supply may be held, on imprest, for use on bulky packages and the like.

It is probable that certain addresses, such as councillors and Government departments, will be due to receive more than one letter from departments of the authority. Correspondence to addresses of this kind should be sorted into marked boxes and sent as a single package in order to avoid waste of postage charges.

FILING

An efficient filing system is an essential ingredient of any businesslike office. The vital principle is that documents must be suitably stored so that they can be found without difficulty when required. As far as possible, the risk of loss or damage must be eliminated. Fireproof safes or strong rooms for the more important documents such as title deeds and contracts, clean and dry cupboards or cabinet space for ordinary business correspondence, suitable and ample accommodation for documents of various shapes and sizes including such things as plans and specifications must be provided.

There is a wide variety of filing systems available of which none can be said to be invariably superior to another. The one chosen should be that best fitted to the particular needs of the office and to the available facilities. If the department is widely scattered in a large building or in several buildings, a centralised filing system might only lead to time-wasting and inefficiency. If the department is compact, on the other hand, the maintenance of several small filing systems should be discouraged. Either some files will be incomplete and therefore a potential source of error or there will be unnecessary duplication and therefore extravagance.

Many forms of sophisticated filing equipment are now on the market and any of the leading manufacturers of office equipment will advise on the most suitable ways of meeting the needs of a particular organisation. The development of visible filing systems, frequently designed on the suspended wallet principle, has greatly facilitated the maintenance of an orderly and up-to-date arrangement. Cupboards with sliding or roller doors obviate the waste of office space caused by the use of old-fashioned filing cabinets with drawers. Another method works on the rotary principle whereby only the required section of the cabinet is visible and the remainder is hidden away somewhere out of sight. It is now possible to move entire banks of filing racks on ball bearings so that access can be achieved to the desired rack. By this means almost the whole of the available floor space can be occupied by filing equipment.

Referencing a filing system

As a means of identification, every file must be given a name and number. The number is usually quoted as a reference on outgoing correspondence in order to ensure that the carbon copy is filed correctly and also to make certain that when the reply is received the earlier correspondence can be readily identified and produced. The use of numbers also facilitates the task of the filing clerk when putting papers safely away.

The number, however, does not indicate the contents or subject matter of the file. Unless the number of files is exceptionally small or the filing clerk has a phenomenal memory, files cannot be identified by number alone. Modern filing systems normally provide that the title of the file shall be typed on the spine of the wallet where it is immediately visible. Unless this is done, it is necessary to maintain a card index in which the title and number of each file are cross-referenced.

Files must be stored in a systematic way so that any one of them may be instantly located when required. The best arrangement can only be decided in the light of local circumstances. If files are most readily identified by a reference number, as might be the case in a rates office where the material information is the house number, the files may conveniently be kept in numerical order. If files are most readily identified by a name or title, such as individual staff files in a personnel department, the files may conveniently be kept in alphabetical order. But in many offices, having a wide variety of files, it may be necessary to devise a more elaborate combination of the numerical and alphabetical principle.

For example, all town planning files may be given the initial letter P or perhaps P1 to distinguish them from, say, publicity (P2). All planning appeals may be given the further distinguishing letter A and then numbered progressively so that the papers concerned with a current appeal may be filed under reference P1A25. This method enables all files concerned with the same general subject matter to be stored in proximity to each other. Furthermore, if a subject expands or proliferates to the extent that one file is insufficient, it is a generally easy matter to introduce further subdivisions.

Visible filing systems provide that the space allocated to any file can be recognised from the title strip even when the folder or wallet is itself missing. A rule should be made and enforced that anyone removing a file must leave in its appointed place a note stating where the file can be found. It is a simple matter to create space for a new file in its appropriate space in the system; likewise when a file is withdrawn, the space allocated to it can be cancelled.

The keeping of registers is strictly unnecessary but there may be advantages in publishing one at regular intervals so that typists and other members of staff may be able to quote correct file references without having to check with the filing clerk. The example given above is a simple one; the possible variations are almost limitless.

Advantage of common filing system

Even if it is inconvenient to maintain a centralised filing system, there is everything to be said for introducing a common referencing system so that all departments and sections store their files according to the same principles. Every file on the same subject matter will thereby bear the same reference but the files of different departments may be distinguished by distinctive colours or other such refinements.

Occasions will arise, for example, when the council will be engaged in legal proceedings and counsel for the authority will wish to be supplied with the relevant files. These may comprise the appropriately numbered files of the legal, financial and technical departments which, when read together, comprise the authority's complete file on the subject. If these departments are permitted to maintain filing systems on differing principles, it may be difficult to identify the files required and they may well prove to be cluttered with a lot of correspondence irrelvant to the matter in hand.

TELEPHONES

For many people, particularly those who live at some distance from the council offices, the telephone will provide the principal source of contact with their local authority. Certainly this is so if they require service in a hurry. For the council's own staff, the telephone represents a vital aid to communication in their daily work.

The telephonists are key officers in more than one sense of the word. They are the first people, and sometimes possibly the only people, to whom members of the public speak and very largely the reputation of the authority may depend upon the impression that they make. They should be carefully chosen for their polite and cheerful manner, their diction, their helpfulness and intelligence and their alertness. The same qualities should be required of the relief staff.

The number of operators should be enough to handle the traffic with reasonable speed at all times even though this may mean that at slack periods they will be underemployed. Nothing is more infuriating to a ratepayer, and therefore damaging to a council's reputation, than to hear a ringing tone which does not produce an answer within a reasonable time.

After office hours, an answering service that will give callers the name and telephone number of the duty officer who may be contacted in emergency is essential. A night extension should be connected to the home of the office caretaker or an emergency service so that urgent messages may be taken or transmitted by these officers if necessary.

CENTRAL RECEPTION

Many people who visit the offices of their local council, either by appointment or for some casual inquiry, may have little or no idea where to go when they arrive. Often they will not know the name of the officer to ask for or even the department that will handle their problem. Even if they have a letter instructing them where to go, they may have difficulty finding their way about a large and strange building.

It is a basic requirement of a well-administered office to provide a reception desk or cubicle as near as possible to the main entrance, with prominent direction signs at strategic points inside and outside the building. These signs should be easily seen by those visitors arriving on foot and those using the official car park.

The reception desk should be staffed by an officer of pleasing appearance and personality with a sound, if superficial, knowledge of the authority's business, a keen acquaintance with the council's staff and their various duties, and a ready familiarity with the geography of the building.

The objective must be to make visitors welcome and to make sure that they are told clearly and accurately where to go. If a porter is available to conduct the visiors or someone can be summoned to meet them in the foyer, so much the better. If a building is very large, further reception points on upper floors, near the lift or staircase, are a good idea.

It is not always necessary for visitors to be directed beyond the central reception area. The receptionist should be provided with a supply of forms, leaflets and other publications and shoul be capable of issuing them to interested persons without reference to higher authority.

From time to time, official documents have to be placed on deposit at the offices of the council for inspection by interested members of the public over a certain period. Examples are compulsory purchase orders or bylaws which are about to be submitted to the confirming authority. Members of the public who wish to speak to an officer handling the matter should be permitted to do so but many will be content just to see the plans or other documentation and, for their convenience, a full set should be kept on deposit at the main reception desk. They should not become mixed with the other flotsam of a general inquiry office but should be carefully deposited in a special drawer in an envelope or wallet clearly endorsed with relevant information such as the title, description of the contents and the name of the officer who is handling inquiries concerning the matter. The receptionist should not be expected to answer detailed questions but should have adequate instructions as to the manner in which general inquiries should be dealt with.

PRINTING

Every local authority needs a wide variety of printing and it is necessary to consider to what extent it is justified in undertaking its own internal printing work.

Minutes and reports have regularly to be printed or duplicuted in some other way. The register of electors has to be prepared. An enormous miscellany of forms is required. A year book and diary may be called for.

Two or three nationally known firms specialise in the production of local government forms. It may prove economical for a local authority to purchase a good supply of those forms that are in common use rather than to print their own, bearing in mind that the use of a copyright form will save the time of the council's staff in preparing a draft of their own.

For other kinds of printing, such as minutes and notices, a local firm may have to be used and the decision may depend on what kind of service local printers are able to give. Other work, such as the register of electors, may be prepared by computer.

The development of offset lithography, coupled with that of the electric typewriter which is supplied with variable type faces, has made it possible for any competent typist to prepare high quality work for reproduction. The required material is simply typed in the required characters on to a paper plate. Any desired art work is added to the plate by a designer and the whole can be reproduced in fairly large quantities by offset lithographic process.

The development of word processors and photocopiers means that there are now adequate facilities for producing the majority of printing and copying work "in house" particularly as the numbers produced are comparatively small. Furthermore the production of agendas and minutes are produced to very tight deadlines.

CENTRAL PURCHASING AND CONTROL OF SUPPLIES

One field in which local authorities often fail to achieve value for money is in the purchasing of supplies. They advertise their wants; they receive offers from interested suppliers who happen to have read the advertisement and they accept the most favourable tender. This system meets the objective of public accountability but it does not ensure the best value for money since it takes no account of relevant market factors. Many local authorities have an inadequate knowledge of their markets and consequently their purchasing policies are ineffective.

This ignorance is often displayed in the preparation of specifications. Sometimes these are written so closely around a particular product that competition is effectively excluded; in other cases they are so loosely written that comparison becomes impossible. Too often it is assumed that suppliers are ready and able to supply any product that is wanted; a shrewder examination of market conditions would sometimes reveal that an alternative product, equally effective, could be purchased much more economically.

The purpose of industry is to make a profit and manufacturers have to study such factors as the availability of raw materials and the cost of labour. Whatever the customer may say, the manufacturer is not going to waste his resources on unprofitable lines. Like other customers, therefore, local authorities need to find out what industry is equipped to make at an economical cost and then to devise their purchasing strategy accordingly.

It is important that purchasing should be undertaken by trained and experienced staff with a thorough knowledge of the essential processes involved in the goods to be purchased. Local authorities buy an exceptionally wide range of supplies and it is impossible for purchasing officers to be expert in every detail. But a large proportion of annual expenditure will probably be concentrated on relatively few items and it is on these major items that the expertise of purchasing staff should be concentrated.

Purchasing officers should have access to a comprehensive library of trade directors, catalogues and periodicals to provide them with the up-to-date information essential to their work.

County Councils or purchasing consortia, would be only too willing to provide a service to District Councils, who may not be able to justify the recruitment of a purchasing specialist.

Stock records and security

The keeping of efficient and accurate stock records is essential both as a check on efficiency and to provide the information necessary for financial budgeting. It is useless to try to keep careful records unless the stock itself is properly stored under lock and key and is issued only in accordance with an organised system.

Every store needs to have its own storekeeper who must be made responsible for checking the delivery notes of all stock placed in his care and for ensuring that all such stock is duly recorded and housed in its allotted place.

The storekeeper should only issue goods for use in exchange for a signed requisition which he must carefully retain and no one should be permitted to take goods from store except from the hands of the storeman. To cover emergencies occurring at week-ends or holidays when the main store is closed, it may be advisable to keep a small stock of essential supplies in a subsidiary store to which the duty foreman would hold the key. The storeman would not, of course, be responsible for this emergency imprest.

It is important that the store shall be large enough and

properly equipped to enable all items to be housed in a separate and distinct place. No effective control can be kept over items that are heaped haphazardly on the floor or in odd corners where they may be easily lost or damaged. Component parts should be kept in bins or racks with a record card showing purchases and issues and the balance of stock in the bin at any given time.

A close watch should be kept on the quantity of each commodity and the speed at which it is used. Orders for replenishment need to be given in good time to avoid an inability to meet requirements. On the other hand, money tied up in stock which is unlikely to be needed in the near future is wasted and, in general, stock should be limited to immediate needs. An exception may be justified if the opportunity occurs to acquire at bargain prices extra supplies of a commodity which is in constant use.

OFFICE MACHINERY AND EQUIPMENT

The range of electronic and electrical equipment available for office use is enormous. There can be few offices that do not make use of some of them. Typewriters, photocopiers, calculators and the like are standard equipment everywhere. Computers, word processors and other sophisticated equipment are now in general use.

The extent to which a local authority can usefully employ any item of equipment depends upon local circumstances. Such appliances are usually expensive and their purchase can only be justified if the benefits to be achieved compare favourably with the cost of installation and maintenance. This usually implies a saving in time and labour of a degree that can only be achieved if there is sufficient work to keep such machines in continuous use.

Financial savings, however, may not be the only consideration. Speed of operation may be another. If by mechanical means, a local authority can print and post all its rate demands on the first day of the financial year, an immediate income may be achieved. On the other hand, if they have to be written by hand over several weeks, the local authority may incur interest charges on money borrowed to meet its commitments before its rate income begins to flow in. Thus, a financial advantage may result even though the actual saving in the cost of clerical labour may not match the cost of installing and maintaining the machine. Furthermore, the cost of electronic equipment is reducing as demands' for more or better information is increasing.

Allowance must also be made for the human factor. People grow tired and their standard of performance tends to fall away as the day wears on. A machine that is properly maintained does not deteriorate in its performance. Clerks make errors; machines that are efficiently operated do not.

Machines, however, do not last for ever. The efficiency of the machine can only be relied upon if it is reasonably new and well maintained. In assessing the value of a purchase, therefore, proper allowance must be made for depreciation and maintenance costs which can be very heavy. But the efficiency and capabilities of electronic equipment are increasing at a very rapid pace, so that the comparative life span of any one piece of equipment is short.

Consideration must also be given to the availability of skilled operators and maintenance engineers. If only one member of staff has the training and skill to operate a machine, the routine of the office can be devastated if that operator is absent through sickness or other cause. Likewise when a fault develops, serious dislocation may result if the maintenance engineer is not at hand. An office should never become so dependent on one piece of mechanical equipment that its temporary failure will being the whole routine to a standstill.

When deciding on office automation, potential savings of money and manpower are important but the possibility of speedier and more accurate work, an increase in the standard of service to the public and improved organisation within the office are other factors to be carefully considered.

OFFICE ACCOMMODATION AND SECURITY

The Offices, Shops and Railway Premises Act 1963, imposes on certain local authorities the duty of ensuring that the minimum standards laid down are observed by all occupiers of office accommodation. If the council's credibility as an enforcement authority is to be preserved, it is essential that the accommodation provided for its own staff should not fall short of statutory standards in respect of such matters us space, ventilation, light and noise.

Another important matter to be considered by those responsible for planning office accommodation is that of security. Local authority premises tend to be extensively used throughout the working day by legitimate visitors who are not known personally to any of the staff but whose right to be there will certainly not be challenged. Sometimes the building will be open for certain limited business, such as committee meetings, outside normal office hours. All this provides a difficult security problem in buildings that often contain large amounts of cash and other valuables.

The crime prevention officer of the local police should be consulted at regular intervals and his reasonable recommendations carried out. All items of value should be kept in private offices and not in places to which the public has access. Where practicable, orders should be given that the more valuable, and easily removable, property should be locked in a safe before the staff leave at night. Doors giving access to cash offices should be fitted with locks, preferably of the mortice type, and should be kept fastened at all times. Cash collection points should be fitted with the best bandit-proof windows.

The authority's insurers will invariably wish to impose conditions regarding security of premises and risks covered by them and normally will provide an advice service on this.

A routine should be established to make sure that all main doors are locked as soon as staff have left at night and are not prematurely opened in the morning. A thorough check needs to be made of the building at the end of the working day, principally to detect windows that have carelessly been left open but also as a precaution against unathorised persons hiding themselves for felonious purposes. A security catch may be fitted to all windows, particularly on the ground floor, and bars may be appropriate in some cases. If the building is used in the evening, special arrangements should be made under the supervision of a responsible person.

Fire drills are an irksome business but they should never be neglected. Loss of life can result from such laxity. Staff should be instructed to leave quickly by the most convenient exit and to assemble at a prearranged point where a roll-call will be made. Specified officers should be made responsible for making sure that corridors, committee rooms, public rooms and toilets are cleared of councillors and members of the public. It should be the duty of the senior telephonist to summon the fire brigade and then to leave the building with all haste.

By arrangement with the local Chief Fire Officer, a fire picket comprising volunteer members of the staff may receive some training in fire fighting, in which case they may attempt to hold the blaze in check until the arrival of the regular brigade.

The importance of nominating reserves to act in the absence of the officers normally responsible for specified tasks should not be overlooked.

CHAPTER 15

COMMITTEE ADMINISTRATION

It is customary practice that the council's Secretary should also act as secretary or "clerk" to each of its committees. The duties of a committee clerk are broadly similar to those of a council secretary and it is usually found convenient for officers of the same department to carry those responsibilities. This system has a number of advantages. Apart from the fact that the Secretary has the particular expertise required to perform the principal duties of committee clerk — the ability to prepare agenda papers, to write clear and concise minutes and so on — additionally, as procedural adviser to each committee enables him to act, as required, in his capacity as chief legal adviser, chief administrative officer, personnel manager or public relations officer.

It is not, of course, necessary that the Secretary should attend every committee meeting in person. Indeed this may be physically impossible. But the duties of committee clerk should always be carried out in the Secretary's name by a well-qualified and senior officer of the department. Some authorities insist that a member of the legal staff shall always be in attendance as committee clerk. In many authorities, having only one or two solicitors or barristers on the staff, such a rule would be impossible to apply. The most important thing to remember is that the committee clerk is acting as proxy for the Secretary and must, by reason of his own status and competence, command the respect of the members and the other officers in attendance some of whom may, of course, be chief officers of considerable experience. The committee clerk must have the ability to intervene in the debate, if called upon, with the same confidence as the Secretary would display if present.

It must also be remembered that the committee clerk is representing the Secretary in all capacities. For example, a solicitor who is acting as committee clerk must be as prepared to advise on matters of civic ceremonial, publicity or staff welfare as on matters of straightforward law. It is very desirable, therefore, that all section heads should see the agenda beforehand and ensure that the officer who is to act as committee clerk is as fully briefed as possible on all matters likely to arise.

The Secretary, as Chief Committee Clerk, also has an unrivalled opportunity to keep abreast of all that is going on or is contemplated by any of the authority's committees. He must insist that committee clerks report to him and to any other chief officer or section head who may be affected so that preliminary steps may be taken, if advisable, in advance of a formal decision by the committee. The position of the Chief Executive, as coordinating officer, must be borne particularly in mind; the committee clerks are in a good position to help sustain in this role.

DUTIES OF A COMMITTEE CLERK

The duties of a committee clerk are many and varied. Dates and times of meetings must be fixed, and sometimes the place also has to be decided. Agenda papers must be prepared and reports circulated. A note must be kept of all decisions and matters of importance. Minutes must be written and the decisions of the committee must be duly promulgated.

It is essential to keep a record of the attendance of members and the times when they arrive and leave the meeting since these facts will be needed to check their subsequent claims for attendance allowances, or may be required to establish who were in attendance when votes were taken. For the most part it will be sufficient to record in the minutes the times at which the meeting begins and ends but a separate note may have to be made concerning any member who is not present throughout the proceedings.

Committee clerk's should know standing orders sufficiently well to be able to deal at once with any point that may be referred to them for advice. They should also be familiar with the detailed terms of reference of the committee and of the history of the various matters for which the committee is responsible. For these reasons it is a good plan to arrange that, sickness and holidays excepted, the same officer or pair of officers should attend all meetings of any particular committee.

The responsibilities of the committee clerk are such that, unless the duties of the committee are light, it is normally a job for two people. The normal practice is for the senior officer to be accompanied by a junior assistant whose task is to attend to most of the paper work, leaving his superior free to concentrate on giving advice to the chairman and the committee as the need arises.

Many chairmen find it helpful to meet their committee clerk and their other professional advisers before each meeting, to go through the agenda and to obtain their advice as to the manner in which each item might best be dealt with. Other chairmen prefer to approach each meeting with an open mind but relying, nevertheless, on the committee clerk to see that they are informed of any difficulties that may arise.

It is the duty of the committee clerk to give the chairman all the help possible to conduct a well-ordered and successful meeting and must adapt methods to fit in with the way in which the chairman likes to work.

PROGRAMME OF MEETINGS

The work of a local authority is greatly facilitated by the production each year of a programme of meetings arranged on a regular cycle.

A proposal of one committee is often required to be

submitted to another committee. A simple example is that a proposal of a "spending" committee may have to be examined by the Finance Committee or by the Policy and Resources Committee before it can be recommended to the council. It is clearly desirable, therefore, that the examining committee should meet to consider the proposal before the next council meeting, otherwise the matter will be unduly delayed.

Councillors are normally busy people with a great many committments to the public service in addition to their responsibilities in private life and it is not easy to convene a meeting of any committee at short notice. It is a convenience to the members if the committees to which they belong meet regularly according to an established routine. This enables them to keep the appropriate dates free in their diary throughout the year.

Some officers have responsibilities to several committees and have to arrange their work accordingly. If they know the dates when each committee is due to meet, they can plan the preparation of reports and plans so that each is ready by the time it is required. If committees met haphazardly, there would be conflicting and irreconcilable demands on an officer's time.

Such a programme also makes it very much easier for the committee clerks to organise their work. It is a useful idea to display a wall chart for the year indicating the dates when each committee is due to meet (including any extra meetings arranged during the year), the dates fixed for the despatch of agenda and reports, the deadline by which draft minutes must be with the printer and any other relevant dates.

By working systematically to a time-table, the committee clerk is able to remind other officers in good time when they are due to report to a committee; and can co-ordinate the work with that of others, such as the printers, typists and postal clerks. Most important too, he can see at a glance when his committments are becoming excessive and either arrange for assistance or even get some minor meeting postponed to a more convenient date.

PREPARATION OF AGENDA PAPERS

The items to appear on the agenda of any committee will fall into several categories. First there are the routine and recurring items such as signing the minutes of the previous meeting and approving accounts for payment. Second are items, such as the resolution to make the rate, which occur regularly at certain times of the year or at the end of some other period. Third is business left over or deferred from some earlier meeting and, fourth, is new business which has arisen since the last meeting of the committee, a category which may include correspondence and reports arising from some earlier decision of the committee. There is no rule which says that business must be taken in this, or any other, order. The committee clerk will strictly observe any provision in standing orders as to the order of business but will otherwise be guided by the usual practice of the committee. It may, for example, be customary to take certain business first in order that a consultant who has been called in for that one item may give his advice and be released. Business in which a member is known to have a pecuniary interest may conveniently be placed last so that the member may participate in the remainder of the business and then go home whilst colleagues deal with the ultimate item. Conversely, items affecting a section of the public might be placed early on the agenda, particularly if they wish to attend the meeting, but do not wish to sit through every item.

It may be convenient to keep an office diary in which annual business is noted against the date when it is due to be transacted. Some committee clerks keep an agenda book in which every item of unfinished business is recorded and is deleted only when it is finally disposed of. An alternative is a card index system in which all "forward" agenda items are included with a note of the date when it is thought they should be brought to the committee's attention. These cards are kept in chronological order so that the cards at the front of the tray are those relating to the next meeting of the committee. Whatever method is used, the committee clerk must make sure that any item due for consideration at the next meeting is picked up. As an additional check, it would be wise to refer to the minutes of the corresponding meeting last year, the minutes of the previous meeting and possibly, if meetings occur at rather frequent intervals, to the meeting before that.

New business will usually comprise correspondence, extracts from proceedings of the council or other committees, and reports or memoranda from officers. Almost all such business will be evidenced in writing. An exception may occur if the chairman telephones to ask that an opportunity be afforded for a particular subject to be discussed. In such a case, the officer concerned would do well to take an immediate note in writing of the instruction.

The customary practice is that documents which are to form the basis of agenda items are kept in a separate folder, box file or drawer, depending on their bulk. When the agenda paper has been prepared, the relevant documents are arranged in order, given a number to correspond with the number on the agenda paper, and clipped together so that they can be taken to the meeting and easily referred to when the relevant number is called.

The presentation of documents

The practices of local authorities vary widely in relation to the presentation of documents to committees and the committee clerk can do no more than follow the accepted practice.

In some authorities, the agenda papers consist of nothing but a bald list of subject headings. As each item is reached, the responsible officer is called upon to give a verbal report or to summarise the correspondence. This puts a heavy responsibility on the officers. The members have really no idea beforehand what they are to be asked to decide and their decisions can hardly be well considered. The system may be tolerable where experience has proved that members do not study documents before the meeting, or where the issues involved are simple.

In other instances, the business of the committee may be so heavy and many documents so long that it would be a physical impossibility for members to read them all and their inclusion would make the agenda paper almost indigestable.

Generally speaking, some form of compromise seems to be preferable. Each agenda item might comprise a short explanation of the matter to be considered and, if further information is needed, a full report might be appended to which suitable reference would be made on the agenda paper.

This is an example of an agenda item of this kind:

12. Hampchester Development Scheme — The Chief Planning Officer will submit the observations of the East Hampset Advisory Panel. (Copy herewith, number TP 12.)

It must be acknowledged that, even though a report may have been circulated, there is no certainty that all members will have read and understood it. An officer will probably be called upon to summarise it but he will at least have the comfort of knowing that the more conscientious members will already have some grasp of the situation. The circulation of reports at the meeting itself is generally unsatisfactory unless they are short enough to be read aloud by the committee clerk whilst members follow the written word. Unless there really is no alternative the practice is best avoided.

Private and confidential matters

It used to be the habit of some committee clerks to mark all committee documents "Private and Confidential". Now that the Press and public have a statutory right of attendance at committee meetings, the practice appears futile since it would be illegal to exclude the Press as a matter of course from all proceedings and improper to ask them to refrain from reporting all matters referred to in the course of discussion. The practice was, in any case, always of doubtful merit since members themselves recognised that much business was scarcely confidential at all and therefore they were encouraged to ignore the endorsement in all cases.

It is, nevertheless, the fact that some public business is confidential and ought not to be disclosed to those who have no public duty to perform in respect of it. If land is to be sold by the council it would prejudice normal tendering procedures if potential purchasers were to be made aware of the valuation placed on the land by the council's surveyor. If the council were to become involved in a law suit it would be prejudicial if the plaintiff were to be supplied with the details of the council's proposed defence.

A widespread practice nowadays is to prepare the agenda in two parts. The first part of the meeting is occupied with business that is not considered confidential. An item is included on the agenda paper to exclude the Press and public when this business has been completed and the confidential matters are then dealt with in closed session. The committee clerk will no doubt be relied upon to identify the items to be placed "below the line" but it is the committee's own responsibility to decide which items should be discussed behind closed doors. These should be as few as possible consistent with the protection of the public interest.

ATTENDANCE AT MEETINGS

When the agenda paper has been prepared and supporting documents have been attached to it, the committee clerk will take steps to ensure that it is sent to all persons entitled to receive it. For this purpose, a distribution list will no doubt be maintained. In addition to the members of the committee, there will doubtless be many officers and consultants who require to be given notice of the meeting and representatives of the Press are entitled to receive information which will enable them to report the meeting properly. It will depend on local practice whether other people, such as councillors who are not members of the committee, are entitled to receive copies. There seems little merit in exclusiveness but the question of expense maybe a material factor.

The committee clerk must also make it his responsibility to ensure that the room is available for the meeting and that the details required for the members' comfort are attended to. The adjustment of the heating and ventilation, the provision of scribbling pads and pencils are points that are often appreciated.

Spare copies of the agenda papers and documents should be taken to the meeting for the benefit of any member of the Press who may arrive unprepared or any councillor or officer who has lost or forgotten the original set. Spare copies of the agenda paper may be distributed, as a courtesy, between members of the public attending the meeting. This will assist them to follow the proceedings more easily.

The committee clerk will also be required to take the minute book containing the minutes of the previous meeting due for signature, the attendance register that members will be required to sign, any letters or documents that are to be considered or are likely to be referred to and, advisedly, a copy of standing orders and financial regulations, including the terms of reference of the committee, in case any doubt should arise.

MINUTES

The minutes of any assembly comprise the official record of the business transacted by the body concerned. Those of a local authority, or one of its committees, are required to fulfil a number of essential purposes.

First, in the case of recommendations that require to be approved or adopted by the council or some other superior authority, they define in precise terms what the confirming authority is being asked to ratify. Second, they give specific instructions to the council's officers and define the limits of their authority. Third, they provide evidence for production to a Court, to the auditor, or to anyone else who may have a duty to verify that any action taken on behalf of the authority was lawfully authorised. Fourth, they are part of the official history of the authority. In later years, they may be the only available explanation of what has gone before.

Minutes represent the corporate mind of the assembly and are not a record of the views of individual members. Any temptation to register the opinions of individuals should normally be resisted. Unless the proceedings are tape-recorded for subsequent transcription — a practice that is both impracticable and unnecessary for routine local authority meetings — it is impossible to record a member's remarks in full. Condensations by committee clerks are unsatisfactory. The member is more likely to complain of being misquoted or inadequately quoted than not being quoted at all. No one else is likely to complain if remarks are omitted. Occasionally it may be necessary to record a member's remarks officially — if, for example, they are to be included in an illuminated scroll to be presented to some distinguished person. In the course of routine they are likely to fulfil none of the purposes listed in the previous paragraph. Almost always it is better to leave them out.

Good minutes should be clear and concise. They should cover all the points that the committee seek to establish and nothing else. It is a sound rule to remember that minutes are written to be read by busy people whose patience will be sorely tried if they are obliged to wade through much verbiage. In some cases it may mean that minutes are not read at all. This risk applies particularly to councillors who, in attempting to glean the important points from unnecessarily lengthy minutes, may miss the vital recommendation altogether.

Recording of resolutions

In theory, minutes consist of a series of resolutions, which comprise motions duly proposed, seconded and adopted by a majority vote. In practice, many committees do not work like that, at least not all the time. Suggestions are made, often in imprecise terms, they are discussed, ideas are adjusted and finally the chairman declares the meeting to be in agreement.

The committee clerk is then left to compose a minute that accurately reflects the decision made by the committee. It is advisable to do this in the form of a resolution, even though one was not formally passed. No doubt the committee would adopt a resolution if someone insisted but it would delay proceedings unacceptably. When the chairman declares that agreement has been reached, it is permissible to infer that the necessary formality is intended.

When a motion has been formally put and approved, the resolution must, of course, be included in the minutes but even in this case there may be an implication that the committee clerk is to "tidy up" the wording to make sure that the true intention of the committee is accurately stated.

Narrative minutes

Although the kernel of the minutes will consist of resolutions and the comments of individuals are to be excluded, a certain amount of narrative cannot be avoided. To be intelligible, many minutes must contain a reference to the letter or report which gives rise to the decision recorded. This is best done by a few well-chosen words of introduction. This is good minute writing provided the narrative matter is brief and to the point and is not allowed to become the pretext for the inclusion of non-essential matter.

There are other items of business which cannot conveniently be expressed as resolutions of the committee. When a member declares a pecuniary interest in some business of the committee, that fact must be recorded. It is not a resolution of the committee, whether by inference or otherwise, and it would be wrong to record it as such. A simple statement that the member declared an interest is all that is required.

The acid tests are these. Was the matter to be recorded as a decision of the committee, whether formally expressed or not? Is the minute, as it is written, intelligible to a person who has no other knowledge of the subject matter? Do the completed minutes omit some essential fact or, on the other hand, do they contain material that is irrelevant?

Practical points concerning minutes

Minutes should be consecutively numbered for ease of reference. Some organisations use a new series of numbers for each meeting. Some continue a series throughout the year. In local authority work it is not uncommon to use one series of numbers to cover the meetings of the council and all committees. In a business organisation, such as a local authority, there is much to be said for avoiding any duplication of minute numbers.

The names of members present at the meeting should be recorded in the minutes and a clear indication given of the person occupying the Chair, even though it is the regular chairman. As previously stated, it may be necessary to record late arrivals and early departures in order that claims for attendance allowance may be checked.

The minutes are required by law to be signed at the same or the next following meeting by the person presiding and, if purporting to be so signed, shall be received in evidence without further proof. For this reason, it is advisable to record that the minutes of the previous meeting were signed by the chairman. It avoids any need to prove before a court that the signature is in fact his. There is no legal need to obtain the committee's approval although, out of courtesy, this is usually done. Signing the minutes, therefore, need not be the subject of a resolution. It would appear that the responsibility for the accuracy of the minutes rests on the person signing them and not upon the committee.

Under Schedule 12 of the Local Government Act 1972, the minutes must be drawn up and entered in a book kept for the purpose. This book may, if desired, be kept on the loose-leaf principle but, if so, each leaf must be separately numbered and initialled.

It is not strictly necessary to record the names of mover and seconder of any motion nor the details of any motion or amendment that is lost. The corporate mind of the committee is not established until a substantive motion is put and carried. What goes before is only part of the mechanics of reaching a decision, comparable with speeches by individual members. There is, however, a school of thought that all motions should be recorded, whether successful or not. If this view is widely held by members, it may be thought needlessly discourteous to refuse to do so.

It is usual for standing orders to provide that, upon the requisition of any member, voting on any question shall be recorded so as to show whether each member present and voting, gave his vote for or against the question. This is a statutory requirement in the case of parish and community councils but is optional in the case of principal councils. Where a requisition is made, the minutes should set out in full the names of members voting for, or against, or abstaining from voting. Accuracy is essential and the committee clerk should not hesitate to ask the chairman to ask members to keep their hands clearly raised until their names have been taken. When this has been done, it is advisable to call the names audibly to make sure that the record is correct. In the absence of a requisition, it is not usual to record the voting, even to indicate the numbers for and against.

If any correction has to be made in the minute book, the alteration should be initialled by the chairman who, by signing, is taking the responsibility for their accuracy. The minute book should be kept in a secure place to discourage tampering by authorised persons. If it is kept in loose-leaf form, it is normal to use a locked binder, the key of which is entrusted to a responsible person.

The minute book is likely to be frequently consulted and time spent in maintaining an up-to-date index will be profitably used. No particular method of indexing appears to have advantages over another but, whatever method is used, adequate cross-references should be made. If sets of minutes are sent for binding periodically, as is the normal practice with loose-leaf minutes, a printed or typewritten index should be bound with them.

Local councils frequently have to consider the minutes and reports of several committees and the use of colour coding has much to command it. It is easier to pick out documents which relate to a particular committee if a different colour of paper is used for each. The minutes of all committees might conveniently be bound together and this helps members find the particular minutes that are being submitted for consideration.

DISTRIBUTING COMMITTEE DECISIONS

As soon as a committee meeting is over, the committee clerk must take steps to ensure that the decisions of the committee are put into effect. Some of these decisions may require the confirmation of the full council, or the completion of some other formality, before they can be put into effect. But action should be commenced on other matters as soon as possible after the decision has been made.

Some decisions may necessitate the writing of letters or the preparation of further reports. An officer who is required to submit a report needs to be told as soon as possible so that he has ample time to put the work in hand. If a letter is to be written for the purpose of obtaining additional information for the committee it should be sent at once, probably by the committee clerk personally. By contrast, a letter which is to convey a decision should not be sent until any necessary confirmation has been obtained.

If an item has been referred to another committee for their consideration, an appropriate extract from the minutes should be placed in the agenda "box" of that committee. Minutes may take several days to prepare and, if an extract is not immediately available, some suitable note of the item must be put in the "box". The clerk of the second committee may be due to prepare the agenda for the next meeting of that committee and justified criticism will ensue if the item is missed.

Similarly, entries should be made promptly in any agenda book or diary concerning matters deferred for future consideration.

Many of the committee's decisions will need to be carried

out by officers of other departments or of other sections of the Secretary's Department. Rather than rely on verbal advice, it will probably be better that the committee clerk should send each of them a memorandum setting out their instructions. It is easy to forget or misunderstand the whole or part of a verbal message. A memorandum acts as a reminder of work to be done and as a check on completion. In default, the committee clerk has the consolation of being able to prove that the committee's instructions were properly transmitted.

From time to time a committee will arive at a decision which is of continuing effect. It is useful if these instructions are filed in a convenient form for ease or reference in the future.

COUNCIL MEETINGS

Council meetings must be conducted in accordance with Schedule 12 of the Local Government Act 1972, which provides that meetings may be held at such place as the council may direct, either inside or outside their area, save only that in the case of parish or community councils the meeting may not be held on licensed premises unless no other room is available.

At least three clear days before the meeting, notice of the intended time and place must be published at the council's offices (or some conspicuous place in the parish or community). In addition, a summons signed by the proper officer of the council, specifying the business to be transacted, must be left or sent by post to the residence of each member. The term "clear days" is not defined in the Act. There have been various judicial interpretations of the term as it has been used in other Acts of Parliament but it is safest to assume that there must be three intervening days (other than Sunday) between the day of despatch and the day of the meeting. If the meeting is called by members of the council, the notice must be signed by them and must also state the intended business.

Meetings of a local authority are usually more formal

than those of its committees but, provided the statutory procedure is carefully followed, they should present no difficulties to a competent committee clerk. The order of business for the agenda paper is normally laid down by standing orders. Some statutory business may need to be transacted but, for the most part, the business is likely to consist of the consideration of the minutes of the various committees and, if so decided, the confirmation of their recommendations.

The motion before the council at any one time, therefore, is likely to be that the minutes of such-and-such committee be approved and adopted. This is unlikely to be negatived since the effect would be to disapprove the whole of the committee's proceedings. It is more probable that an amendment will be moved to disapprove a particular recommendation, or to vary it, or to refer it back to the committee for further consideration. If such an amendment is carried (and, incidentally, it should be noted that the mover of the original motion and not the mover of the amendment has the right of reply), the substantive motion will be put to the council in the ordinary way and will be minuted after the following fashion: "The minutes of the Housing Committee, dated 14th May, were approved and adopted, with the exception of Minute No. 49, which excepted minute was referred back to the committee for further consideration".

If this precept is carefully applied, and provided the same practical principles are followed as were discussed earlier in this chapter in relation to committee meetings, few difficulties are likely to be experienced.

Statutory business — making of general rate

A good example of statutory business that must be performed at a council meeting is the making of the general rate. Every rating authority, which is to say every district council, must make and levy a general rate for the whole of its district including suitable provision for any payments due to other authorities, such as the county council, under precept. This task must be performed by the full council and may not be delegated to any committee.

The preliminary work of considering and approving estimates will, of course, be done by the spending committees and, ultimately, by the Finance Committee or its equivalent. These preliminaries will doubtless be handled by the Treasurer and the Secretary is only indirectly concerned. At length, the Finance Committee will decide upon the rate that it is necessary to levy and will resolve to recommend the council accordingly.

At this stage the Secretary, in consultation with the Treasurer, will draft a suitable form of resolution which, if and when adopted by the council, will give effect to the recommendation. A resolution to make a rate must state the amount of the rate levy, any special or concessionary charge and the area to which it applies, and the period to which the rate applies. For the benefit of ratepayers wishing to pay by instalments, the resolution must declare the number and amount of such instalments and the date on which each of them will become payable. It is not strictly necesssary to seal the rate book but, if it is intended to do so, the council's authority must be obtained.

The summons and agenda paper for the council meeting at which the rate is to be made will be made up in the ordinary way but the resolution to make the rate will be included as a separate item. It is not sufficient merely to adopt the recommendation of the Finance Committee. Standing orders will determine the point at which the business will be taken but it is a widespread custom to take statutory business as early in the meeting as possible, that is to say after the previous minutes have been signed but before committee and routine business is considered.

The draft resolution should be set out on the agenda paper in full. No risk should be taken of the mover of the motion omitting some essential wording. The subject might be introduced on the agenda paper in the following manner: "To consider and, if thought fit, to adopt the following resolution to make and levy a general rate." The Secretary's draft would immediately follow.

If the motion is carried, the resolution will, of course, be repeated exactly in the minutes of the council meeting and a copy of it, either sealed or authenticated by the signature of the proper officer, will be inserted as the first page of the rate book.

Within seven days after the date of the formal resolution of the council making the rate, notice must be given in a manner prescribed by law and the rate will not be valid unless this is done. The law does prescribe some choice in the manner of giving notice but the usual practice is to place an advertisement in one or more newspapers circulating in the area and also to display a notice in the accustomed place at the council's offices.

Notice of motion

Because no business may be transacted at a meeting of a local authority unless the prescribed notice has been given, it is customary for the standing orders of local authorities to specify a method whereby one or more members may indicate their intention to move a motion on some relevant subject at the next convenient meeting of the council.

This usually requires the sponsors of the motion to give written notice to the Secretary, signed by the mover and possibly by a given number of committed supporters, before the meeting at which it is intended to be moved. The purpose is that the Secretary must give the required statutory notice that the business is to be considered and it is vital, therefore, that the notice of motion is received before the prescribed deadline.

When the Secretary receives a notice of motion it is normal to date it, number it progressively to establish the order in which such notices have been received and to enter it in a book which is kept open for the inspection of any member of the council.

Any motion of which due notice has been received must

be included on the agenda paper of the next council meeting at which it can lawfully be considered. The custom is to put notices of motion last on the agenda paper in the order in which they have been received. The date and order of receipt may, therefore, be of material significance.

Any other business

It is not permitted to take business without notice and therefore the item "Any other business" should never appear on the agenda paper of any council meeting. Some local authorities attempt to circumvent this rule by including an agenda item such as "Business of an urgent character, at the discretion of the chairman". It is highly questionable whether this practice is legal but there are long-established precedents for it and no one is likely to object as long as the chairman limits the exercise of his discretion to items of genuine urgency and to which, if possible, there is no opposition.

The object is that, in public affairs, all points of view should receive a fair hearing and the purpose of the rule would appear to be a prevent supporters of a contentious course of action from forcing a "snap vote" at a time when their opponents happen to be inadequately represented. A chairman of a local authority, therefore, should be firmly advised of the duty to close the meeting immediately the advertised business has been completed and never canvass members to raise topics of which statutory notice has not been given.

CHAPTER 16

PUBLIC RELATIONS

The modern local government system is complex and is imperfectly understood by the average citizen. Too often people have no proper idea of the services available to them or how they can best make use of them and consequently are apt to complain that they do not get value for their rates and taxes. In this way a gulf tends to develop between the county and district councils and the public they are seeking to represent and this is a potential cause of inefficiency and error in the administration of local affairs.

In recent years, many local authorities have sought to reverse these trends by promoting public relations, that is to say they have attempted to explain the local authority to the public and to secure for themselves a more accurate impression of public opinion.

Many local authorities have recognised the importance of public relations by appointing a specialist Public Relations Officer, with or without staff to help and it seems that the remainder have added public relations to the responsibilities of one of their existing officers.

The Institute of Public Relations Local Government Group in their evidence to the Bains Working Group included a list of functions performed by public relations units in local government. This list was reproduced as Appendix K of the Bains Report and will repay study.

PRESS RELATIONS

The best avenue of information to the public is still, as it always was, a good local Press and the Public Relations

Officer who should give the highest priority to ensuring that local reporters are able to do a first-class job.

The Press now have a statutory right of attendance at all council and committee meetings and the authority should ensure that editors are supplied with all the documents to which they are entitled and which their reporters will need to follow the proceedings intelligently. Steps should be taken to make sure that every reporter has a comfortable place to sit, can see and hear distinctly all that is going on, with adequate light and table space in which to write notes.

The discussion will not always be intelligible to a reporter who lacks essential background information and arrangements should be made for the Press to have ready access to an officer of sufficient knowledge and stature to deal with their enquiries both before and after the meeting.

This officer should be vested with sufficient authority to make a full and frank disclosure of relevant facts. A reporter who has incomplete information can hardly be blamed if a story contains inaccuracies unfavourable to the council. There will be times when the significance of a story can only be understood in the light of certain information which cannot be released for publication. In these circumstances a reporter will appreciate a statement "off the record", which carries with it an undertaking not to publish the proscribed information. Any responsible reporter will respect a confidence; after all, the Press may want assistance again tomorrow. But the Public Relations Officer must play fair. Reporters should never be given information "off the record" if they can get the same information, without restriction, from elsewhere. The object of the exercise is to help reporters to write complete and well-balanced stories, not to prevent them from writing stories at all.

On occasion, it may be mutually helpful to arrange a press release or a press conference to explain some complex matter of special interest. However, this device should be used sparingly. Newspaper editors are the people to decide what will interest their readers and it is generally better to leave their reporters to follow up a story in the manner they think best. Nevertheless there will be times when a reporter will need expert help and it will be appreciated if this is made conveniently available.

The needs of the sound broadcasting and television news editors are largely the same as in the newspaper world but they have the additional complication that their stories must have immediate impact, either in sound or vision. Unlike the newspaper reader, the listener or viewer cannot take the news items away to read at leisure. It will be helpful, therefore, if the council can supply a personality with the ability to explain an item in a brief and interesting fashion for broadcasting. Most local politicans are willing to do this but sometimes training is necessary to make them good presenters.

Editors know their own needs best. They will understand the council's point of view even if it does not coincide with their own. It is a good plan to have meetings from time to time to exchange ideas and clear up areas of difficulty, always bearing in mind that the two sides are partners, and not rivals, in the public information business.

Press monitoring

Any officer concerned with the public relations of a local authority will need to read the local newspapers to keep abreast of news items and expressions of opinion concerning council's activities. It is a useful practice to mark those features which concern the local authority, to have them cut out and pasted into a file or press cuttings book. A press cuttings agency will supply such a service if required but it may be advantageous from the points of view of both convenience and economy to have the work done internally. A telephonist or an information desk clerk might handle this work during quiet periods.

There are several benefits to be gained from monitoring the Press in this way. Criticisms can be answered in letters to the editor. Depending on the council's policy in these matters, such letters can be written by the chairman of a committee, by a chief officer or by the public relations officer. In any event, the public relations officer will assist, if asked, in gathering the necessary information for a complete answer.

Newspaper editors like to publish letters from readers if they are brief and to the point. They stimulate interest in the material appearing in the paper and help to ensure that both sides of a question are given a fair hearing. Some councillors are less enthusiastic. Their reasoning is that answering criticism only invites further argument from those people who are discontented. This attitude is to be discouraged. A grievance that is ignored remains a grievance still, even if it is not repeated in the newspaper. A reasoned answer will satisfy some critics even if it cannot hope to persuade everyone.

Newspaper comment, whether it appears in the editor's own leader column, in featured articles or on the correspondence page, is the most reliable guide to public opinion. It is a remarkable fact that, in formulating their own views, people are heavily influenced by the printed word. Press cuttings supply the members of a local authority with a valuable barometer into the way that public opinion is shaping.

Sometimes a news item may present an officer with the first indication of a problem that has not arisen through the normal channel. Drastic action should never be taken on the strength of an unverified newspaper story. People do not always tell the whole truth when speaking to a reporter. But attention to a press cutting may begin a line of inquiry that will lead to some necessary action being taken and some useful public service being thereby rendered.

Defamation in newspaper reports

Any fair and accurate report published in a newspaper of the proceedings of a local authority or any of its committees is privileged unless the plaintiff is able to prove that the publication was made with malice. The effect is to exempt the reporter and his editor and publishers from liability for libel. The exemption does not apply to proceedings during a time when the Press are excluded from the meeting nor to private publication otherwise than in a newspaper report. Privilege would be lost if the newspaper refused, after request, to publish in the newspaper a reasonable and adequate letter or statement by way of contradiction or explanation of the report. If any newspaper report is complained of by the council, the appropriate course for the public relations officer to take is to communicate with the editor to seek his agreement to the publication of a suitable correction or rebuttal.

Civic newspapers

Several local authorities publish their own newspaper or bulletin, particularly those who employ a specialist public relations officer with experience of journalism. Such newspapers are rarely self-supporting and enjoy a limited circulation. Before founding one it is necessary to decide whether the publication will serve any useful purpose apart from its prestige value. However, some councils may feel that their policies, views or philosophy can only be put across through their own newspaper and that this is well worth the cost involved. But the dividing line between information and political propoganda is a very difficult one to draw.

If the newspaper serves the purpose of enabling the public to read in greater detail particulars of the council's activities, this is very much to the good. However, the question may need to be asked why the local Press cannot do the same job at least equally well.

Editing a newspaper of any quality is a job for a professional journalist and it is doubtful whether any administrator, however gifted, could conveniently combine the task with other duties.

PREPARATION OF LOCAL GUIDE

Some county councils and the vast majority of district and parish councils publish a guide to their district. There is a consistent demand from reference libraries for copies and information officers of local authorities find that many of their correspondents are seeking the kind of intelligence that is conveniently included in a publication of this kind.

There is handful of publishing houses that specialise in the production of local authority guides and the chosen firm will gladly place its expertise at the disposal of its customer authority. The success of the venture invariably depends upon the amount of advertising revenue obtained from local tradespeople. The publisher's own representative will undertake the canvass but may well ask to be supplied with some evidence, by way of a letter or pass from the sponsoring authority. It is desirable to agree beforehand the period during which the guide is to be valid and to let that fact be known. The advertiser will wish to be assured that displays will continue to appear in the official guide throughout the period agreed upon; if it is to continue to appear after that, the publisher will naturally be looking for the payment of an additional advertising premium.

Many local authorities issue their guide free and expect to derive no revenue from it. Others make a small charge for each copy or they require the publisher to make some payment for the concession. The imposition of a charge will tend to restrict the circulation and may be unfair to advertisers as well as detrimental to the publicity value of the guide. A charge to the publisher has to be passed on to advertisers in the form of higher advertisement rates. It is questionable, therefore, whether many local authorities are justified in seeking more than the considerable publicity value that they receive from their guide.

The editorial content is, if possible, best supplied by the local authority itself. The size of the guide will depend upon the amount of advertising revenue obtained. When the canvass has been completed, agreement should be reached with the publishers as to the approximate length of written matter and the number of photographs to be included. The subjects to be covered in the next and the scenes to be photographed are essentially matters for local decision.

Short notes on the history and geography of the place and its facilities, together with names and addresses of local organisations, are the kind of thing normally included. The work can be entrusted to a local journalist and photographer or to a member of the staff with the required flair. Any fees will be defrayed by the publisher.

PUBLICITY FOR HOLIDAY RESORTS

Those towns and districts which hope to attract tourists and holiday-makers in large numbers will undoubtedly employ their own publicity department and their principal publication is likely to be a holiday guide of much greater sophistication than the modest booklets favoured by other authorities. It is highly likely that this will be professionally produced and will describe and illustrate in detail the attractions offered by the resort. It will hardly suffice to wait for librarians and others to write for copies. Instead, enterprising publicity officers will arrange an advertising campaign in the national press, inviting potential visitors to write for the guide and other resort publicity.

The resort may be offering special attractions during the season in the form of conventions, musical or sporting festivals and the like and special publicity material may be prepared for visitors expected to attend these events. Other matter may be intended to publicise special features available at the resort, such as the championship golf courses in the vicinity.

The principal guide may include a section devoted to holidays and guest houses although it is probably better to publish a separate list of available accommodation. Some resorts maintain an accommodation bureau to which hoteliers are encouraged to notify their vacant rooms; intending visitors are then invited to approach the bureau in case of difficulty.

COUNCIL DIARY AND YEAR BOOK

Local authorities frequently find it useful to supply their members and principal officers with a year book giving the information which they will need from time to time if they are to do their jobs properly. If this is combined with a diary in which the various council and committee meetings and other official appointments can be recorded, the value of the publication will be greatly increased.

Certain information is common to most year books and might well be looked upon as the minimum content of any satisfactory manual. The names, addresses and telephone numbers of all members of the council are in this category, together possibly with their year of retirement. The membership of all committees and sub-committees is usually shown, with details of the programme of meetings. Particulars of the council's officers and their representatives on other bodies are also included among the essential information. Some statistics are normally given. The area, population, rateable value, penny rate product and rate levy are typical.

Some councils include details such as standing orders and financial regulations, details of local bylaws and extracts from Acts of Parliament, which hardly ever vary from year to year. It is no doubt sometimes convenient for members to have this information printed in their diaries but the cost of annual reprinting is excessive. It is probably better to print this kind of information in a separate booklet; if it is possible at reasonable cost to provide a pocket for it in the cover of the year book, this may represent a satisfactory compromise.

INFORMATION CENTRES AND LOCAL OFFICES

If the area of the local authority is large and it is not always easy for members of the public to visit the council's principal offices, consideration may have to be given to the provision of information centres or sub-offices in other parts of the locality.

It must be recognised that it is difficult if not impossible to staff every sub-office with officers of the same rank and qualification as are available at headquarters. Members of the public may need detailed professional advice on, for example, the planning condition with which they will have to comply if they apply for permission to extend their house. They will wish to discuss their problem with the senior planning officer concerned; it is unlikely that anyone at their local sub-office will be able to satisfy them.

Some councils take the view that it is necessary to provide a service locally, even if it costs more, since it will be a better service. Others do not think that this cost can be justified and would regard such sub-offices as going part of the way towards a local service. In which case staff at these offices need to be all rounders capable of dealing sympathetically and sensibly with a miscellany of complaints, inquiries and requests for information. They must be cautioned from going into detail that is beyond their capability but must exercise considerable tact if the public is not to complain of inadequate attention.

The use of terminals linked to the authority's control computer can provide information locally that previously required a visit to the Town Hall. The use of "View data" terminals also provides information on council and other services at a local level.

An ample supply of the basic forms for which the public may ask should be provided, such as applications to be placed on the housing waiting list. Publicity information should be freely available for the public to take from the inquiry desk. Basic reference works, at least, should be provided such as municipal and trade directories, maps of the district, the current register of electors and the council year book. Cash collection facilities might be made available to tenants and ratepayers.

PUBLICATIONS, FILMS AND EXHIBITIONS

The methods by which the activities of a local authority can be presented to its own public are varied and the choice will depend upon local circumstances and the amount of money which the authority feels able to afford.

Many departments prepare annual reports of their work but these are too often dull and uninteresting to the general public. Efforts are sometimes made to make them more attractive by the use of colour and the inclusion of pictures, and by the use of pithy and less formal language. Many authorities place great emphasis on the production of the annual report, which they are required to produce, and make it an attractive and readable document that can be used either as a promotional document for the area, or for publicising the work of the council among local organisations.

Informative leaflets concerning the facilities available at the local industrial estate or the municipal airport and things of that kind may serve a useful purpose. These can be distributed through libraries and information centres or by private arrangement with people having an interest in publicising the locality, such as estate agents.

Promotional material on industrial and other development opportunities is now a feature at many authorities.

Films are expensive to make and require expertise of a high standard. Nevertheless some local authorities have sponsored documentary films related to their work. The purpose which the film is intended to serve and the type of audience to which it is to be shown must be settled at the outset. The possibility of amateur cine-photography enthusiasts being encouraged to produce such a film might be worth exploring. Video recording however, now makes this type of presentation much easier and less costly.

Exhibitions often create quite a lot of interest, particularly if they are concerned with a current project which has already caught the public's attention, such as the submission of a town or village plan or the choice of route for a by-pass. These may be limited to the display of still photographs and diagrams, with a few models, otherwise the expense is likely to be considerable. The choice of the right hall for the exhibition is important and it is often advisable to arrange for a well-informed officer to be present to speak to visitors and to answer questions.

PROVISION OF LECTURERS AND SPEAKERS

Most localities have a number of private or community organisations who are constantly on the look-out for interesting speakers to address their meetings. The public relations officer may care to establish a panel comprising officers of the local authority who have the ability to talk interestingly about their jobs. He will then be in a position to approach programme secretaries with an offer to help them in their search for suitable speakers. Personal contact of this kind is often worth far more than reading matter; a person who would not cross the road to see an exhibition may be agreeably surprised by a well-presented talk.

Arrangements might be made for officers of the council to visit schools for the purpose of talking to pupils on the subject of civic affairs. Many schools find it difficult to fit such activities into their curricula but the short period between the completion of the sessional examinations and the end of term is a time schoolmasters are often grateful for some variety in the programme. The public relations department can help by the provision of visual aids such as slides and transparencies.

"WELCOME TO CITIZENSHIP"

An inspired public relations idea of a few years ago, which is still popular, was named "Welcome to Citizenship". The idea is that all young voters coming on to the electoral register for the first time on reaching the age of eighteen are invited to a reception at the civic centre. They are usually greeted, with some show of ceremony, by the civic head and are offered some suitable refreshment. If numbers permit, it will be greatly appreciated if the young people are individually introduced to the civic head by name and given the opportunity of a short, personal conversation.

The subsequent programme will depend upon the facilities available but interest is usually shown in the council chamber and the civic plate. If someone is available to relate the history of the latter, the young people might be invited to sit in the councillors' places whilst this is done. Another idea is the creation of a dummy polling station with volunteer staff in which the young visitors might receive some instruction on the procedure for casting their vote.

Special arrangements can be made for organised groups of all ages to attend council meetings or to visit council establishments.

PUBLIC MEETINGS

From time to time, issues of deep public concern may arise and it is then a good public relations exercise to hold a meeting in a local hall or cinema to which the general public will be invited by an announcement in the local Press. Members and officers of the council may occupy the first hour of the meeting in the explaining the project and the way in which the council propose to handle it. The meeting can then be open to comment from the floor.

It is extremely difficult to estimate the numbers who may attend a meeting of this nature but the attempt must be made. A handful of people meeting in a large hall are sure to be disappointed; a large number trying to crowd into a hall that is too small will create chaos. Microphones and amplifying equipment should be provided and the chairman should insist on their use.

Much good may accrue from meetings between local authorities, as for example between a district council and its constituent parish councils. In this case it is possible to ascertain how many people will be attending and it is a wise precaution to do so. The opportunity may be taken to invite questions to be submitted to the organisers beforehand. These questions can be answered by the appropriate people in the early part of the meeting and whilst they are doing so, it is likely that people present will be reminded of other matters they would wish to raise for discussion. People tend to be self-conscious and embarrassed when invited to speak too early in a meeting and, if an attempt is made to start a discussion from "cold", the meeting may never really get off the ground.

STAFF ATTITUDES

Finally, it must be stressed that the best public relations are the ways in which "front line" staff relate to the general public that they serve. Most people's knowledge of council services is acquired at first hand through refuse collectors, cashiers, telephonists, reception staff, planning assistants etc. Their attitude to the public is crucial for good public relations. Ensuring that such people are aware of their value in this respect needs to be re-inforced through training and by encouragement from senior and top management of the authority.

CHAPTER 17

LAND CHARGES

A series of Acts of Parliament passed in 1925, which is commonly called "the property legislation", had as one of its major aims the protection of purchasers of land. The Local Land Charges Act, 1975, furthers that object by requiring the registration of certain charges and incumbrances relating to land and it facilitates searches in the registers maintained for that purpose.

In general, the charges which are registrable under the Act are those that run with the land so as to be binding on subsequent purchasers. Such charges are known as "land charges", a term that is not defined, but registrable charges are expressly specified in the Act or have been so specified in subsequent legislation. Tables of registrable land charges are published and it is obvious that a registrar must be familiar with the various charges he is under a duty to register.[1]

Certain land charges are registrable at H.M. Land Registry by the Chief Land Registrar. Broadly speaking, these are incumbrances that run with the land but which may not be revealed when title is being investigated. Other charges, are registrable by a local registrar, and are known as "local land charges". Under subsequent legislation, certain other matters are registrable in the local land charges register even though, strictly speaking, they are not local land charges at all. The distinction is of importance inasmuch as it affects the degree of protection afforded to a purchaser.

The registrar of local land charges, outside Greater

London, was formerly the Clerk of the Council of the district in which the land is situated. Since that statutory office was abolished by the Local Government Act 1972, the responsibility now falls upon the "proper officer" of the district council. Notwithstanding the normal provision, which makes the local authority responsible for appointing its own "proper officer" for any purpose, the registrar of local land charges is to be a proper officer prescribed by rules made by the Lord Chancellor under the provisions of the Land Charges Act 1925.

THE DUTIES OF THE LOCAL REGISTRAR

The responsibilities of the Registrar of Local Land Charges fall under two distinct headings. One is to ensure that all charges, burdens and incumbrances which are registrable as local land charges are, in fact, so registered. The other is to ensure that searches requisitioned are promptly and accurately made and the appropriate certificate is despatched. There has grown up, alongside the system of local land charges, a complementary system of Supplementary Enquiries which the proper officer will normally answer. He does so in his capacity as an officer of the local authority and not as Registrar of Local Land Charges but, as an administrative convenience, he invariably performs both duties simultaneously.

It is not intended here to discuss what is or is not registrable nor what is the appropriate part of the register in which a particular charge should be registered. The general point must be made, however, that all local land charges (as specified) are registrable, together with certain other charges already referred to; any other charge on land is not registrable. The local registrar is under a duty to study new legislation with care so as to ensure that newly created local land charges are duly registered whilst making certain that his register is not cluttered with entries that should not be there.

Many registrable land charges will be enforceable by the local authority of which the registrar is an officer and it is his duty to register all such charges without application. For this purpose the Registrar of Local Land Charges will need to maintain close co-operation with other departments to ensure that relevant matters are brought to his attention as part of a recognised procedure.

A close watch must be kept by the local registrar on action taken by his council or any committee as it is most important that any land charges that may be created by their action should be registered forthwith. Every official certificate of search must be correct and complete as at close of business on the day of issue even if a new charge has been created on the same day. To this end, the committee clerk must be firmly instructed on his responsibilities towards his colleague, the local land charges clerk.

It is worth remembering that, if any record maintained by a local authority contains the relevant particulars of a charge, a reference in the land charges register to such a record is sufficient if the relevant particulars can thereby be easily traced even by a member of the public making a personal search. A good example is the statutory register maintained under the Town and Country Planning Acts. A high proportion of restrictions on land nowadays arise under these Acts. It seems wasteful to record these details in full in two statutory registers maintained by the same authority. When handling searches, it is maintained by the same authority. When handling searches, it is a valuable precaution to check minute books and other appropriate registers or records whether or not a cross-reference appears in the local land charges register.

Other authorities, such as a county council, may make application for the registration of a local land charge and the registrar must immediately make the appropriate entry provided the prescribed fee has been paid.

Anyone who requires a search to be made in the register may submit a requisition to that effect, together with the prescribed fee, and the registrar must thereupon make the search required and issue a certificate setting forth the result. This does not in any way impair the right of any person to make a personal search in the register.

LIABILITY OF THE REGISTRAR

If the registrar or any other person employed in the registry is wilfully negligent in relation to an official certificate of search, or is party to an act of fraud or collusion, he will be guilty of a misdemeanour punishable by a fine or imprisonment.

If the register is inadequately maintained, or false entries are disclosed attributable to the personal carelessness of the registrar, he may be subjected to a civil action for negligence by any person who has incurred damages thereby.

A member of the staff who is negligent in performing a search may be similarly liable, as may his employing authority, but not the registar unless he committed the tort in person. Such actions are unlikely to occur often in practice since a purchaser for value will take the land free from any charge that ought to have been disclosed on search. Action will still lie with the person or authority which could otherwise have enforced the charge but this will be, in most cases, the same local authority which is vicariously liable for the error of its officer.

If a charge which is not properly registrable is nevertheless registered and someone suffers loss thereby, an action for damages would lie against the authority which applied for the registration of the charge in addition to any cause of action against the registrar for carelessness.

It is most important that registrars and their staff should be adequately insured against common law claims but it is even more important to take the most thorough precautions against the possibility of error since the result of a mistake is more likely to be a serious administrative embarrassment for the authority itself rather than a civil or criminal action.

FORM OF REGISTER

The Local Land Charges Rules, require that the register shall be divided into numbered parts, each containing entries of the type and in the form specified in the rules.

In addition to his duty to register local land charges and other matters that are statutorily registrable, the local registrar must make any incidental variations to the entries in his register which may from time to time be necessary and, where any charge has been discharged or become unenforceable, the local registrar must thereupon cancel the appropriate entry in the register.

Loose-leaf registers, with hardboard covers, have long been popular and suitable registers and pages with appropriately ruled and titled columns are obtainable from leading local government law stationers. Strictly speaking, the various parts of the register should be kept in separate volumes or, if the number of entries does not justify the use of separate volumes, in different sections of the same volume. For this purpose, dividers will be provided by the stationer.

This requirement is not administratively convenient for the registrar who may have to search in several parts of the register for entries in respect of the same property or parcel of land. It is not unknown, therefore, for a registrar to maintain the whole of his register on the basis of an alphabetical or numerical order of property. All entries relating to the same property are grouped together, irrespective of the part of the register to which they belong. The latter will, of course, be apparent from the title and columnar ruling of the entry in question.

Card index systems have hitherto been less popular and have been used mainly in densely populated districts where the predominant use of street names and numbers has lent itself to a self-indexing method. The land charges system has now been in operation for half a century and control, of development — which has caused a vast increase in the number of land charges — for more than half of that time.

Local land charges registers are thus becoming voluminous and local registrars are seeking alternatives to the traditional bound registers. As card index systems have become more sophisticated they, or methods based on similar principles, have come to present an attractive alternative.

For example, large cards or folios can be filed in cabinets, possibly by suspended visible filing methods, each card bearing the official reference of the land or property, usually in relation to the index map, and its name or description, if any. Space on each card is allotted to every part of the register and charges are entered in the appropriate space. Entries relating to any one parcel of land are thus contained on the same card. Photographed copies of entries may serve as schedules to a certificate of search.

Such patent systems are not inexpensive but the work of modernising a local land charges register is likely to take a number of years and the cost can be spread accordingly.

FORM OF INDEX

To enable entries in it to be traced, the register of local land charges is required to have an index, which has to be in the form of a map or a card-index or in any other approved form.

Originally, the index had to be in the form of a map unless the Minister approved otherwise. In towns and cities, where many entries related to single urban properties, the use of a map index was wholly inappropriate and the rule was either totally disregarded or given only token acknowledgement. For practical purposes, registrars relied upon alphabetical indices compiled by reference to street names. In the cases of loose-leaf registers, index sheets were included at the front of the register with columns relating to the various parts of the register. Upon finding the required address in the index, the searcher could immediately ascertain the various parts of the register in which entries occurred. A similar system was incorporated into card index systems.

Nevertheless a map index remains indispensable by any local registrar whose district includes any rural or undeveloped components. This must be on a fairly large scale in order that boundaries of individual properties may be clearly defined and references plainly written. The use of the Ordnance Survey maps may be found satisfactory. This means that the map index will, in many districts, comprise perhaps a hundred sheets or more.

RECEIPT OF REQUISITIONS

Any person who wishes an official search to be made in the local land charges register may lodge a requisition with the registrar on payment of the prescribed fee. Every requisition must be made on the prescribed form and must be signed by the person making it or by his solicitor. It must identify the land in respect of which a search is to be made, either by the submission of a scale plan or by any other sufficient means.

A separate requisition is necessary in respect of each parcel of land in respect of which a search is desired except where, for the purpose of a single transaction, an official certificate is required in respect of two or more parcels of land having a common boundary or which are separated only by a road, river, railway, stream or canal.

Details of requisitions received for searches should be entered in a special book with cash columns to record the fees paid. This money will have to be accounted for and it may be found convenient, by agreement with the Treasurer, for fees to be totalled each day or at some other acceptable interval and paid over to the cashier, who will sign the entries in the book or affix an official receipt. The auditors will certainly wish to verify that the fees so accounted for correspond to those expressly due and received.

The requisition should be examined as soon as possible and certainly before the official search is attempted. Requisitions are sometimes addressed to the wrong registrar. If the land is not within the district of the registrar to whom the requisition is addressed, the requisition with the accompanying fee should be readdressed without delay to the correct registrar. As a precaution and a courtesy it is advisable to notify the sender that his requisition has been redirected.

Sometimes the fee paid is incorrect. In this case the sender must be asked to remit the balance or a refund must be made as the case may be. An official certificate should never be issued until the correct fees have been paid.

It is the responsibility of the person making the search to define the land in respect of which a search is to be made and the duty of the registrar to check it. The registrar may believe that he can identify the land but if he has the slightest doubt he should return the requisition and insist on being supplied with a better plan and particulars. He is never justified in guessing since, if the certificate is in respect of the wrong property, he may render himself liable to an action for negligence.

ISSUE OF CERTIFICATE

Since the absorption of the former registers maintained by Clerks of county councils into those of the proper officer of the district council, all requisitions for official certificates of search are made to the latter officer. Provided that the register and index are properly maintained and the property is properly identified in the requisition, the official search should present no difficulty. Official schedules to the certificate of search are prescribed by the Rules and can be obtained from law stationers. If no entry appears on the register, all that is necessary is to complete an Official Certificate of Search stating that no subsisting entries have been revealed. On the other hand, if one or more entries are discovered the appropriate schedules will be completed, signed and attached to the certificate, which will indicate the number of schedules annexed.

For some years to come, entries may be revealed in the local land charges register which refer to some public record maintained by the county council. It will then be necessary for a schedule to be completed from the county council's record and this is likely to be a cause of delay, particularly if County Hall is some distance from the district council's offices. Otherwise there seems to be no good reason why an Official Certificate of Search should not be ready for despatch on the same day, or at the latest on the day following the receipt of the requisition. The registrar's staff need to be capable of handling an average day's work, since no headway can be made if they are not, and requisitions do not tend to seasonal fluctuation. Delays used to occur before the reorganisation of 1974 because the registrar's staff often did have other duties which were subject to seasonal pressures impinging on the time available for performing searches. With the creation of larger authorities, this trouble has been largely eliminated.

The prinicipal cause of delay nowadays is the system of supplementary enquiries. Agreement has been reached between the Law Society and the local authority associations concerning a series of stock questions which solicitors will normally submit to a local authority at the same time as they submit a requisition for search and for which they will pay an additional fee. This is really a private arrangement between the solicitor and the council and officially it has nothing to do with the statutory system of land charges. The registrar handles the supplementary enquiries in his capacity as an officer of the district council; indeed, if the solicitor wishes to add further questions not in the agreed series, and to pay a further fee, and the proper officer of the local authority is able and willing to answer, this is quite in order.

The problem is that the answers to the supplementary questions are not in the local land charges register and, for the most part, are not within the personal knowledge of the proper officer. The answers are within the knowledge of different officers of the council, such as the Engineer, Surveyor, Environmental Health Inspector or Treasurer. Some have to be referred to officers of the county council.

The usual practice is to send an internal memorandum to

each officer concerned asking him to answer, so far as he is able, the usual supplementaries and any special enquiries in respect of the land or property specified. Most of them will do so quite quickly but, unfortunately, there is often one who is unable to supply the desired information immediately, with the result that the whole process is delayed.

A speedier method is to arrange with the heads of department concerned for an officer of the local land charges registry to obtain the information in person, either by exercising permission to search the department's records or by interviewing the officers who are doing the work.

Although the district council is asked to obtain the information required from the county council, it is a waste of time and money for the latter to send it to the district council for onward transmission. The better plan is to arrange for the county council to send their replies direct to the enquiring solicitor. If the latter is unfamiliar with the procedure, it may be necessary to explain why replies from the district council are incomplete.

In replying to supplementary enquiries, officers should attempt to be as helpful as possible and to avoid stereotyped and over-cautious answers. If the answer to a special enquiry is not known it is honest to say so and to return the fee.

The Official Certificate of Search, the schedules and the supplementary enquiry form will be returned, duly signed by or on behalf of the proper officer, together with a receipt for the fees. It is probably better that the official receipt of the council should be sent to the applicant in which case the local registrar will be content with the cashier's signature in his Requisitions Received Book.

Copies should be filed of all documents issued, both originals and duplicates bearing a reference number corresponding to that in the Requisitions Received Book.

CHAPTER 18

ELECTORAL REGISTRATION AND ELECTIONS

THE REGISTRATION OF ELECTORS

The Representation of the People Act 1983, provides for the preparation of an annual register to be published not later than the fifteenth of February each year. Each register is to be used for elections at which polling day falls within the period of 12 months from February 16th in the year of publication.

The qualifying date for inclusion on the register, so far as Great Britain is concerned, is the 10th of October in the preceding year.

The preparation of the register for each constituency, or the appropriate part of it, is the responsibility of the electoral registration officer who, in England and Wales, is an officer appointed as such by the corresponding district council or London Borough Council or by the Common Council of the City of London.

The manner in which the registration officer is to carry out his duties is strictly controlled by directions from the Secretary of State.

The register, so far as practicable, combines the list of parliamentary electors and that of local government electors, the names of those who qualify only as local government electors being marked to indicate that fact. Special provision is made in the regulations for the registration of those persons who will attain the age of 18 during the currency of the register and for the registration of service voters and merchant seamen.

219

It is the duty of the electoral registration officer to have a house-to-house or other sufficient inquiry made as a persons entitled to be registered (otherwise than as service voters) and to publish "electors lists" (which may take the form of a draft register) stating the names and qualifying addresses of the persons who appear to him to be entitled to be registered. For this purpose, the registration officer has authority to require information to be given to him.

The electors lists are to be made available for public inspection on or before November 28th each year and any person aggrieved by an omission or entry may formally lodge a claim or an objection with the electoral registration officer. There is provision for appeals against a decision of the registration officer.

The canvass

It was at one time the common practice of electoral registration officers to organise a house-to-house canvass throughout their districts. This appears to be no longer the case. The use of the postal services is considered sufficient for the straightforward inquiries, the time and energies of canvassers being largely reserved for visits to those houses and other premises that present cases of difficulty.

The choice of reliable and energetic canvassers is essential to the success of the operation. Many registration officers employ members of their own staff, or other officers of the council, on a part-time basis working in the evenings or at week-ends. Others prefer to engage canvassers on a temporary, full-time basis.

The desired information is required to be set forth on a prescribed form, known as Form A. This form is usually sent by post to the occupier of every dwelling in the district. This task does not often present any difficulty since the district council normally has the basic information in its rating records and arrangements can be made for Forms A to be addressed by computer, addressing machine or other available mechanical means.

It is often convenient for one canvasser to be allocated responsibility for one ward or polling district. The envelopes in which Forms A are despatched are so printed that, by sealing down the flap, they can be used as pre-addressed, postage paid, envelopes in which the completed forms are to be returned to the electoral registration officer. The canvasser will be instructed to endorse each envelope with the polling district letter or the reference number allocated, either by hand or by the use of a rubber stamp which will be supplied. This will facilitate the sorting of the envelopes when they are returned.

The despatch of the forms and the return of many of them at the peak period, around the 10th of October, will place extra strain on the postal services and it is wise to make advance arrangements with the local postmaster for their handling.

It should be emphasised to every canvasser that it is their first duty to ensure that Form A is delivered or left at every dwelling in the ward. Newly built houses, caravans and other temporary homes may not yet have been incorporated in local rating records. The canvasser must be relied upon, notwithstanding the use made of the post office, to survey the territory and do the best he can to make sure that no eligible voter is overlooked.

The method of canvassing

Each canvasser must be provided with the equipment necessary to do the job thoroughly and accurately.

The existing Register of Electors may be printed with margins wide enough to enable it to be used as working copy but it is more likely to be convenient to require the canvasser to cut the register into columnar strips and to paste each column on the left hand side of a sheet of paper. These sheets of paper may then be clipped into a file cover to form a loose-leaf working copy register. The right hand side of the pages of the loose-leaf register may be ruled to prescribe space for particular entries or, if preferred, may be left as a wide blank margin to give maximum flexibility. Another form, entitled "Canvasser's Return", may be affixed to the inside front cover.

Form A will already have been addressed but canvassers must ensure that a form is sent to every residential address within their territory, including any new or temporary properties. A number of spare copies of Form A and envelopes will be supplied for this purpose. A tick or similar mark should be placed against each address on the working register to indicate that Form A has been sent and the number of forms despatched should be entered on the Canvasser's Return. When forms have been prepared, checked and placed in envelopes, they should be made up into bundles of a convenient number, as agreed beforehand with the post office, and returned to the registration officer for bulk despatch according to the approved procedure.

When a form is returned, another appropriate mark should be made in the working register to indicate that the completed form has been received. The details given must then he compared with the entries in the previous register, as recorded on the left hand side of the working copy. Where these are the same, a small tick may be placed against each elector's name in the left hand column. If there is to be an addition, the new name (and address, if required) should be distinctly printed on the right hand margin opposite the point at which it is to be inserted. Any required deletion should be boldly ruled through.

In the case of anyone who is to reach the age of eighteen during the currency of the register, the date of birth should be shown in brackets after the name. Such entries should be deleted automatically after one year and it should not be necessary for a canvasser to rule them through.

In the interests of brevity, it is normal to register the first name, extra initials and surname of each voter but, wherever ambiguity would ensue, a longer entry is necessary. This may comprise the use of two or more Christian names or the use of the expressions "senior" and "junior".

Whenever Form A is returned by the post office as unde-livered, a visit will be necessary as near as possible to the qualifying date (October 10th) to ascertain whether the property has been re-occupied in the meantime.

Once Forms A have been checked they must be filed, in correct sequence, on a file to be provided for the purpose. A lever-arch file is usually considered suitable. It is necessary to be particular about this as complaints are always received about alleged errors in the register, particu-larly under the stress of polling day, and it is most important that the returning officer should at that time be able quickly to turn up the completed Form A in question.

The completion of the canvass

Canvassers will be supplied with certain additional forms to enable to follow up Form A where such action is necessary.

One form is used to obtain further information from the householder wherever it appears that Form A has been inaccurately or incompletely filled up. For example, where several additional names appear in the same year in the same household it is to be suspected that the householder has mistakenly included children under voting age.

Another form is sent as a reminder when Form A has not been returned by the qualifying date, and a final reminder may be sent five days later, together with another Form A in case the first one has been lost.

If this does not produce the required result, further meas-ures are urgently necessary. Perhaps a telephone call may suffice but usually a personal call to the property by the canvasser will be needed. Householders may have difficulty in completing the form and the canvasser must be prepared to write down the details on their behalf. If the householder is away, information may be obtained from a neighbour; this may be no more than confirmation that there has been no change from the previous year. The canvasser should always attempt to obtain a signature to the completed Form

A, but if this is not possible, should make an endorsement stating the source of his information. If the details are later disputed, the registration officer may wish to quote authority for the entry.

Members of the Armed Forces must not be registered by the canvasser; they are eligible only on their own Service Declarations. A person who has left the services since the previous register was compiled, however, will be eligible for his civilian address. In such a case, the letter "S" must be deleted.

Merchant seamen are entitled to be registered as electors for any address at which they would be residing but for their occupation. The prefix letter "M" must be entered against their name in the register.

All persons between the ages of 18 and 65 are now eligible for jury service unless they are in one of the exempted occupations. Any elector who claims to be over 65 should be identified.

The electors lists

The electors lists, which the registration officer is required to prepare and publish, are to be framed in separate parts for each ward or parish.

There are, strictly speaking, three electors lists for each such unit. List A is the register currently in force, List B is a list of newly qualified voters and List C is a list of persons who have ceased to be qualified. However, the electors lists may now be prepared as a single draft register showing only the names and addresses of the persons whom the registration officer thinks are entitled to be registered. This is a great advance on the traditional method, which was expensive in terms of both time and money, and it facilitates the use of computers or modern methods of printing.

The draft register or the electors lists must be published by November 28th by making a copy available for inspection at the office of the registration officer. It is also necessary to make a copy of the appropriate part of the register available for inspection in each electoral area; the custom is to arrange for the electors lists to be displayed in post offices or other buildings to which the public have access. They must be kept so available until the new register is published.

The registration officer must publish a notice in the prescribed form of the publication of the draft register or electors lists, which must be combined with a notice relating to the making of claims and objections.

Correction of errors

By Section 11 of the Representation of the People Act 1983, an electoral registration officer is empowered to make a necessary correction to the register at any time, subject to a rule that any alternation made after a notice of election has been given shall not have effect for the purposes of that election. This is a great change for the better; a long-standing cause of injustice has been removed, largely because of the development of modern printing processes and other means of reproduction, such as computers.

This power enables the registration officer to make amendments of many kinds in addition to those arising as a result of formal claims or objections. The names of dead electors can be deleted and clerical errors can be corrected without formality but, if it is proposed to make an alteration for the purpose of ensuring that a person shall not be incorrectly registered or registered when not so entitled, he must be given an opportunity to object.

Service voters

The procedure relating to service voters is laid down in the relevant regulations. To qualify for inclusion on the register, service declarations are to be received by the registration officer by December 16th. On or shortly after that date, the registration officer should compile a list of service voters and make appropriate arrangements with the printer or computer manager for their names to be incorporated in the register.

Absent voters, proxies and postal proxies

The rules governing the registration of absent voters and their proxies are contained in the regulations. The records and lists of absent voters, proxies and postal proxies are to be kept in such form as the registration officer may decide. As soon as they are prepared, copies are to be made available for inspection at his office and a copy is to be supplied, without fee, to each candidate or his election agent.

Publication and sale of the register

The register is to be published by making a copy available for inspection at each of the places at which the electors lists were displayed. A copy is to be sent to the Secretary of State and to the British Museum. The electoral registration officer must also supply, on request and without fee, one copy of the appropriate part of the register to every councillor and candidate for local government election.

The returning officer for the parliamentary constituency must supply one free copy to the Member of Parliament and other copies to the persons specified in the regulations.

It will be convenient to supply a copy to the Crown Court in which those electors known to be ineligible for jury service, namely those over 65, will have been suitably marked.

So long as sufficient copies are available, they are to be sold at a prescribed fee to any of the people specified or to the public at large.

THE CONDUCT OF ELECTIONS

The returning officer at a parliamentary election is to be the sheriff in a county constituency and the mayor or chairman of the district or borough council in a borough constituency. The functions which the returning officer performs in person are, however, somewhat limited being normally restricted to receiving the writ, declaring the result, returning the name of the successful candidate to the clerk of the Crown and signing the public notice of the result. The remaining duties are performed by the acting returning officer. In a borough constituency he will be the same person who was appointed electoral registration officer by the appropriate borough or district council. Otherwise he will be a registration officer designated by the Secretary of State.

As regards local elections, a county council appoint an officer to be the returning officer for the county and a district council appoint one for the district and for the parishes and communities within its boundaries. The returning officer at an election of London borough councillors is the proper officer of the borough.

All parliamentary and local government elections are conducted in accordance with the various Representation of the People Acts and rules made by the Secretary of State. Every returning officer or acting returning officer needs to be thoroughly familiar with the election rules, and it is not practicable to attempt to summarise them in this chapter.

Provision as to time

The proceedings at any election must be conducted to a strict timetable. Various steps have to be taken before a given date before polling day and the returning officer should compile a list of the essential acts to be performed noting the last date for their performance in each case. A calendar of this kind is often provided by law stationers but, in a case of a by-election, the returning officer might find it desirable to compile one for himself.

There are a number of provisions dealing with polling hours and, if an election is to be contested, the returning officer will need to give attention to determining the correct hours of poll.

Prepatations for an election

The returning officer at an ordinary local government election has the advantage of knowing well beforehand the date chosen for the poll (if any) and can make preparations accordingly. A casual vacancy may arise unexpectedly but even so the returning officer may well be in a position to influence the choice of polling day and can thus make preparations in an orderly way.

The returning officer for a parliamentary constituency has no such advantage. The Prime Minister of the day will undoubtedly time the announcement of a General Election to maximise political advantage and the announcement may well be delayed until as late as three weeks before polling day. The acting returning officer is therefore obliged to keep election machinery in full working order so that only the minimum remains to be done after the day of election has been announced.

The choice of polling station

The polling station to be used for each polling district needs to be chosen well in advance. Indeed, for a number of good reasons, the same polling station should be used, if possible, at every election, whether it be a parliamentary election or a local election of any kind.

The electorate becomes accustomed to voting at a particular place. If the station is changed, it is virtually certain that some electors will go to the old place and not vote.

The staff of the school or other building used for the purpose will be used to the interruption and will know the routine steps to take but at a new place there may be difficulty and resentment.

The crew delivering election equipment to polling stations will know where to go if they have been before and this will certainly expedite their work. Likewise, the polling staff will probably know what facilities are available for their use At a new station they might have to go to considerable trouble to find out beforehand.

Every possible consideration should be afforded to the owners or staff of the building chosen as a polling station with the intention of minimising the inconvenience to them. They should be told the date chosen for polling day as soon as it is known and, if it is practicable to divide the building, only as much should be taken for polling as is strictly necessary.

It must be remembered that the polling staff will be on duty all day, possibly for a continuous period of 13 hours, and in that time they will not be permitted to leave the station. Adequate toilet facilities are therefore essential and it is also highly desirable that they should have some means of making themselves hot drinks. Some thought should also be given to questions of heating, lighting and ventilation, particularly in the winter months.

Preparation of poll cards

The acting returning officer is responsible for the issue to electors of poll cards at parliamentary elections and it is generally considered advisable to have to least two sets of cards in stock as a precaution against one snap election following another.

The cards may be printed with certain standard information such as the name of the constituency and the voting instructions. A number can be overprinted with each polling district letter and the address of the corresponding polling station. Two details cannot be inserted until an announcement of a pending election is made; one is the date of polling day and the other is the elector's number on the register (unless it is a certainty that an election will be held on the current register as is the case in a Government's fifth year of office).

Most Electors lists and poll cards are now produced by computer, so that production is greatly facilitated compared with the previous clerical exercise.

Purchase of stationery

Measures may be taken in good time to replenish stationery stocks and avoid last-minute demands to harassed suppliers. Some stationery and equipment, like stamping instruments, are used at one election after another but these should all be checked to ensure that they are still complete and in working order.

The smaller items of stationery tend to be consumed and need to be replaced. The leading stationers supply a standard pack containing all the sundry items of small stationery that a presiding officer will need.

Selection of staff

A considerable amount of work will need to be done in a short period prior to polling day, the returning officer will probably wish to second members of his regular staff from other work and will delegate responsibilities to each of them.

In addition, he will provisionally recruit staff to run the polling stations on election day. Whilst he may leave the choice of poll clerks until a late stage, when it is known who will be available, he will certainly want to ensure that the presiding officers are people with previous election experience, preferably at the polling station allocated to them.

Final preparations

Once an announcement of a parliamentary election has been made or, in the case of a local election, in the last month or so before polling day, a great deal of work will have to be done in a short space of time. One of the most urgent tasks is the organisation of the postal vote and it is very advisable that one or two thoroughly reliable officers should concentrate their efforts entirely on this.

Arrangements will need to be made with the printer to give absolute priority to election work. The Notice of Election will require to be printed straight away. The notice of Poll and the ballot papers cannot be completed until the close of nominations and the period allowed for withdrawal. The period between then and the despatch of ballot papers to postal voters is only a few days and it may be necessary to ask the printer to provide a small supply of ballot papers for this purpose in advance of his bulk order. The printer is also likely to have urgent work from the candidates in the form of election addresses and the like.

Liaison should be established with the police, the press and the post office. Security arrangements at the polling stations and the counting hall should be agreed with the superintendent of police, an escort may be needed to get some ballot boxes through to the counting hall in good time, some traffic control may be needed near the counting hall or a busy polling station.

Poll cards and, to some extent, postal votes will put extra pressure on the post office and the postmaster may be grateful if the former at least can be released in batches.

Letters will now be sent confirming the booking of polling stations and arrangements will be made for polling screens, tables and other equipment to be taken from their store and delivered to the various locations.

The selection of polling station and counting staff will be completed and letters of appointment sent to them. Steps will be taken to ensure that everyone concerned with the election makes the necessary Declaration of Secrecy.

One officer should be made responsible for assembling and equipping the ballot boxes. Each box should be legibly marked with the name of the polling station at which it is to be used. The box must contain the relevant part of the register, the absent voters and proxy list, an adequate supply of ballot papers, the stamping instrument and all the stationery and notices required. It is a good idea to have the presiding officers collect their own ballot boxes on the previous day and to check the contents.

Postal votes

The procedure for the issue and receipt of postal ballot papers is prescribed in Part V of the Representation of the People Regulations, 1983 which must be precisely followed.

The count

There are a number of provisions in parliamentary and local election rules relating to the counting of votes but a good deal is left to the discretion of the returning officer.

The success of the operation may well depend upon the choice of hall in which the count is to be held, the arrangement of furniture and the selection of staff. The transportation of the ballot boxes from the more remote polling stations is critical if the completion of the count should not be unduly delayed.

The best way to organise the furniture in the counting hall is the shape of a horseshoe or hollow square with the counting assistants seated inside and the counting agents overseeing them from the opposite side of the table. The acting returning officer and his supervisory staff may be seated at a table looking into the horseshoe. Counting staff can be distracted by people coming up behind them and this, if permitted, is a common cause of error.

As the ballot boxes arrive, an assistant will receive them at a reception desk near the door and as near as possible to the acting returning officer's table. The ballot paper account will be passed to the table and the ballot box may be passed along the horseshoe and its contents emptied for counting. The empty boxes will eventually be passed on and stacked at the far side of the room. The parcels containing unused stationery and the like will have been heaped in a space allocated for the purpose near the reception desk. By these arrangements the count may proceed in an orderly fashion.

The first stage of the procedure is the verification of the ballot paper account, that is to say to discover whether the number of papers in the ballot box coincides with the number of ballot papers recorded as having been issued by the presiding officer.

The second stage, which is never commenced until all ballot papers have been accounted for, will vary according to the number of seats to be filled. In a contest for a single seat the matter is easy. The votes are simply sorted into piles for each candidate and made up into bundles of 25 or 50 by the use of clips or elastic bands. Bad and doubtful votes are passed to the head table for scrutiny. When sorted, the bundles of ballot papers are passed back to a table inside the horseshoe where the number of votes cast for each candidate is ascertained.

If votes are permitted to be cast for more than one candidate the use of a clerical procedure is required. Usually this involves each counting assistant in copying the votes cast on each ballot paper on to a master copy under the supervision of the counting agents. Ruling the horizontal columns on the master copy carefully to coincide with those on the ballot paper minimises the possibility of error.

Essential nature of further references

The foregoing are merely practice notes on some of the work which the Secretary and his electoral registration and elections staff may be called upon to perform. They do not remotely cover all the responsibilities of this section of the department. Reference to statutes and regulations and to the various standard works on election law is indispensable.

CHAPTER 19

CIVIC AFFAIRS

Any book dealing with the responsibilities of a local authority could not claim to be complete unless some reference were made to civic affairs and ceremony. It is, unfortunately, a subject that is incapable of precise definition. Practices vary between one authority and the next, reflecting local circumstances and local traditions. The most that can be said is that the customs described have been followed by some councils but not by others. Each follows its own inclinations.

Council meetings

Most of the former boroughs and county boroughs introduced some ceremonial colour into their council meetings. The practice was less common in county councils and in urban and rural district councils but appeared to be spreading. The post 1974 local authorities, are inclined to less ceremonial than their predecessors.

It is a widespread practice for a mayor or the chairman of a council to wear a chain or badge of office in the course of public duties, particularly when presiding at council meetings. In almost all boroughs it was the custom for the mayor to wear a robe in addition; and the Town Clerk to be dressed in wig and gown. In some cases, ceremonial dress was worn at all council meetings; in others it was worn quarterly or solely at the annual meeting.

The chairman and vice-chairman of a local authority would normally enter the council chamber after the other members had taken their places and the other members would rise and remain standing until they were seated. They might have been preceded by a uniformed attendant — the mayor's officer and mace bearer if there were one — and certainly would have been accompanied by their clerk and chief executive.

The practice gives form and dignity to the proceedings. The chairman commands respect from the beginning and is able to start the proceedings in a quiet and orderly way, which is much more difficult if he has to exert himself to obtain the attention of the meeting before the business can commence.

The annual meeting is often the showpiece of the civic year. The installation of a new mayor or chairman is treated as a significant occasion. Special invitations may well have been sent beforehand to representatives of local organisations and to the new civic leader's family and personal friends. The opportunity may be taken to impress the importance which attaches to civic office. It is legitimate to choose beforehand the proposer and seconder of the motion in order that they might be allowed to prepare their remarks with some care. When elected, the chairman should be invited to read the declaration of acceptance of office in an audible voice before formally signing it and being invested with the chain of office and handed the key to the council's seal. Attention should be devoted to the remainder of the proceedings — the vote of thanks to the retiring chairman and the declaration of acceptance of office by new councillors are examples — and it may be worth while to prepare and circularise a memorandum for the guidance of members as to the procedures recommended.

From time to time, opportunities will occur to introduce civic pride into the ordinary business meetings of the council. Presentations of safe driving awards or gifts to long-serving employees are examples. Such pleasing ceremonies do not have to be confined to the council's own staff. The opportunity might be taken to honour other local people who have made a significant contribution to the authority.

Some think that these practices are worth retaining.

Others take an opposite view with few of these traditions being observed.

Royal visits

Arrangements for the reception of a Royal Visitor require to be made with the most minute care. The details must be settled beforehand with the Private Secretary to the Royal Visitor and must be strictly adhered to. The advice of the Lord Lieutenant of the county may be invaluable, particularly if he is to be present himself. It is also important to make sure that everyone who is to be presented or is to take any part whatsoever in the proceedings is fully briefed and occupies the allotted place at the prescribed hour.

Processions and church services

Many local authorities attend a church service at least once a year. It is a common practice to hold a civic service on the Sunday following the annual meeting of the council, either at the parish church or at the church to which the new civic leader belongs. At some authorities it is the custom for the civic party to assemble at the council offices and to walk in procession to the church. If this is so, certain protocol may need to be observed in organising the order of the procession.

People are often offended if they are not given the priority they expect. The order of procession should be settled beforehand and notified to those who are to take part in an effort to reduce confusion and misunderstanding on the day.

Remembrance day

In most places, a religious service is held on the Sunday set aside as a National Day of Remembrance. This is held either in church or at a local war memorial. In the latter case the service is likely to be interdenominational. For many years such services were organised by the Royal British Legion but nowadays they are more often the responsibility of the local authority, although members of the Legion continue to take part. Similar arrangements regarding this procession may be necessary as are applied to Church services.

Assistance to the chair

One of the important duties of the chairman or mayor of a local authority is the conduct of meetings of the authority and in performing this task he will expect the support and advice of the Secretary of the council who is (or, certainly should be) professionally trained in such matters. A secondary duty of the chairman, but nevertheless a highly important one, is to represent the county or district on many ceremonial and other civic occasions. It is natural that he will continue to turn to the Secretary for advice in cases of doubt and the Secretary should seek to become expert in matters of this kind. In some cases it may be considered appropriate or indeed essential to appoint a member of the Secretary's staff as private secretary to the chairman or mayor in order that a regular source of advice and assistance may be available. The Secretary should, however, be careful not to press unwelcome advice. Within the law and accepted tenets of good behaviour, it is the chairman's privilege to do things in this own way. The Secretary's duty is to sustain, not to usurp.

If asked to do so, the Secretary may advise the chairman whether or not to accept certain invitations, help him to prepare his speeches (or even write them in their entirety on request), or make enquiries about applicants for charitable donations.

Advice is often sought as to the precedence to be accorded the civic heads at various functions such as dinners and receptions. Where the council is the host, no difficulty should be encountered; the civic leader will normally take the Chair. At a private function at which the chairman is to be a guest, there is no strict right of precedence but the organisers may nevertheless be encouraged to give him a position which will reflect the dignity of his office. Factors to be taken into account are, who is to be the guest of honour, who is to be asked to speak and whether the function is taking place in the area of his own authority. As a rule, the chairman is expected to wear the chain and badge of office at a function within the county or district but elsewhere only when invited, expressly or by inference, by the civic head of the area concerned.

Conferences

Most local authorities will, from time to time, find themselves responsible for organising a conference or seminar and much of the detailed preparation is likely to fall upon the Secretary. In larger authorities and seaside resorts such events are likely to form a regular part of the council's activities and may comprise a major function of a separate department. Other authorities may merely act as occasional hosts to meetings of local authority provincial associations or meetings of other bodies or societies which they desire to encourage.

It is important to make an accurate estimate of the size of the proposed conference since this will affect the choice of venue and the arrangements to be made in the hall for the accommodation of the delegates. If the council is simply providing hospitality to a regularly constituted association, the secretariat of the association may be expected to provide the answers to questions of this nature. If, however, the council is convening a meeting of parties who are interested in the proposed subject matter but who are not bound together in a formal society, the council will itself have to organise the event, and decide on.

a) Who is to be invited?

b) whether it is to be attended by member or officers?

c) The business to be discussed.

d) Who is to take the Chair?

A record of the proceedings will probably be needed and, unless there is a regular secretariat, arrangements will have to be made by the host authority. The use of tape recordings should be considered since there is always a real risk that a summary of proceedings, however well written, may be challenged by somebody.

Marches past

On occasion, particularly if a military unit is stationed locally, the civic head may be invited to take the salute at a march past of troops or at the conclusion of the ceremony of Beating the Retreat. A meeting should be arranged with the military officers responsible and with the local police. They are the experts in ceremonial of this kind. It is unlikely that the duties of the Secretary of the local authority will be very onerous. The main value to the discussion is likely to be local knowledge in selecting the best time and place for the ceremony.

Union flag

A number of public occasions have been prescribed at which the national flag is to be flown from Government buildings, either at the masthead or at half-mast as is appropriate. It may be thought fit to fly the flag on civic buildings on the same occasions. A list of relevant dates may be obtained from the Department of the Environment for the use of the officer who is responsible for flying the flag. Some initiative will be required when the flag is to be flown at half-mast on the death of a distinguished person.

There is a proper way to fly the flag which must be strictly adhered to if the council is not to appear sloppy and incompetent.

Armorial bearings

The possession of armorial bearings by a local authority is often a source of civic pride.

Once the council has resolved to apply for a grant of armorial bearings, the Secretary should write to the College of Arms expressing their wish. A memorial will be prepared by a Herald of Arms for the signature of the chairman. This memorial represents an official petition to the Earl Marshal for his warrant to the Kings of Arms to grant and assign Arms in exercise of the Royal Prerogative delegated to them.

Designing arms is an art which is best left to professionals but it might be a good idea to involve the public by inviting them to suggest a suitable motto.

Logos

Many authorities, in addition to using a traditional coat of arms also adopt a more simple, easily recognizeable symbol which appears on notepaper, buildings, vehicles etc, which publicises the council and allows its various services to be quickly recognized.

The aim of this is to provide the quick recognition that would not be given by a Coat of Arms.

Civic receptions and other functions

It is commonly a part of a Secretary's duties to organise social functions on behalf of his municipality although the nature of the events may vary from place to place. Some authorites hold an annual civic lunch and others a civic dinner. The object is sometimes to pay tribute to a particular guest of honour. In some parts of the country it is customary to hold an annual Chairman's Ball to which are invited the civic heads of neighbouring authorities and the leaders of local voluntary organisations.

Some of these events are financed from the Chairman's allowance and are looked upon as a form of public relations exercise. In suitable circumstances a charge may be made to those persons attending (with the obvious exception of the Chairman's official guests) and any profits given to local charities.

The organisational work which will fall upon the

Secretary's department is unlikely to vary in substance from the work undertaken by any private individual or organisation undertaking a similar venture but there will be points of detail which will require careful attention. As most local authorities seem to repeat their social programmes year after year, it is a good plan to maintain a detailed file ennumerating the steps that need to be taken by the responsible staff.

If one or more guests are to be asked to speak, it is important to settle the programme, in consultation with the Chairman, well beforehand. Each speaker should be advised as early as possible what subject to speak about stating the length of time this might appropriately take. It is thoughtful to provide speakers with background colour and local information.

Information about style of dress is always wanted. Visiting civic heads should be expressly invited to wear their chains of office, if this is desired. If this is not appropriate, a tactful word of advice to their own Secretary is called for. The need to provide a suitable robing room should not be overlooked and reserved parking spaces should be set aside for mayoral cars or their equivalent. It is essential to discover whether any official guest will be accompanied by a chauffeur or attendant and proper facilities should be provided for this officer to obtain rest and refreshment during the official function.

Town twinning

Now that foreign travel is so much easier than it used to be, a new development has occurred in international relationships. Contacts and friendships are established between cities and towns in this country and places of similar size and interests elsewhere, particularly in France and other parts of Western Europe. The great value of the twinning movement, is that it places international links largely in the hands of ordinary people who travel to foreign countries during their holidays meeting and making friends. They are no longer solely the business of statesmen and professional diplomats.

A criticism commonly levelled at the twinning movement — usually, it seems, by people who have no practical experience of it — is an accusation of "civic junketing". If any municipalities have used twinning as an excuse for unnecessary revels they have done a great disservice to the majority of honest and purposeful liaisons. Civic delegations are essential in establishing the initial link, in keeping contact alive at the right level, in helping to identify partners for their own schools, societies and organisations and generally in fostering an atmosphere in which wide exchanges between citizens of the two communities can take place. There are twinning links in which annual conferences are held, by rotation, between citizens of several associated towns, for the purpose of discussing political and economic problems of common concern.

But if a twinning link is to be worthwhile it must depend predominantly on the active support of the townspeople. Where successful links have been established, local authorities have encouraged town twinning associations to be formed from representatives of local organisations and from the population at large. These associations and their executive committees should be represented on them. If the Secretary of the council is co-operative, the local authority can give valuable backing in the form of administrative assistance, such as the free use of a committee room, duplicating and postal services and the like. A small grant to defray a proportion of the overheads would certainly be appreciated. The twinning association ought to have its own formal constitution and the council's legal staff can be of great assistance in this matter.

The local authority will have its own role to play. The Chairman of the council might be invited to be Patron or President of the Association to maintain a close alliance between the local authority and the town twinning association. The Chairman will certainly wish to extend a personal welcome to his opposite number whenever there is a formal visit, and may also wish to extend some hospitality to organised groups from the twin town, to receive parties of school children at the Council Chamber and other courtesies of that nature which help to oil the wheels of international friendship.

Twinning associations should be expected to raise money themselves to meet the cost of twinning activities, either by annual subscriptions from members or by fund-raising efforts, and to encourage individual organisations to arrange and pay for their own exchange programmes. Twinning activities are supported when they can be seen to be a genuine effort by the community for the community.

In order to get the maximum initial publicity for the twinning and to emphasise to the people of both towns that it is intended for their participation — without which the twinning would serve little purpose — it is usual to launch it with some considerable ceremony.

CHAPTER 20

MISCELLANEOUS
FUNCTIONS

There is a tendency to place with central administrative departments responsibility for a miscellany of services which are provided on too small a scale, or on too few occasions, to justify a separate department.

Such duties vary from time to time and from one authority to another. The professional administrator in local government must be prepared to apply his skills to the service of the authority in a variety of ways.

Archives and official records

Some County Secretaries have overall responsibility for the supervision of the County Records Office and the general principles referred to in the opening paragraphs of this chapter are well illustrated in this kind of work.

It is impossible, and quite unnecessary, to keep everything, but, unless a sensible scheme is drawn up much rubbish may be hoarded while many priceless records are thrown away. The appointment of a skilled archivist as curator is essential and the co-operation of local historical societies is highly desirable. It is not enough to select the right records for retention. Premises must be selected where they can be kept clean, dry and readily accessible to students and historians. Some records will require expert restoration.

The selection of records for permanent preservation is not a task to be left exclusively to experts. The administrative records of local authorities offer considerable scope for future research. There are files about the organisation of rationing and air raid precautions in the Second World War and material concerning public celebration of Coronations and the Silver Jubilee of King George V. There are plans of early housing, lighting and drainage schemes, possibly going back to the late nineteenth century. This kind of thing will provide valuable information to future historians about the social conditions of the recent past which it will eventually be impossible to discover from personal recollection.

Some of the records of our own generation will one day acquire the same historical value. All staff should be instructed to take proper care of plans and registers and similar items in their charge. They should never be stored in conditions of dirt and disorder. Before any document is destroyed, the advice of the County Archivist should be sought so as to ascertain whether it possesses sufficient historical value to be worthy of permanent retention.

Burials and Cremations

When the council is a burial authority and maintains a cemetery, the Secretary may hold the appointment of Registrar of Burials. Somewhat similar provisions apply where the authority operates a crematorium. The work involved is straightforward but it is particularly important that it should be performed with care and accuracy. Even small errors can cause much distress to bereaved families and more serious mistakes can lead to acute difficulties.

The recognised procedures will probably be prescribed in the local Cemetery or Crematorium Regulations and should be strictly adhered to. If the rules are always observed, funeral undertakers will know exactly how to organise their work; if all manner of exceptions are made, uncertainty and error can easily creep in.

Applications for burials or cremation should be made at the office of the Registrar during normal business hours but it is essential to provide an opportunity for urgent applications to be made during public holiday periods. Every application should be made on a standard form which needs to be carefully designed to make sure that all essential information is given. Telephoned instructions should be discouraged as they are a common source of mistakes; if they are accepted at all they should require to be confirmed in writing at the first opportunity. The death certificate and, in appropriate cases, the certificate of the coroner will require to be produced. For cremation an additional certificate by the Medical Officer to the Crematorium Authority is necessary.

All burials in grounds maintained by burial authorities are required by statute to be registered. Two such records should be kept by the registrar. One is a chronological record of interments taking place in the cemetery, the other is a serial record of the interments which have taken place in each numbered grave. Both records need to be fully detailed. The compelling importance of ensuring that these records are accurate and up to date at all times is underlined.

Emergency planning

From time to time a local authority finds itself faced with the task of coping, or helping to cope, with some civil emergency. Floods, unhappily, have too frequently brought disaster or distress to particular parts of the country. Colliery and factory accidents have caused suffering to individual communities. Aircraft and railway accidents may bring special problems to the areas in which they happen.

In the ordinary way, the responsibility does not rest solely on the local authority. The police are trained to deal with emergencies, the factory or railway managements will have their crisis routine, the central authorities may take charge. But a good deal will be left to the initiative of the local authority.

Considerable experience in dealing with serious emergencies, acquired during the Second World War, used to be available in the Civil Defence Corps. When the corps was wound up in 1965, the Home Office recommended that all local authorities should appoint their Clerk as Controller Designate for purposes of home defence planning in the event of a further threat of war. This tacitly recognised that in any emergency situation of that kind much would depend upon the skill and initiative of the permanent staff of the local authority. The Clerk's position as organiser and controller has been inherited by the Chief Executive.

So far as time permits, it is a good scheme to have an emergency plan prepared for immediate use. To be effective this needs to be kept continuously up to date and written copies need to be in the hands of all who may have some duty to perform or kept at locations where they can be easily recovered and studied by others.

Of course, no one can predict the nature or details of the emergency and the exercise of considerable initiative is essential. But certain basic provisions can be made. Homelessness, temporary or otherwise, is commonly the aftermath of a catastrophe. Schoolrooms or other public buildings can be earmarked for temporary accommodation. Bedding, toilet equipment and other essentials can be stored and their location recorded. By prior arrangement with the medical authorities, arrangements can be made to set up and equip dressing stations. Vehicles and drivers can be designated to provide additional ambulances. In short, much can be done with foresight and enterprise. The contribution that can be made by clerical workers, properly directed, should not be undervalued. Orderliness in the distribution of assistance is to be preferred to chaos and confusion and proper organisation can do much to relieve suffering.

It needs to be recognised that, in a war emergency, communications could be so badly disrupted that normal services could cease to exist altogether and small communities could find themselves thrown back entirely on to their own resources. What is needed to meet this dire possibility is a basic survival routine, a copy of which should ideally be in the hands of a recognised leader in every community. This is not easy to achieve. A true understanding of the problems can only be gained from specialised training and, in normal times, people are reluctant to give their time and energies to training for responsibilities in war-time. None the less, emergency planning units need to provide short study courses for as many people as can be persuaded to attend.

Licensing and registration

There are nearly 50 statutory provisions imposed on local authorities licensing or registration functions and the the list is subject to continual variation. Pawnbrokers, refreshment houses, small lotteries and hackney carriages are varied examples of activities that must be licensed or registered with a local authority.

In practice, some of these enactments make no demand on the local authority at all. Others do create work which may be of a seasonal kind as annual licences fall due for renewal. Bound registers can be purchased for every kind of need but for many authorities a single binder will suffice for all purposes, with dividers and ruled pages to meet the requirements of various statutes. Local government law stationers are geared to meet all demands for licences and registers.

The work must be organised systematically. Licensees are not usually very good at remembering to renew their licences unless they receive a reminder. A diary should be kept of dates when licences are due for renewal and appropriate reminders sent in good time. This not only helps to secure compliance with the law but brings income, by way of licence fees, into the council's coffers.

Enforcement is not always easy since the scale of operation is often too small to justify the employment of an inspectorate.

Registration of births, marriages and deaths

It is a statutory responsibility of county councils, Metropolitan Districts and London Borough Councils to prepare schemes for the registration of births, marriages and deaths in their area and to arrange for supervision by a proper officer. The officer in charge of a registration district is the superintendent registrar who is appointed by the council but who holds office at the pleasure of the Registrar-General.

Rent control

Another responsibility that has been placed on the proper officer of a county council, Metropolitan District and London Borough Council, but which is not related to his normal duties is the appointment of a Rent Officer whose principal duty is to fix a fair rent for a regulated tenancy under the Rent Acts and generally to give advice to private landlords and tenants.

Although, in some cases, rent officers are housed physically with the Secretary's Department, they function independently and are not, strictly speaking, officers of the department.

Secretarial services to members

The Bains Group, in their report, drew attention to the work done by councillors in following up requests for information or complaints and in stimulating public interest in local affairs. It was suggested that this work benefited the local authority sufficiently to justify assistance being given with the requisite correspondence.

The provision of this varies from authority to authority but where it is the approved practice of the local authority, it seems appropriate for the Secretary's Department to undertake the facility.

SPECIMEN STANDING ORDERS AS USED BY THE CITY OF BRADFORD METROPOLITAN COUNCIL

(The following specimen is reproduced with the kind permission of the City of Bradford Metropolitan Council, who retain the copyright)

PART A — COUNCIL MEETINGS

A1 Meetings

(a) At the Annual Meeting, the Council will decide the dates and times for ordinary meetings during the year. The Lord Mayor or five members may, by giving written notice to the Director of Legal Services, call extraordinary meetings, and the date and time shall be fixed by the Director of Legal Services after consulting the Lord Mayor.

(b) The Director of Legal Services, with the support of the Leader of the Council may cancel an ordinary meeting if not enough business has arisen to justify calling it.

A2 Chairing the Meeting

The Lord Mayor, (or in his/her absence) the Deputy Chair of Council shall chair meetings of Council. In their absence, the Council shall select a person to chair the meeting.

A3 Quorum

No business shall be dealt with unless there is a quorum of 23 members present. If there is no quorum, the meeting must be adjourned immediately and any remaining business postponed to the next ordinary meeting.

A4 Order of Business at Ordinary Meetings

At ordinary meetings, business will usually be dealt with in the following order:

(a) choice of a person to chair the meeting if the Lord Mayor and Deputy Chair are absent

(b) disclosures of interest from members and officers

(c) agreeing the minutes of the last meeting and signing them

(d) receive any apologies for absence.

(e) consideration of any appeals from the public against "Not for Publication" reports or documents

(f) any written announcements from the Lord Mayor which will be circulated to all members and placed in the public galleries before the meeting starts

(g) any deputations or petitions

(h) to answer questions at Public Question Time (which will be circulated to all members and placed in the public galleries before the meeting starts)

(i) any business remaining from previous meetings

(j) recommendations from Committees

(k) motions (in the order in which they were notified)

(l) any other business on the agenda

(m) questions to Chairpersons

(n) questions to nominated spokespersons of Joint Authorities

(o) comments.

The order of items (e) to (o) may be changed by the meeting by means of a motion passed without discussion.

A5 Annual Meeting — Restrictions on Business

At the Annual Meeting, the following matters cannot be considered:–

(a) deputations, petitions and Public Question Time

(b) business remaining from previous meetings

(c) recommendations from Committees

(d) motions

(e) questions to Chairpersons

(f) questions to nominated spokespersons of Joint Authorities

(g) comments

A6 Motions and Amendments which can be moved without notice

Notice is not required to move motions and amendments:

(a) to propose a person to chair the meeting

(b) about the accuracy of the minutes

(c) to take an item of business before other items on the agenda

(d) to refer an agenda item to the next ordinary meeting or to a Committee, Sub-committee or Advisory Group

(e) to accept a Committee recommendation

(f) to withdraw an agenda item

(g) by the mover of a recommendation or motion to seek the meetings permission to amend it or in the case of a motion only to withdraw it

(h) by the mover of an amendment to seek the meetings permission to withdraw it

(i) to go to the next business

   (j)   to put the question to a vote immediately

   (k)   to adjourn the debate or the meeting

   (l)   to exclude the public

  (m) to suspend particular Standing Orders

   (n)   not to hear a member further or to require a member to leave the meeting

   (o)   to obtain the agreement of the meeting where a particular Standing Order requires that it be obtained

   (p)   to record the Council's appreciation or condolence

   (q)   to consider the constitution of Committees, Sub-committees and Advisory Groups

   (r)   to receive a deputation or petition

   (s)   to refer a matter raised by a deputation, petition or question to the appropriate Committee, Sub-committee or Advisory Group of the Council; or to an external body.

A7 Minutes

The person chairing the meeting will move that the minutes be signed as a correct record. The only part of the minutes which can be discussed is their accuracy. This must be raised by motion and as soon as any motion (if any) is dealt with, the person chairing the meeting shall sign the minutes.

A8 Deputations and Petitions

   (a)   Deputations and petitions may be received at ordinary meetings of Council, provided that written notice has been given to the Director of Legal Services no later than mid-day three working days before the day of the meeting. The notice must also give the subject of the deputation or petition and will be entered in a book open to public inspection.

   (b)   The Director of Legal Services must not accept a request for the Council to receive a deputation or petition:

     (i) from a political party or organisation or in connection with the activities and aims of such a party or organisation without first consulting the Leader of the Council or in his/her absence the Deputy Leader.

     (ii) either from an individual or in furtherance of an individual's particular circumstances.

     (iii) about any matter where there is a right of appeal to the Courts, a tribunal or to a Government Minister.

(c) No more than five deputations and petitions will be received at a meeting. They will be heard in the order in which notice was received by the Director of Legal Services. The names of the organisations or persons attending and the subject of the deputation or petition will be included on the agenda for the meeting.

(d) Any deputations or petitions which are not received because of the limit on numbers will be heard at the next meeting or subsequent meetings in the order in which notice was received.

(e) Every deputation or petition must be about a matter for which the Council have a responsibility or which affects the district. A deputation or petition will not be received where the subject of the deputation or petition has been the subject of a decision made by a Council meeting within the previous six months or is about an issue arising from that decision.

(f) A deputation must consist of not less than three and no more than five people. A petition must be signed by at least 50 persons residing in the district. Only one person may speak to the meeting and the speech (including reading any written material) must not last longer than five minutes.

(g) At the meeting, the person chairing the meeting will move that the deputation or petition is received. After being seconded, the motion will be voted on without discussion.

(h) No discussion will take place on any issue raised by a deputation or petition. Any member may move that a copy of the speech is referred to the appropriate Committee, Sub-committee or Advisory Group, or to another body. Once seconded, the motion will be voted on without discussion.

A9 Public Question Time

(a) at ordinary meetings of Council, a maximum of 20 minutes will be allowed for Public Question Time.

(b) any elector for the district may ask a question of any member of Council who will have up to five minutes to reply.

(c) questions must be about matters for which the Council have a responsibility or which affect the district.

(d) all questions must be given in writing to the Director of Legal Services no later than mid-day one week before the day of the meeting. The questions will be referred to the appropriate members and entered in a book open to public inspection.

(e) details of questions to be asked will not appear on the agenda but will be circulated to all members and placed in the public galleries before the meeting starts.

(f) the person chairing the meeting will ask the person who gave notice to put the question to the member concerned. The questioner may be accompanied by a friend. The friend may ask the question on his/her behalf if this is notified to the Director of Legal Services at the time when the question is submitted.

(g) the member may reply at the meeting, reply after the meeting in writing, ask some other member to reply on his/her behalf or refuse to reply (such refusal to be notified to the Director of Legal Services).

(h) any questions which cannot be dealt with during Public Question Time will be referred to the member concerned to reply as mentioned in (g) above.

(i) no discussion will take place on any question but any member may move that a matter raised by a question is referred to the appropriate Committee, Sub-committee,

Advisory Group or external body. Once seconded, the motion will be voted on without discussion.

(j) a question cannot be asked about a matter which has been the subject of a decision made by a meeting of Council within the previous six months.

(k) once a question has been brought to the Council, the subject cannot be brought again for six months.

A10 Recommendations of Committees

Any recommendations of Policy and Resources Committee will be submitted for approval first. Recommendations of other Committees will be considered by the meeting in the order in which they appear on the agenda. The Council may change the order in which they consider the Committees' recommendations if this will help business to be dealt with more efficiently.

A11 Committee Recommendations — Rules of Debate

(a) A recommendation cannot be discussed until it has been formally moved and seconded.

(b) An amendment to a recommendation must be in writing and contain the name of the mover and seconder. It must be delivered to the Director of Legal Services at least six hours before the start of the meeting. Copies of every amendment received will be made available to every member at the meeting.

(c) An amendment must be relevant to the recommendation and may:–

    (i) refer the recommendation back to the Committee from which it was referred for reconsideration or to a Committee, Sub-committee or Advisory Group

    (ii) delete words

    (iii) add words

    (iv) delete words and add words

But deletions or additions must not simply nullify the recommendation before the meeting.

(d) An amendment may be moved and seconded either by the members who submitted it or by other members on their behalf.

(e) The mover of an amendment may, without discussion, withdraw it with the permission of the seconder and the meeting. If the mover asks to withdraw an amendment, there shall be no discussion on the amendment until the vote has been taken.

(f) The meeting may agree to allow two or more amendments to be discussed together if it will help business to be dealt with more efficiently.

(g) Every amendment must be voted on separately unless two or more amendments are discussed together in which case the first amendment to be carried will become the substantive motion. If an amendment is carried, the amended recommendation takes the place of the original.

(h) The order of speeches on a Committee recommendation and amendments (if any) shall be:
  (i) mover of the recommendation
  (ii) seconder of the recommendation
  (iii) mover of first amendment
  (iv) seconder of first amendment
  (v) mover of second amendment
  (vi) seconder of second amendment and so on until all movers and seconders of amendments have spoken
  (vii) any member (excluding the above)
  (viii) right of reply movers of amendments in reverse order until:–
  (ix) right of reply mover of second amendment
  (x) right of reply mover of first amendment
  (xi) right of reply mover of recommendation

(i) A member may only speak once on a recommendation except:–
  (i) in exercising a right of reply
  (ii) on a point of order
  (iii) in personal explanation

    (iv) if the first speech was formally to move or second a recommendation or an amendment.

(j) The chairperson of the Committee from which the recommendation comes or his/her nominee shall have the right to move the recommendation on the agenda.

(k) A member may nominate another member to exercise any of the above rights to speak.

(l) When a recommendation is being debated, the only motions which may be moved are:–
    (i) to amend the recommendation
    (ii) to put the question to a vote immediately
    (iii) to refer the matter to the next ordinary meeting or to a Committee, Sub-committee or Advisory Group
    (iv) to move to the next business
    (v) to adjourn the debate or the meeting
    (vi) to exclude the public
    (vii) to move that a member is not further heard

(These motions may only be moved by members who have not spoken on the recommendation under debate or by a Group Chief Whip) and
    (viii) on a motion by the person chairing the meeting to require that a member leave the meeting.

A12 Motions

(a) Except for motions which can be moved without notice written notice of every motion must be given, signed by at least two members and be delivered to the Director of Legal Services not later than mid-day eight days before the date of the meeting. These will be entered in a book open to public inspection;

(b) Motions for which notice has been given will be listed on the agenda in the order in which notice was received unless the member giving notice stated, in writing, that s/he proposed to move it at a later meeting or it is withdrawn in writing.

(c) The Director of Legal Services will arrange for one or more

Committees to consider a motion if it is within their province, so that the meeting can receive a report when the motion is discussed. No motion will normally be discussed until this report is received. The meeting may, however, agree to deal with the motion without a Committee report if the matter is urgent.

(d) Motions about a decision which has been made under powers or duties delegated by the Council cannot be referred to Committees under paragraph (c) above.

(e) Motions must be about matters for which the Council have a responsibility or which affect the district.

A13 Motions — Rules of Debate

(a) Motions must be formally moved and seconded as set out on the agenda, either by the members who gave notice, or if they do not do so by other members on their behalf. If a motion is not moved and seconded, it is treated as withdrawn and cannot be moved without fresh notice.

(b) If the meeting agrees on a motion put without discussion, the mover of a motion with the permission of the seconder may alter a motion of which s/he has given notice if the alteration could have been made as an amendment; and may withdraw a motion. If a motion is withdrawn, a member cannot speak on it.

(c) Usually only one motion may be discussed at a time but the person chairing the meeting may allow two or more motions to be discussed together if it will help business to be dealt with more efficiently.

(d) An amendment to a motion must be in writing and contain the names of the mover and seconder. It must be delivered to the Director of Legal Services at least six hours before the start of the meeting. Copies of every amendment received will be made available to every member at the meeting.

(e) An amendment must be relevant to the motion and may:–

    (i) refer the motion to a Committee, Sub-committee, or Advisory Group for consideration

    (ii) leave out words

    (iii) add words

    (iv) leave out words and add words

But omissions or additions must not simply nullify the motion before the meeting.

(f) An amendment may be moved and seconded either by the members who submitted it or by other members on their behalf.

(g) The mover of an amendment may, without discussion, withdraw it with the permission of the seconder and the meeting. If the mover asks to withdraw an amendment, there shall be no discussion on the amendment until the vote has been taken.

(h) The meeting may agree to allow two or more amendments to be discussed together if it will help business to be dealt with more efficiently.

(i) Every amendment must be voted on separately unless two or more amendments are discussed together in which case the first amendment to be carried will become the substantive motion. If an amendment is carried, the amended motion takes the place of the original motion.

(j) The order of speeches on a motion and amendments (if any) shall be:–

    (i) mover of the motion

    (ii) seconder of the motion

    (iii) mover of the first amendment

    (iv) seconder of first amendment

    (v) mover of second amendment

    (vi) seconder of second amendment and so on until all movers and seconders of amendments have spoken

    (vii) any member (excluding the above)

    (viii) right of reply movers of amendments in reverse order until:–

    (ix) right of reply mover of second amendment

    (x) right of reply mover of first amendment

(xi) right of reply of chairperson of the Committee about whose work the motion is concerned (whether or not s/he has spoken previously)

(xii) right of reply mover of motion

(k) A member may only speak once on a motion except:
  (i) in exercising a right of reply
  (ii) on a point of order
  (iii) in personal explanation
  (iv) if the first speech was formally to move or second a recommendation or amendment.

(l) A member may nominate another member to exercise any of the above rights to speak.

(m) When a motion is being debated, the only motions which may be moved are:–
  (i) to amend the motion
  (ii) to put the question to a vote immediately
  (iii) to refer the matter to the next ordinary meeting or to a Committee, Sub-committee or Advisory Group
  (iv) to move to the next business
  (v) to adjourn the debate or the meeting
  (vi) to exclude the public
  (vii) to move that a member is not heard further

(These motions may only be moved by members who have not spoken on the motion under debate or by a Group Chief Whip) and

  (viii) on a motion by the person chairing the meeting to require that a member leave the meeting.–

A14 Ending Debates — Recommendations and Motions

At the end of any speech, a member who has not spoken in the debate, or a Group Chief Whip, may move:–

(a) that the meeting move to the next business. If seconded, the vote will then be taken to move to the next business

(b) that the vote is taken immediately. If seconded, such a motion will be put to the meet straightaway. If carried, there are no rights of reply

(c) that the debate or the meeting is adjourned. If seconded, the person chairing the meeting will put the motion to the vote. If carried, there are no rights of reply.

A15 Speeches of Members

(a) No speech shall last more than five minutes except for the mover of a recommendation or motion or amendment who may speak for 10 minutes.

(b) Before the start of the meeting the Chief Whip of each political group may give the person chairing the meeting in advance in writing the name of one member who will be entitled to speak for 10 minutes on the recommendation or motion or an amendment to a recommendation or motion.

(c) A member when speaking must stand and address the meeting through the chair. If more than one member stands, the person chairing the meeting will ask one to speak and the others must sit. Other members must remain seated whilst a member is speaking unless they wish to make a point of order or of personal explanation. Members must refer to one another in meetings by their correct title.

(d) A member may only speak about the matter under discussion or on a point of order or in personal explanation.

A16 Point of Order

(a) A point of order is a request by a member to the person chairing the meeting to rule on an alleged irregularity in the constitution or conduct of the meeting.

(b) The member must rise to take the point immediately s/he notices it and state the Standing Order or procedural rule in question and how it is broken.

(c) A ruling must be given by the person chairing the meeting before the debate continues. There is no discussion on the ruling.

A17 Point of Personal Explanation

(a) A member may find that s/he has made a mis-statement which is quoted by a later speaker or that another member has misunderstood or misquoted what was said.

(b) If this happens, s/he may rise on a point of personal explanation and with the permission of the person chairing the meeting interrupt the speaker to correct the misunderstanding.

(c) There is no discussion on the ruling of the person chairing the meeting.

A18 Conduct

(a) When the person chairing the meeting stands during a debate, any member speaking at the time must stop and sit down. The Council must be silent.

(b) If a member persistently disregards the ruling of the person chairing the meeting by behaving improperly or offensively or deliberately obstructs business, the person chairing the meeting or any member may move that the member is not further heard. If seconded, the motion will be voted on without discussion.

(c) If the member continues to behave improperly after such a motion is carried, the person chairing the meeting or any member may move that either the member leave the meeting or that the meeting is adjourned for a specified period. If seconded, the motion will be voted on without discussion.

(d) If there is a general disturbance making orderly business impossible, the person chairing the meeting may adjourn the meeting for as long as s/he thinks necessary.

A19 Rescinding Previous Resolutions

(a) A motion to rescind a decision made at a meeting of Council within the past six months cannot be moved at a meeting unless the notice of motion is signed by at least 30 members.

(b) A motion or amendment in similar terms to one which has been rejected in the past six months cannot be moved unless the notice of motion or amendment is signed by at least 30 members. Once the motion or amendment is dealt with, no-one can propose a similar motion or amendment for six months.

(c) A recommendation of a Committee to rescind a decision made at a meeting of Council within the past six months cannot be moved without this standing order being suspended.

A20 Voting

(a) Members will vote by a show of hands. Members votes will only be counted if they are sitting in seats reserved for members.

(b) Either before or immediately after a vote has been taken, any member may require a recorded vote which will supersede any vote taken under (a). At least seven other members must support the request.

(c) Before a recorded vote, a bell will be rung for one minute to warn members.

(d) The recorded vote will be taken immediately afterwards and recorded in the minutes. A member's vote will only be recorded if the member is sitting in a seat reserved for members and answers "Yes" or "No" immediately after his/her name is called.

A21 Questions to Chairpersons

(a) A member may ask the chairperson of a Committee or Advisory Group a written question about any matter which relates to the work of the Committee or Group, or which affects the district. The question must be delivered to the Director of Legal Services at least three clear working days before the meeting.

(b) The person chairing the meeting will ask for questions about the work of each Committee and Advisory Group. Questions cannot be asked about subjects covered by Committee recommendations at the meeting.

(c) An answer may be written and circulated to members at the meeting, given orally by the chairperson at the meeting, or a combination of both. The chairperson may decline to answer or ask someone else to answer.

(d) The person chairing the meeting may give permission for a supplementary question at the meeting about the written question or its answer. A supplementary question and its answer (if any) shall not last more than three minutes each.

(e) Questions will be asked and answered without discussion.

A22 Questions to Nominated Spokespersons of Joint Authorities

(a) A member may ask the nominated spokesperson of Joint Authorities a written question about any matter which relates to the work of the Joint Authority. The question must be delivered to the Director of Legal Services at least five clear working days before the meeting.

(b) The person chairing the meeting will ask for questions about the work of each Joint Authority.

(c) An answer may be written and circulated to members at the meeting, given orally by the nominated spokesperson, or a combination of both. The nominated spokesperson may decline to answer.

(d) The person chairing the meeting may give permission for a supplementary question at the meeting about the written question or its answer. A supplementary question and its answer (if any) shall not last more than three minutes each.

(e) Questions will be asked and answered without discussion.

A23 Comments

(a) A member may comment once about any matter which

relates to the work of each Committee or Advisory Group, or which affects the district.

(b) The person chairing the meeting will ask for comments about the work of each Committee and Advisory Group. Comments cannot be made about subjects covered either by Committee recommendations or questions at the meeting.

(c) The chairperson of a Committee or Advisory Group (or nominee) may reply to any comments.

(d) A comment and the reply to each comment shall not last more than three minutes each.

(e) Comments will be made and replied to without discussion.

A24 Referring to a Committee etc.

The Council may refer a matter to a Committee, Sub-committee or Advisory Group and may also take away the rights of members to send up a decision as a recommendation only to the parent body.

A25 Disturbances at the Meeting

(a) If a member of the public interrupts proceedings, the person chairing the meeting will warn the person concerned. If s/he continues to interrupt, the person chairing the meeting will order removal from the Council Chamber.

(b) If there is a general disturbance in any part of the Council Chamber open to the public, the person chairing the meeting may call for that part to be cleared.

A26 Record for Attendances

Except for the person chairing the meeting, all members must sign their names on the attendance sheets. Their attendances will be recorded from these lists.

PART B — STANDING ORDERS — GENERAL

B1 Changing or Deleting a Standing Order

Any motion to change or delete a standing order adopted at the Annual Meeting must, after being proposed and seconded, be adjourned without discussion to the next ordinary meeting.

B2 Suspension of a Standing Order

(a) Any standing order may be suspended for all or part of the business of a meeting at which suspension is moved by a motion.

(b) Such a motion cannot be moved without notice unless at least 45 members are present.

(c) This provision does not apply to standing orders A2, A3, A16, A17, A18, A20, A26 or F2.

B3 Interpretation of Standing Orders

In ruling how these standing orders are interpreted or applied, or on Council proceedings, the person chairing the meeting must ascertain and reflect the mood of the meeting.

PART C — COMMITTEES ETC.

(Note: Part C relates to Committees, Sub-committees, Select Committees and Advisory Groups).

C1 Membership

(a) Membership of each individual body under Part C must be allocated according to the proportion of the membership of each Political Group, including the Lord Mayor, to the total number of members.

(b) The appointment of co-opted members of the Educational Services Committee (excluding the teachers' representatives) must accord with the principle in (a) above.

(c) A member may sit on no more than two Committees but may substitute for occasional meetings of other Committees.

(d) Standing Committees (except the Educational Services Committee) will consist of 17 Council members appointed by the Director of Legal Services on the nomination of the political groups as follows:
    10 by the majority group
    7 by the opposition group

(e) The Educational Services Committee will consist of 38 members appointed by the Director of Legal Services from nominations as follows:

    14 Council members by the majority group
    10 Council members by the opposition group
    1 Council member by the Liberals
    6 co-opted members by the majority group
    4 co-opted members by the opposition group
    3 teacher representatives

(The Lord Mayor is an ex-officio member included within a group's allocation).

(f) Standing Sub-Committees and Select Committees will consist of up to eight members appointed by the Director of Legal Services on the nomination of the political groups in accordance with the provisions of Standing Order C1 (a) except that the membership of the joint arrangement Sub-Committee in C4(e) shall be in accordance with arrangements made between the five West Yorkshire Metropolitan District Councils.

(g) Co-opted members of the Educational Services Committee may be appointed to its Sub-Committees and Select Committees in addition to the Council members.

C2 Chairing

(a) The Director of Legal Services will appoint on the nomination of the majority group, the chairpersons and deputy chairpersons of Committees and Sub-Committees.

(b)   If a vacancy occurs in the office of chairperson or deputy chairperson, the Director of Legal Services will make a fresh appointment as soon as practicable.

(c)   The opposition group will nominate the spokespersons and deputy spokespersons of Committees and Sub-Committees.

C3 Political Groups

(a)   In these Standing Orders the majority group is the group with the largest number of members on the Council and the Leader and Deputy Leader of the majority group are the Leader and Deputy Leader of the Council.

(b)   In these Standing Orders, the opposition group is the group with the second largest number of members on the Council.

C4 Standing Committees and Sub-Committees

(a)   The Council's standing Committees are:–

> Policy and Resources
> Educational Services
> Employment and Economic Affairs
> Housing Services
> Public and General Services
> Social Services

(b)   The Standing Sub-Committees are:–

Educational Services:
> Further Education
> Further Education Grant Appeals
> Leisure Services
> School Benefit Appeals
> Schools Buildings
> Schools Education
> Schools Special

Employment and Economic Affairs:
> Grants and Loans

Housing Services

Housing
Public Health and Protection

Public and General Services:
Direct Works
General Services
Planning
Public Services

Social Services:
Access and Parental Rights
Children and Services to the Handicapped
Elderly and Mental Health Services
Private Residential Care Establishments

(c) The **Advisory Groups** are:–

Disability
Health
Race Relations
Sex Equality

(d) The **Select Committees** established by these Standing Orders
are:–

Policy and Resources
Community Programme
Disciplinary and Grievance
Ilkey Campus
Personnel (Authority Wide)
Resource and Forward Planning
Sports Stadia
Strategic Policy Issues
Under 5s

Educational Services
Adult Education
Personnel
13–19

Employment and Economic Affairs
Employment and Economic Initiatives
Personnel
Service Delivery

Youth Training Scheme

Housing Services
Personnel

Public and General Services
Personnel

Social Services
Child Abuse
Drug Abuse
Personnel

(e) The following joint arrangement Sub-Committee of Policy and Resources Committee is established:–
Superannuation, Debt Management and Computer Joint Advisory

C5 Casual Vacancies and Substitutions

(a) The Director of Legal Services may appoint members to fill casual vacancies on Committees, Sub-Committees and Advisory Groups for the remainder of the municipal year.

(b) Substitutes for members unable to attend particular meetings may be appointed by the Director of Legal Services on the nomination of the appropriate Group Whip provided that the proposed substitution is notified to the Director of Legal Services before the meeting begins.

(c) Councillors may be appointed to substitute for co-opted members at meetings of the Educational Services Committee and its Sub-Committees.

(d) Co-opted members of the Educational Services Committee may not substitute for Councillors at meetings of the Committee's Sub-Committees.

C6 Observers

(a) Any Council Member can attend meetings of Committees, Sub-Committees and Advisory Groups as an observer.

(b) An observer may speak with the permission of the chairperson.

(c) A co-opted member of the Educational Services Committee may attend meetings of their Sub-Committees as an observer and may speak with the permission of the chairperson.

(d) The chairperson and opposition spokesperson for a Committee may attend and speak at any meeting of the parent Committee's Sub-Committees.

C7 Convening Meetings

(a) The Council, at the Annual meeting will decide the dates of meeting of Committees for the year.

(b) The Director of Legal Services will call all meetings of Committees, Sub-Committees and Advisory Groups.

(c) The chairperson of any Committee, Sub-Committee or Advisory Group can instruct the Director of Legal Services to call a special meeting of that body if possible within 10 working days of the instruction being given.

(d) If at least one quarter of the members of any Committee, Sub-Committee or Advisory Group inform the Director of Legal Services in writing that they wish a special meeting to be called, the Director of Legal Services must do so.

(e) The instruction to the Director of Legal Services in (c) and (d) must specify the business to be dealt with. No other business may be considered at the special meeting.

C8 Meetings in District Locations

(a) Each Committee must consider the desirability of holding meetings at district locations and review their policy during the course of the year. When district meetings are held, a public question time will be included in the agenda for a maximum period of 15 minutes and the provisions of

Standing Order A9(b) to (i) will apply with the substitution of "Committee" for "Council".

(b) The Planning Sub-Committee will organise their business so as to meet in area locations relevant to the items on the agenda.

(c) Every Advisory Group and Standing Sub-Committee must consider the desirability of holding meetings in district locations and review their policy during the course of the year.

C9 Order of business at meetings

The first items to be dealt with at meetings will be to receive disclosures of interest by members and officers, sign the minutes of the previous meeting and consider public access to internal documents.

C10 Quorum

The minimum number of members necessary for business to be dealt with is:–

(a) seven members of a Committee

(b) for a Sub-Committee: four members or one half of the voting membership whichever is the lesser

(c) four members for an Advisory Group

(d) for joint meetings, the sum of the required members for each constituent body.

C11 Voting

Voting is by show of hands, unless the majority of members decide to vote by ballot on a particular item.

C12 Powers of Policy and Resources Committee

(a) The Policy and Resources Committee will operate within

the broad policy of the Council and any directions given by the Council and will exercise the powers and duties of the Council (apart from certain legal exceptions such as levying a rate) in the following areas:–

allocation and distribution of financial, personnel, land and property resources

major policy planning and strategic development

major across-the-district issues

reviewing the work of other Committees, Sub-Committees and Advisory Groups

reviewing the base budget and directing policy implementation

consultations and negotiations with Trades Unions

review of overall capital implementation

control and direction of advertising, publicity and campaigning

(b) The Committee will not establish any standing Sub-Committees but will establish Select Committees, as and when necessary, to look at specific issues.

C13 Powers of other Committees

(a) Committees will operate within the broad policy of the Council and, subject to any directions given by the Council and the Policy and Resources Committee, the Committees will exercise the powers and duties of the Council in the following areas:—

Educational Services
Archaeology and Archives
Culture
Education
Leisure and Recreation

Employment and Economic Affairs
Tackling poverty and unemployment by economic and other

measures. Directing efforts to tackle unemployment and promote economic development and co-ordinating resource allocation in these areas. Major policy planning on unemployment, economic development and municipal enterprises. Service Committee for central services and Unemployment Unit.

Approving and monitoring expenditure and policy for civic ceremonial matters and using the ceremonial engagements of the Lord Mayor in order to use to best effect the Lord Mayoralty to promote the District and further the overall policy aims of the Council.

Housing Services
Environmental Health
Housing
Public Protection

Public and General Services
Architectural, Engineering and Planning Services
City Works Organisation
Highways and Transportation Services
Municipal enterprises including Airport
Public Works
Licensing
Member Services
Coroners, Local Valuation Panels, Probation and Rent
    Officer Services
Emergencies
Waste Disposal

Social Services
All Social Service functions, personal social services and social care.

(b) Committees must review constantly the Council policy affecting their particular services to promote efficiency and effectiveness. They may also take time to debate important matters affecting their services. Major policy matters will be referred to Policy and Resources Committee.

C14 Powers of Sub-Committees and Select Committees

(a) Except as provided in Standing Order C12(b) all Committees are empowered to establish Sub-Committees and Select Committees during the year for any purpose and to fix their membership and functions.

(b) Select Committees are for all purposes Sub-Committees of the Council and any references in these Standing Orders to Sub-Committees will include all Select Committees.

Select Committee may have powers delegated to them by the Committee; others will report their findings and recommendations.

(c) The terms of reference, powers, duties and the continuing need for all Sub-Committees are always subject to review and alteration by the appropriate parent committee during the year.

(d) Persons serving on Sub-Committees do not necessarily have to be members of the appointing Committee but only members of Council and co-opted members of the Educational Services Committee may vote.

(e) Unless otherwise decided by the parent committee all Sub-Committees are empowered to take decisions on matters within their responsibility and where specifically authorised by the parent Committee.

C15 Powers of Officers

(a) The only officers who are empowered to act in the name of the Council are:
   Chief Executive
   Directors

(b) The officers in (a) are empowered to take action in the following areas:
   (i) in cases of emergency
   (ii) on matters of day to day professional or managerial responsibility

(iii) to put into effect approved schemes of general Council policy

(c) In exercising delegated powers in cases of emergency, officers must consult with and obtain the prior agreement of the chairperson of the appropriate Committee or Sub-Committee. Emergency action should be reported to the next meeting of the Committee or Sub-Committee concerned.

(d) Where an officer mentioned in (a) above is to be absent for any period, the Chief Executive or the officer concerned may nominate in writing another officer to act during the period of absence and exercise any powers delegated by the Council under this provision.

C16 General Delegations

(a) All Committees and Sub-Committees may take decisions where authorised by these Standing Orders, by Standing Orders for Contracts, by Financial Regulations, and where authorised by their parent body.

(b) All delegated powers and duties are performed on the Council's behalf and in the Council's name.

(c) All Committees may delegate to their Sub-Committees and officers mentioned above any of the powers and duties of the Committee.

(d) Sub-Committees may delegate any of their powers and duties to the officers mentioned above.

(e) Any decisions taken using delegated powers or duties can be acted on immediately except where the agreement of any other body with relevant powers or duties is also required.

(f) A Committee or other body cannot without the approval of the Council exercise delegated powers or duties to act contrary to a Council policy agreed within the past six months.

C17 Removal of Delegation (Sending Up)

(a) This Standing Order enables the specified number of members to remove a power to make a decision delegated to a Committee or Sub-Committee. By "sending up" a decision to the parent body, members remove the delegated power and make any "decision" merely a recommendation to the parent body.

(b) If the appropriate number of members require immediately after a decision has been taken, the decision becomes only a recommendation to the parent body.

(b) If the appropriate number of members require immediately after a decision has been taken, the decision becomes only a recommendation to the parent body.

(c) The recommendation will then be put to the next ordinary meeting of the parent body, or in special cases to a special meeting.

(d) A decision taken at a joint meeting will be sent up to a joint meeting of the parent bodies for decision.

(e) The number of members required to send up an item from a meeting (including a joint meeting) is: for a Committee, 2, for a Sub-Committee, 1.

(f) If a Committee delegates a specific item or class of items, they may also take away the right of any member to send up a decision, that is to require that any decision must be submitted to the Committee as a recommendation only.

C18 Decisions which cannot be "Sent Up"

The following decisions cannot be "sent up":

(a) A decision to give effect to Council policy made within the last six months.

(b) A decision which will form part of a recommendation either to the parent Committee or to the Council.

(c) A decision on an item or class of items where the "sending up" power has been specifically removed when the matter was delegated.

(d) The following procedural items:
    (i) approval of minutes
    (ii) exclusion of the public
    (iii) dates and times of meetings

(e) Decisions on specific cases dealt with by the following Sub-Committees or Select Committees:

Policy and Resources:
    (i) Disciplinary and Grievance Appeals
    (ii) Personnel (Authority Wide) in respect of issues considered at Joint Consultative Committee meetings

Educational Services:
    (i) Further Education Grant Appeals
    (ii) School Benefit Appeals

Housing Services:
Housing Benefit Appeals

Social Services:
Access and Parental Rights
Private Residential Care Establishments

C19 Appeals against Officer Decisions

(a) Where a specific appeals procedure does not exist, any officer decision taken under delegated powers can be the subject of appeal to the appropriate Sub-Committee.

(b) Such an appeal shall not however invalidate any action taken on the decision which has been made nor (pending consideration by the Sub-Committee) remove the power delegated to the officer to take the decision in question.

(c) There is no right of appeal against an officer decision which is merely the implementation of a Council policy determined within the past six months.

C20 References to Policy and Resources Committee

A Sub-Committee (other than one which reports directly to the Policy and Resources Committee) cannot refer a matter to the Policy and Resources Committee without the support of the parent Committee unless:–

(a) the Sub-Committee decide that the matter cannot wait for the next meeting of the parent Committee

(b) the Sub-Committee are otherwise directed by the Policy and Resources Committee.

PART D — MISCELLANEOUS

D1 Powers of Individual Members

(a) A member cannot by law exercise powers or duties on behalf of the Council.

(b) In particular, a member must not issue any order relating to work being done by or for the Council or claim any rights to enter or inspect property where the Council have the right or duty to enter or inspect. A member must not issue any communication to the media pending the outcome of any internal inquiry or investigation into the business of the Council or its employees which could be prejudiced to the interests of any employee or the activities of the Council.

D2 Members Expenses and Allowances

Members are entitled to allowances for the performance of approved duties. Details of the allowances and how to claim are set out in the Year Book.

D3 Staff Vacancies

(a) All permanent vacancies must be publicly advertised unless:
  (i) the post is filled by promotion or transfer from another permanent post or
  (ii) the post is filled from an approved register or
  (iii) Policy and Resources Committee decide otherwise.

(b) If a similar vacancy occurs again within six months of the post being publicly advertised, one of the original applicants may be appointed without further advertisement.

(c) If there is a vacancy in the post of:
Chief Executive
Director
Assistant Director,
Policy and Resources Committee must consult any Committee concerned before any action is taken on the vacancy.

(d) In the case of vacancies in (c) above, Policy and Resources Committee will then decide whether to fill the post and on what terms and conditions. If Policy and Resources Committee decide not to fill the post, they must determine how the duties of the post are to be performed.

D4 Attempts to Influence an Appointment

(a) Candidates for any appointment will be disqualified if they canvass members in their favour.

(b) A member may give a written reference to accompany an application but must not in any way try to influence improperly the choice of candidate for any appointment. Under no circumstances must people who have agreed to act as referees for a candidate take any part in the recruitment process.

D5 Candidates Related to Members or Officers

(a) Candidates for any appointment must state in their application if they are related to a member or any person listed under "Top Management" in the Year Book. Anyone who fails to do this will be disqualified, or if appointed liable to instant dismissal on grounds of gross misconduct.

(b) Members and the above officers must inform the Director of Personnel if they know that any candidate is related to them. The Director of Personnel must ensure that the appointing body is made aware of the relationship.

(c) Members and the above officers must inform the Director of Personnel in writing if a relative is appointed. The Director of Personnel will inform the appropriate Committee.

(d) All candidates must be made aware of these rules.

(e) For the purposes of this Standing Order, relative means:–
        husband or wife
        parent or child
        grandparent or grandchild
        brother or sister
        uncle or aunt
        nephew or niece

or if any of these relationships apply to the married partner of the candidate.

D6 Custody of Seals

(a) The Director of Legal Services must keep the Common Seal in safe custody.

(b) The Conditioning House Manager must keep the special seal of the Conditioning House in safe custody.

D7 Sealing of Documents

(a) Council decisions (including those made under delegated powers and duties) are authority to seal documents needed to put those decisions into effect.

(b) The impression of the Common Seal must be witnessed by the Director of Legal Services or a senior officer named by him/her.

(c) A record of every sealing must be entered and consecutively numbered in a book and signed by the officer who witnessed the sealing.

The impression of the Conditioning House Special Seal must be witnessed by the Conditioning House Manager or an authorised representative. Any copy must be certified by the signature of one of these officers.

D8 Authentication of Documents for Legal proceedings

Only the Director of Legal Services or a senior officer named by him/her can sign documents needed for legal proceedings on the Council's behalf unless:

(a) an Act of Parliament requires or authorises some other person to do so, or

(b) the Council give authority to some other person.

PART E — INTERESTS

E1 Disclosure of Interest

(a) As soon as practicable at the beginning of a meeting, members and officers must disclose any interests in matters to be discussed.

(b) A member or officer who has an interest must leave the meeting room whilst that matter is being discussed unless:
  (i)   the interest arises only on an aspect incidental to the main subject of debate and the matter in which the interest arises is not itself under consideration as such, or
  (ii) the interests arises solely because the member or officer has been appointed as the Council's representative on an outside body, or
  (iii) the Secretary of State for the Environment has issued a dispensation allowing members to discuss and vote on a particular matter.

(c) A member of officer who has disclosed an interest must notify the chairperson immediately before leaving the meeting.

(d) For the purposes of this Standing Order, "interest" includes not only pecuniary interests as defined in the Local Government Act 1972 but also the types of non-pecuniary interest referred to in the National Code of Conduct.

E2 Register of Members Interests

The Director of Legal Services will keep a register of interests disclosed by members. This will be open for public inspection during normal office hours.

E3 Interests of Officers in Contracts

Officers must inform the Director of Legal Services in writing if they have any interests in a contract. These interests will be recorded in a register open for public inspection during normal office hours.

E4 Membership of Clubs, etc.

(a) Members must notify the Director of Legal Services of their membership of associations, societies, Trades Unions, Clubs, secret societies and other bodies such as the Freemasons and a register of such declarations will be kept by the Director of Legal Services which will be open to public inspection.

(b) Officers who make appointments or take part in disciplinary proceedings (other than by way of providing information for such proceedings) must notify the appropriate Director of their membership of associations, societies, Trade Unions, Clubs, secret societies and other bodies including the Freemasons and a register of these declarations will be kept by the Director and will be open to public inspection. The Chief Executive and Directors must also disclose any of the above memberships and these will be kept in a register maintained by the Chief Executive and open to public inspection.

PART F — OPEN GOVERNMENT

(Note: Part F relates to meetings of Council, Committees, Sub-Committees, Select Committees and Advisory Groups)

F1 Open Meetings

(a) The public are entitled to attend all meetings.

(b) They may only be excluded from meetings by the passing of a resolution at the meeting itself under the Local Government Act 1972 as amended by the Local Government (Access to Information) Act 1985. These provisions are set out for ease of reference in the Council's booklet "A Code of Practice About Public Access to Reports and Internal Documents."

F2 Items affecting Employees

Before any discussion takes place on the appointment, promotion, dismissal, salary, superannuation, conditions of service, or the conduct of a Council employee, the appropriate meeting must decide whether or not the public should be excluded from the meeting whilst the whole (or part) of the item is discussed. Where the conduct of an employee is being considered, the person chairing the meeting will allow the employee concerned (if present) to address the meeting on the proposed exclusion of the public.

F3 Rights of the Media

The Media will on request receive copies of the agenda and reports for meetings, any further statements or particulars as are produced to indicate the nature of items and, if the Chief Executive or appropriate Director thinks fit, copies of any other documents supplied to Members in connection with items on agenda.

F4 Recordings at Meetings

(a) Any person attending a meeting may take written notes of the proceedings.

(b) No one may make recordings of any other kind unless the person chairing the meeting has given permission. If anyone does so without permission, the person chairing the meeting can either require the person to leave at once and/or adjourn the meeting for as long as s/he thinks fit.

F5 Agenda and Reports

(a) Agenda items and reports (except reports marked "Not for Publication by reason of . . .") must be available for public inspection at all reasonable hours at least four clear working days before the day of the meeting.

(b) If, however, a meeting has to be called at short notice, the agenda items and reports (except reports marked "Not for Publication by reason of . . .") must be available for the time the meeting is called.

(c) Meetings may only consider agenda items if they have been included in an agenda which has been made available for public inspection.

(d) In special circumstances, however, the person chairing the meeting has power to allow an item to be considered which has not been on a publicly available agenda but only if s/he is of the opinion that it is a matter of urgency. An explanation of the "special circumstances" must be given in the minutes of the meeting to justify this action.

(e) Members of the public may receive at their own expense a copy of the agenda and reports which are available for public inspection.

(f) A reasonable number of agenda and open reports must be available free of charge to members of the public attending meetings.

F6 Reports for Agenda Items

(a) When preparing a report on an agenda item, the Chief Executive or Director responsible for the Report must ensure that the Report contains a list of background documents unless the officer has designated the report as "Not for Publication by reason of . . ." under F7.

(b) The list of background documents must set out all the documents which disclose facts or matters on which the report or an important part of it is based and which have been relied on to a material extent in preparing the report.

(c) The background documents which are available for public inspection do not include documents which fall within the confidential or exempt categories of documents specified in the Local Government Act 1972 and set out in full in the Code of Practice.

F7 Not for Publication Reports

(a) The Chief Executive or a Director may mark a report or any part of it "Not for Publication by reason of . . ." provided that s/he is of the opinion that the item to which the report relates is likely to be considered by the meeting with the public excluded.

(b) All reports marked "Not for Publication by reason of . . ." must specify the grounds which justify the restriction and the report itself must contain a brief statement explaining the reason for restriction.

(c) Any person may challenge the "Not for Publication by reason of . . ." by applying to the Chief Executive or Director concerned as the Proper Officer who made the restriction. The Proper Officer may either maintain the restriction after hearing any representations or decide to lift the restriction.

Where an unsuccessful application has been made to lift a restriction, the Proper Officer should advise the Chairperson either before or at the meeting. The member of the public may by completing the appropriate appeal form, ask the meeting to review the decision to restrict the document.

(d) Where the Proper Officer restricts publication of a report, s/he must ensure that the restriction itself and the grounds justifying it are stated on every copy of the report.

F8 General Access to Documents

(a) A member of the public may ask the appropriate Proper Officer for permission to inspect and copy any specified document which is in the possession or control of the Council. The Proper Officer may only refuse access to such a specified document on one or more of the grounds set out in the Local Government Act 1972.

(b) A member of the public who is refused access to any document by the Proper Officer may on completing the appropriate form complain against the refusal to the member body for the service in question. On receiving the form, the Director of Legal Services will arrange for the matter to be put to the appropriate meeting as soon as practicable.

(c) This Standing Order applies to all documents which are background documents to reports for agenda items as specified in the Local Government Act 1972 and as from 1 January 1987, except for officer reports prepared specifically for and at the request of a political group, to any other document produced by the Council after that date.

F9 Agenda Items Proposed to be taken in Private

(a) The Chief Executive or the appropriate Director may with the agreement of the Director of Legal Services indicate on an agenda item (by an asterisk against that item) that it is recommended that the item be dealt with in private session. The Director of Legal Services may only do this for items raised by him/her with the agreement of the Chief Executive.

(b) When an agenda item is marked in this way, it must also state the grounds for such a recommendation.

F10 Inspection of Background Documents

After any agenda item for a meeting has been published, if the report is available for public inspection under F5, members of the public are also entitled to inspect the Proper Officer's list of background documents and a copy of each of the documents in that list.

F11 Members' Rights of Inspection

(a) Any member of Council is entitled to inspect any document in the possession or under the control of the Council which relates to any business to be transacted at a meeting unless the document is certified by the appropriate Proper Officer as "Not for Publication" by reasons of paragraphs 1 to 6, 9, 11, 12 and 14 of Schedule 12A to the Local Government Act 1972 (see the Code of Practice for details of these).

(b) Members of Council are also entitled to inspect other documents in the possession or under the control of the Council subject to certain qualifications set down by the Courts. The Director of Legal Services will provide detailed advice on request.

F12 Minutes

Minutes of meetings must be available for public inspection at all reasonable times. Anyone may copy these at their own expense.

F13 Personal Files — Employees

Any employee of the Council about whom information is held by the Council may request in writing to inspect that information. The Chief Executive or a Director shall be entitled to refuse to allow inspection of any information where s/he certifies that disclosure would prejudice the Council on the grounds that:

(a) the particular document has been received in confidence and disclosure would breach that confidence, or

(b) disclosure would infringe personal privacy, or

(c) disclosure might prejudice the Council's position in legal proceedings.

There shall be a right of appeal by an employee to an Appeals Sub-Committee against a refusal to allow inspection of any piece of information.

F14 Housing Tenants' Files

Tenants of Council property administered by the Directorate of Housing and Environmental Health Services shall have the right to inspect the file maintained in respect of their tenancy in accordance with a scheme/arrangements drawn up by the Housing Services Committee.

The Director shall be entitled to refuse inspection of any document where s/he certifies that:

(a) the particular document has been received in confidence and disclosure would breach that confidence, or

(b) disclosure would infringe personal privacy, or

(c) disclosure might prejudice the Council's position in legal proceedings.

The arrangements shall provide a right of appeal to the Housing Sub-Committee against a refusal by the Director to allow inspection of any piece of information on the file.

F15 Personal Files — Social Services

Any person in respect of whom a file is maintained by the Directorate of Social Services has the right to inspect that file in accordance with a scheme/arrangements drawn up by the Social Services Committee. There shall be a right of appeal to the appropriate Social Services Sub-Committee against a refusal by the Director of Social Services to allow inspection of any particular document or piece of information on the file.

POWERS AND DUTIES

POLICY AND RESOURCES COMMITTEE

A. COMMITTEE

The Policy and Resources Committee will operate within the broad policy of the Council and any directions given by the Council and will exercise the powers and duties of the Council (apart from certain legal exceptions such as levying a rate) in the following areas:–

allocation and distribution of financial, personnel, land and property resources

major policy planning and strategic development

major across-the-district issues

reviewing the work of other Committees, Sub-Committees and Advisory Groups

reviewing the base budget and directing policy implementation

control and direction of advertising and publicity

Debt Management, Superannuation compensation

Matters listed under Select Committees set out below.

B. SUB-COMMITTEES

(NIL)

C. SELECT COMMITTEES

(a) Community Programme

To look at future policy in relation to the Community Programme and other similar grants to voluntary organis-ations with delegated powers to make decisions within the existing policy guidelines to protect existing on-going jobs and projects but will report to Policy and Resources Committee on proposals for future policy options with regard to the Community Programme generally.

(b) Disciplinary and Grievance

To hear employee disciplinary and grievance appeals. ("Upping" powers removed).

(c) Strategic Policy Issues

(1) to consider the effects of major changes in national legis-

lation which affect the Council as a whole, or which are not the obvious responsibility of one service committee, and where relevant to be responsible for the Council's response.

(2) to be responsible for the input to regional and national organisations where the Council has inherited a responsibility or lead role following the abolition of the West Yorkshire Metropolitan County Council or which are not the obvious responsibility of one service committee.

(3) to be responsible for the Council's overall advocacy role with the European Community, Central Government, Members of Parliament etc.

(d) **Personnel (Authority Wide)**

To deal with personnel matters in the following three categories:–

(i) The Joint Consultative Committees for each of the four main groupings of employees. (The management side of each JCC comprises the Personnel (Authority Wide) Select Committee). ("Upping" powers removed).

(ii) Authority-wide issues, or where there are Authority-wide implications.

(iii) Directorate establishment matters where there is a "failure to agree" between the Director of Personnel and the Director(s) concerned.

(e) **Resources and Forward Planning**

To deal with resources and forward planning.

(f) **Under 5s**

To oversee the development of provision for Under 5s in the District and to make recommendations to the appropriate member bodies and meet with Under 5s Forums representing the voluntary sector.

(g) **Sports Stadia**

To make recommendations to the Policy and Resources Committee on policy issues relating to sports stadia and professional sport in the District.

(h) **Ilkley Campus**

(1) To examine all alternative uses for the Ilkley Campus and to make recommendations on alternative uses of the Campus to both the Educational Services and the Employment and Economic Affairs Committees before reporting back to the Policy and Resources Committee.

(2) To be responsible for identifying both the costs of pursuing different courses of action and the savings accruing to the Educational Services Committee's base budget as a result of withdrawal from the Campus.

D. **JOINT ARRANGEMENT SUB-COMMITTEE**

(a) **Disability**

The Advisory Group will act to:–

    (i) publicise, promote and popularise disability issues in the Bradford Metropolitan Area;

    (ii) rectify disadvantages of the disabled in the community;

    (iii) promote and influence disability issues at national and local level, via the media, Government Departments and other appropriate channels;

    (iv) eliminate areas of unequal treatment relating to the disabled;

    (v) ensure that the Council's Equal Opportunities Employment Policy relating to the disabled is implemented, particularly by identifying and attempting to eliminate, the disadvantages which disabled people suffer in employment and service areas of Council activity.

(b) **Health**

The Advisory Group have the following terms of reference:–

(1) To co-ordinate responses to Health Authority initiatives and decisions where these do not fall within the remit of any single Directorate.

(2) To co-ordinate the Council's responses to health care issues affecting the District.

(3) To investigate methods of promoting preventative health care in the District.

(4) To investigate and examine those factors which could have a detrimental effect on the health of the people of the District and co-ordinate and correlate responses to those factors.

(5) To provide back up and briefing for Local Authority members on Health Authorities and Community Health Councils.

(6) To liaise closely with voluntary and non statutory groups involved in the promotion of Health Care and with Community Health Councils.

(c) **Race Relations**

The terms of reference are as follows:–

(1) To consider what are the obstacles for the attainment of greater racial harmony and equality.

(2) To examine in what ways the Council's policies might be extended or altered so as to contribute towards overcoming these obstacles.

(3) To establish priorities in any such policy development.

(4) To consider the reasons for any apparent low rate of take up of Council services by ethnic minority groups and to recommend accordingly.

(5) To liaise with those outside bodies and organisations having an interest in the promotion of community development and good race relations.

(6) To monitor the action taken by the Council services to ensure the fulfilment of the recommended actions.

(7) To ensure that ethnic minority viewpoints and values are given fair and adequate expression within the Council's policy making arrangements.

(d) **Sex Equality**

The Advisory Group will act to:–

(1) publicise, promote and popularise sex equality issues in the Area;

(2) rectify disadvantages of women in the community;

(3) identify sex discrimination in employment and service areas;

(4) promote and influence sex equality issues at a national and local level, via the media, Government Departments and other appropriate channels;

(5) eliminate areas of unequal treatment relating to sex or sexual orientation.

EDUCATIONAL SERVICES COMMITTEE

A. COMMITTEE

Archaeology and Archives
Culture
Education
Leisure and Recreation
Matters listed under Sub-Committees and Select Committees set out below.

B. SUB-COMMITTEES

(a) **Further Education**

Maintaining the District's colleges
Making grants to students to enable them to attend courses
Youth and community facilities

(b) **Further Education Grant Appeals**

To deal with appeals against the refusal of the Director of Educational Services to make further education awards in accordance with the Council's policy. ("Upping" powers removed).

(c) Leisure Services

The collection, management, presentation and interpretation of articles of cultural and educational interest in the District's galleries and museums; the Museums Loans Service to Schools; the Community Arts Centre and the West Yorkshire Ecological Advisory and Information Service; Archaeology and Archives.

The provision of a comprehensive library service throughout the District.

The provision and organisation of sporting and recreational facilities.

Maintaining the Authority's parks and recreational land. The provision, management and development of countryside activities.

Management of the District's theatres, public halls and concert halls as well as the promotion of various musical and dramatic presentations.

(d) Schools Buildings

The Sub-Committee is responsible for the development of all school buildings within the District and also for maintaining, repairing, furnishing and cleaning the existing buildings.

(e) Schools Education

The Sub-Committee is responsible for all aspects of educational development in schools (excluding schools for the handicapped) ranging from the under fives in nursery schools to the provision of in-service training courses for teachers. Provision of a comprehensive careers advisory service for school leavers and unemployed youngsters. Provision of educational supplies and equipment.

(f) Schools Special

The Sub-Committee is responsible for ensuring that the special educational and related needs of pupils are provided for.

Welfare and psychological needs of children at school, the provision of a specialist remedial service for those children with learning difficulties, a child guidance clinic for children with emotional and behavioural problems, and the initial education and welfare of ethnic minority children. The administration of all manner of individual pupil aid schemes, including home to school travel, assistance with boarding education, provision of school clothing and applications for free school meals.

School crossing patrols.

(g) School Benefit Appeals

To deal with appeals by parents against the refusal of the Director of Educational Services to award benefits or grants provided for in the Education Acts 1944 to 1984 applicable to the attendance of any pupil at school. ("Upping" powers removed).

C. SELECT COMMITTEES

(a) Adult Education
  (i) to formulate an adult education policy;
  (ii) to involve and co-ordinate the work of the local authority, Colleges, and voluntary sector provision;
  (iii) to produce a coherent policy for the District which avoids duplication and fills in any areas of shortfall in existing service provision.

(b) Personnel

To deal with personnel matters for the Committee's service.

(c) 13–19

To consider the draft policy document on 13–16 curriculum and to submit to the Committee policy proposals for a 13–16 curriculum within the wider 13–19 context in accordance with the remit set out in Educational Services Committee Document "M", namely:
  (i) approve and recommend a policy document for 13–16 curriculum and its development;

(ii) recommend on the future and follow-up to Technical and Vocational Education Initiative (TVEI) and Skills Foundation Course (SFC) which are time expiring projects with dissemination requirements;

(iii) give consideration to the costs, implementation and monitoring of General Certificate of Secondary Education (GCSE), Certificate of Pre-vocational Education (CPVE), Northern Partnership for Records of Achievement (NPRA), work practice and other work-related initiatives;

(iv) recommend on the co-operative roles which will be required of different parts of the system in achieving an efficient, effective and viable delivery, 13–19;

(v) consider the mechanisms and resources necessary for ensuring appropriate staff development;

(vi) look into the question of Education Support Grant (ESG) and other external funding.

EMPLOYMENT AND ECONOMIC AFFAIRS COMMITTEE

A. COMMITTEE

Tackling poverty and unemployment by economic and other measures.

Directing efforts to tackle unemployment and promote economic development and co-ordinating resource allocation in these areas.

Major policy planning on unemployment, economic development, development of tourism and municipal enterprises.

Administration of the Chief Executive's Office and the Directorates of Finance, Legal Services and Personnel and the Unemployment Unit.

Central Purchasing — matters relating to the Yorkshire Purchasing Organisation.

Inter-town twinning.

Matters listed under Sub-Committees and Select Committees set out below.

B. SUB-COMMITTEES

(a) Grants and Loans

To deal with applications for grants and loans and concessionary rents.

C. SELECT COMMITTEES

(a) Employment and Economic Initiatives

To consider employment and economic initiatives.

(b) Personnel

To deal with personnel matters for the Committee's service.

(c) Employment and Economic Affairs Service Delivery

To examine how the Council delivers services to unemployed persons and promote economic development.

(d) Youth Training Scheme

To consider and make recommendations to the Employment and Economic Affairs Committee on the implementation of the two-year Youth Training Scheme by the Council.

HOUSING SERVICES COMMITTEE

A. COMMITTEE

Environmental Health
Housing
Public Protection
Matters listed under Sub-Committees and Select Committees set out below.

B. SUB-COMMITTEES

(a) Housing

All matters relating to Council housing
Clearance and closing/demolition orders
General Improvement Areas (in consultation with Planning
Sub-Committee)
Housing Action Areas
Housing Advice Centre
Homelessness
Housing Associations
Improvement Grants
Mortgage Loans
Supervision of sheltered housing schemes
Gypsies

(b) Public Health and Protection

Certain legislation relating to health and safety in
employment
Environmental control, including food and drugs, infectious
diseases, stray dogs, stray horses, diseases of animals
Rodent and pest control, noise, air pollution and public
nuisance
Health education and home safety
Keeping of animals
Public Mortuaries
Trading Standards

C. SELECT COMMITTEES

(a) Personnel

To deal with personnel matters for the Committee's service.

PUBLIC AND GENERAL SERVICES COMMITTEE

A. COMMITTEE

Architectural, Engineering and Planning Services
Directorate of Works
Highways and Transportation Services

Municipal enterprises, including Airport
Public Works
Waste Disposal
Matters listed under Sub-Committees and Select Committees set out below.

B. SUB-COMMITTEES

(a) Direct Works

Cleaning and Caretaking — Public Offices
Direct Works Organisation
Operational maintenance of District Roads
Public Conveniences
Refuse Collection
Street Cleansing
Vehicle Provision
Waste Management

(b) General Services

Coroners
Licensing
Local Valuation Panel
Management of administrative buildings not within ambit
of another Sub-Committee
Management of City Hall
Member Services
Probation Services

(c) Planning

Administration of Planning Section of the Directorate of
Development Services
Closure and diversion of footpaths and bridleways
Compensation for planning restrictions
Conservation areas and listed buildings
Control of Development through consideration of planning
applications and use of enforcement procedures
Countryside planning
District Planning
Environmental improvement programmes

General Improvement Areas
Industrial Improvement Areas
Local Plans and Unitary Plans
Planning input to transportation studies
Purchase notices
Reclamation of derelict land
Tree preservation
Green Belt
Minerals

(d) **Public Services**

Administration of the Directorate of Development Services (except the sections under the control of another Sub-Committee)
Abattoirs and cold stores
Airport
Architectural Services
Cemeteries and crematoria
Conditioning House
Engineering Services
Licensing of hackney carriages and private hire vehicles
Off-street car parks
Markets

C. SELECT COMMITTEES

(a) **Personnel**

To deal with personnel matters for the Committee's service.

SOCIAL SERVICES COMMITTEE

A. COMMITTEE

All Social Services functions, personal social services and social care.

Matters listed under Sub-Committees and Select Committees listed below.

B. SUB-COMMITTEES

(a) Elderly and Community Health Services

Responsibility for all Domiciliary, Residential and Day Care, and specialist Social Work services to the Elderly and the Mentally Ill.

Registration and supervision of private residential care establishments.

Services to clients who live at home but need care and occupation during the day at special centres.

(b) Children and Services to Disabled People

Responsibility for all Domiciliary, Residential and Day Care and specialist social work services to Children and the Handicapped.

Boarding Out of Children.

Special facilities for groups with special problems.

Supervision of registered private day care provision.

(c) Access and Parental Rights

Decisions on questions of parents access to children and the taking or rescinding of Parental Rights.

Other additional confidential and complex appeals might be considered at this Sub-Committee with the agreement of the Chairperson.

("Upping" powers relating to specific cases removed).

(d) Private Residential Care Establishments (Appeals)

To determine appeals relating to the licensing of Registered Homes.

("Upping" powers relating to specific cases removed).

C. SELECT COMMITTEES

(a) Child Abuse

To consider the implications of a report of the Director of Social Services submitted to the Social Services Committee on 15 January 1986 (*Document "S"*) with terms of reference which acknowledge the responsibilities of the Area Review Committee and require the Select Committee to report back to the Social Services Committee in six months time on the progress made towards implementing resolutions approved by the Committee (*Minute 43 (1985–86)*).

(b) **Drug Abuse**

To report to the Social Services Committee with the following terms of reference:–

"To monitor the work of the Working Party on services for Drug Misusers and make recommendations to the Social Services Committee and to any other appropriate Council body to ensure that

    (i) implications for the Council's services of issues identified by the Working Party on Services for Drug Misusers are fed into Directorates quickly to facilitate policy changes

    (ii) appropriate issues are raised by the Council at meetings of the Joint Consultative Committee with Health Authorities

    (iii) the Council representatives on the District Health Authority are fully briefed on any implications of the work of the Working Party on Services for Drug Misusers to assist them in their contribution to District Health Authority meetings".

(c) **Personnel**

To deal with personnel matters for the Committee's service.

(d) **Operations and Service Delivery**

To deal with the following issues

    (i) Issues relating to Area Offices

    (ii) Management and Planning Issues

    (iii) Grants to voluntary organisations and subscriptions

    (iv) Other operational issues not clearly defined under the two Standing Sub-Committees.

MODEL STANDING ORDERS WITH RESPECT TO CONTRACTS

STANDING ORDERS RELATING TO CONTRACTS

Compliance with Standing Orders and European Economic Community (EEC) Directives

Note 1 **1.** Every contract made by the Council or by a committee, sub-committee, or officer acting on their behalf shall comply with the EEC Treaty and with any relevant Directives of the EEC for the time being in force in the United Kingdom and, except as hereinafter provided, these standing orders.

2. It shall be a condition of any contract between the Council and any person (not being an officer of the Council) who is required to supervise a contract on their behalf that, in relation to such contract, he shall comply with the requirements of these standing orders as if he were a chief officer of the Council.

Notes **3.** Exemption from any of the following provisions
2 & 4 of these standing orders may be made by direction of [the Council] [a committee or sub-committee duly authorised in that behalf] [an officer of the Council duly authorised in that behalf] where [they] [he] [are] [is] satisfied that the exemption is justified in special circumstances.

4. The [Council] [appropriate committee] shall be informed of the circumstances of every exemption made by a sub-committee or by an officer.

5. A record of any exemption made in accordance with standing order 3 shall, if not made in the minutes of the Council, be made in the minutes of the committee or sub-committee to which the report referred to in that standing order is made.

Invitation of Tenders

Notes 2, **6.** Where the estimated value or amount of a
3 & 5 proposed contract exceeds [£   ], and in any other case where [the Council] [the appropriate committee or sub-committee] determine, tenders shall be invited in accordance with either standing order 7, 8 or 9.

Selective Tendering

AD HOC LIST

Notes 4, **7.** i. This standing order shall apply where the Council,
5 & 6 or a committee or sub-committee duly authorised in that behalf, have decided that invitations to tender for a contract are to be made to some or all of those persons or bodies who have replied to a public notice.
ii. For the purposes of this standing order, public notice shall be given:
a. in at least one local newspaper, and

Note 5 b. where the estimated amount or value of the contract exceeds [£   ], in at least one newspaper or journal circulating among such persons or bodies who undertake such contracts, and

c. at the discretion of the [Council] [appropriate committee or sub-committee] to all or a selected number of persons or bodies named in the list maintained under standing order 8.

iii. The public notice shall:

a. specify details of the contract into which the Council wish to enter,

b. invite persons or bodies interested, to apply for permission to tender, and

Note 4   c. specify a time limit, being not less than [14] days, within which such applications are to be submitted to the Council.

iv. After the expiry of the period specified in the public notice invitations to tender for the contract shall be sent to:

Note 4   a. not less than [4] of the persons or bodies who applied for permission to tender, selected by [the Council] [the appropriate committee or sub-committee] [an officer of the Council duly authorised in that behalf] or

Note 4   b. where fewer than [4] persons or bodies have applied or are considered suitable, those persons or bodies which [the Council] [the appropriate committee or sub-committee] [an officer of the Council duly authorised in that behalf] consider(s) suitable.

STANDING LIST

Note 6   **8.** i. This standing order shall apply where the Council, or a committee or sub-committee duly authorised in that behalf, have decided that invitations to tender for a contract are to be limited to those persons or bodies whose names shall be included in a list compiled and maintained for that purpose.

Note 7   ii. The list shall:

a. be compiled and maintained by the [Council] [appropriate committee or sub-committee];

b. contain the names of all persons or bodies who wish to be included and who are approved by [the Council] [the appropriate committee or sub-committee] [an officer of the Council duly authorised in that behalf]; and

c. indicate in respect of a person or body whose name is so included, the categories of contract and the values or amounts in respect of those categories for which approval has been given.

Note 4   iii. At least [4] weeks before a list is first compiled, notices inviting applications for inclusion in it shall be published:

a. in at least one local newspaper; and

b. in at least one newspaper or journal circulating among such persons or bodies as undertake such contracts.

Note 8   iv. The lists shall be reviewed at regular intervals of not less than [1] year or more than [2] years.

v. Invitations to tender for a contract shall be sent to:

Note 4   a. not less than [4] of those persons or bodies selected by [the Council] [the appropriate committee or sub-committee] [an officer of the Council duly authorised in that behalf], from among those approved for a contract of the relevant category and amount or value, or

Note 4   b. where fewer than [4] persons or bodies are approved for a contract of the relevant category and amount or value, all those persons or bodies.

Open Tendering

Note 3   **9.** i. This standing order shall apply where the Council, or a committee or sub-committee duly authorised in that behalf, have decided that tenders

for a contract are to be obtained by open
competition.

Note 4

ii. At least [14] days public notice shall be given
in one or more local newspapers and also,

Note 5

wherever the values of the contract exceeds
[£   ] in one or more newspapers or journals
circulating among such persons or bodies as
undertake such contracts. The notice shall express the
nature and purpose of the contract [state where
further details may be obtained], invite tenders for its
execution and state the last date and time when
tenders will be received.

Submission of Tenders

Notes
2 & 4

10. i. Where in pursuance of these standing orders
invitation to tender is made, every invitation shall
state that no tender will be received unless it is
enclosed in a [plain] sealed envelope which shall
bear the word "Tender" — followed by the
subject to which it relates [but no other name or
mark indicating the sender].

ii. The tenders shall be kept in the custody of the
Chief Executive Officer or such other officer of
the Council as may be duly authorised in that
behalf until the time and date specified for their
opening.

Note 9

iii. No tender received after the time and date
specified in the invitation shall be accepted or
considered [under any circumstances] [unless
there is clear evidence of it having been posted
by first class post at least the day before tenders
were due to be returned].

Opening and Acceptance of Tenders

11. Tenders received under either standing order
7, 8 or 9 shall be opened at one time and only in
the presence of:

    i.   such member or members, or

    ii. such member or members and officer or officers, or

    iii. such officer or officers

as the Council may determine.

12. All tenders received shall be recorded.

13. A tender other than the lowest tender if payment is to be made by the Council or the highest tender if payment is to be received by the Council shall not be accepted except as authorised by the Council or a committee or sub-committee authorised in that behalf, having considered a report by the appropriate chief officer or other authorised person.

14. A registrar of all contracts placed by the Council shall be kept and maintained by such officer or officers as the Council may determine. Such register shall for each contract, specify the name of the contractor, the works to be executed or the goods to be supplied and the contract value. The register shall be open to inspection by any member of the Council.

Nominated Sub-contractors and Suppliers

Note 11   **15.** Where a sub-contractor or supplier is to be nominated to a main contractor, the following provisions shall have effect:

    i. Where the estimated amount of the sub-contract or the estimated value of the goods to be supplied by the nominated supplier does not

Note 5   exceed [£   ] then, unless the appropriate chief officer is of the opinion in respect of any particular nomination that it is not reasonably practicable to obtain competitive tenders, tenders shall be invited for the nomination.

Note 5

ii. Where the estimated amount of the sub-contract or the estimated value of the goods to be supplied by the nominated supplier exceeds [£   ] then, unless the Council or a committee or sub-committee duly authorised in that behalf determine in respect of any particular nomination that it is not reasonably practicable to obtain competitive tenders, tenders shall be invited in accordance with either standing order 7, 8 or 9 as the case may be.

iii. The provisions of standing orders 10, 11, 12, 13 and 14 shall apply to tenders received under this standing order.

Contract Conditions

Notes
2 & 5

16. i. Every contract which exceeds [£   ] in value or amount shall:

a. be in writing and signed by an officer of the Council duly authorised in that behalf;

b. specify the goods materials or services to be supplied and the work to be executed; the price to be paid together with a statement as to the amount of any discount(s) or other deduction(s); the period(s) within which the contract is to be performed and such other conditions and terms as may be agreed between the parties, and

Notes
5 & 12

c. in appropriate cases, where a contract exceeds [£   ] in amount or value, provide for the payment of liquidated damages by the contractor where he fails to complete the contract within the time specified.

Note 13

ii. The Council may also require a contractor to give sufficient security for the due performance of any contract.

Note 14

17. Where an appropriate British Standard Specification or British Standard Code of Practice issued by the British Standards Institution is current at the date of the tender, every contract shall require that all goods and materials used or supplied, and all the workmanship shall be at least of the standard required by the appropriate British Standards Specification or Code of Practice.

18. There shall be inserted in every written contract a clause empowering the Council to cancel the contract and to recover from the contractor the amount of any loss resulting from such cancellation, if the contractor shall have offered or given or agreed to give to any person any gift or consideration of any kind as an inducement or reward for doing or forbearing to do or for having done or forborne to do any action in relation to the obtaining or execution of the contract or any other contract with the Council, or for showing or forbearing to show favour or disfavour to any person in relation to the contract or any other contract with the Council, or if the like acts shall have been done by any person employed by him or acting on his behalf (whether with or without the knowledge of the contractor), or if in relation to any contract with the Council, the contractor or any person employed by him or acting on his behalf shall have committed any offence under the Prevention of Corruption Acts 1889 to 1916, or shall have given any fee or reward the receipt of which is an offence under section 117(2) of the Local Government Act 1972.

NOTES

1. Standing order 1 requires compliance with the EEC Treaty (the Treaty of Rome) and with any relevant EEC Directives. In particular, attention is drawn to Article 30 of the Treaty which prohibits quantitative restrictions on imports between Member States and measures having equivalent effect to such restrictions. This provision has effect in United Kingdom law by virtue of section 2(1) of the European Communities Act 1972.

The relevant EEC Directives in the context of public sector construction contracts are:

i. Directive 71/304, which requires the abolition of any restrictive or discriminatory practices which might prevent contractors from other Member States from participating in public works contracts on equal terms with national contractors.

ii. Directives 71/305 and 72/277, which lay down common advertising procedures and award criteria for public works contracts with an estimated value above the prevailing threshold.

Advice on the application of these Directives to local authority works contracts is given in DOE Circular 4/73 (Welsh Office 4/73) and in DOE Circular 59/73 (Welsh Office 109/73) as amended by DOE Circulars 102/76 and 67/78 (Welsh Office 158/76 and 118/78). With regard to public sector supplies contracts, the relevant EEC Directives are:

iii. Directive 70/32 which applies the same principles of free competition to supplies contracts as Directive 71/304 applies to works contracts.

iv. Directive 77/62 which lays down common advertising and award criteria for public sector supplies contracts with an estimated value above the prevailing threshold.

Advice on the application of these Directives to local authority supplies contracts is given in DOE Circulars 4/73, 46/78 and 27/81 (Welsh Office 4/73, 81/78 and 40/81). These model standing orders do not conflict with the provisions of the EEC Directives, but in the case of contracts exceeding the thresholds, there will be instances where both Directive 71/305 and Directive 77/62 impose requirements additional to those set out in the model. Those authorities whose standing orders are not based on this model or its predecessor should ensure that there is no conflict with the provisions of the Directives. The requirement to comply with the Directives cannot be suspended, but the Directives themselves provide for exemption from their provisions in specified circumstances.

2. i. The provisions of Part III of the Local Government, Planning and Land Act 1980 ("the 1980 Act") and the Regulations and Directions made thereunder cannot be affected by anything contained in a local authority's standing orders. Thus construction or maintenance works to which Part III of the 1980 Act applies cannot be exempted from competition under a standing order in the form of standing order 3 if competition is required under the 1980 Act.

ii. Similarly any financial limit fixed by a local authority in its standing orders is subject to any financial limits or prescribed amounts in relation to construction or maintenance work of different descriptions as provided in Part III of the 1980 Act and any Regulations and Directions made under it.

iii. A local authority cannot enter into a contract with its own direct labour organisation, thus where a direct labour organisation competes for construction or maintenance work with outside contractors for one of its own authority's projects it does not "tender" for the work. A direct labour organisation is required by Part III of the 1980 Act to prepare a written statement for any job of functional work which it wishes to undertake and to which Part III of the 1980 Act applies.

iv. In applying standing orders, therefore, in these circumstances the terms "job" and "written statement" are to be treated as being synonymous with the words "contract" and "tender".

3. i. The three recognised tendering procedures are selective tendering (standing orders 7 and 8), open competition (standing order 9) and negotiation based on a contract won in competition. Use of the latter procedure in cases where the estimated value or amount of a proposed contract exceeds the threshold prescribed in standing order 6 would require formal steps to be taken under standing order 3. Generally, negotiation is acceptable where it is based on some preliminary form of price competition such as obtains in two stage tendering, or continuation contracts where the earlier contract, for broadly similar work, was won in competition within a year or two of the later contract.

ii. In deciding which method is most suitable for particular works contracts local authorities should bear in mind that the use of open competition is not recommended. Open competition has been widely criticised in successive reports because it is wasteful of resources and may lead to employment of unsuitable contractors, and indiscriminate tendering may lead to bad building. The disadvantages of open competition can be obviated by the use of selective tendering procedures which are recommended.

4.   i. Throughout the model, various designations, periods and other references are shown in brackets. The designations, as in standing order 3 and elsewhere, are the options open to authorities, the choice of which will depend upon the nature of the arrangements they have made under section 101 of the Act for the discharge of their functions. Some references in brackets are either options as in standing order 10(iii) or may be deleted as in standing order 10(i).

ii. Periods shown in brackets as in standing order 7(iii)(c) are suggestions and may be amended. In considering whether or not to depart from the periods suggested in 7(iii)(c) and 9(ii), it is recommended that 14 days should be regarded as the minimum period. Four weeks notice, however, should normally be given for the preparation of tenders other than for minor contracts. The suggested period of 4 weeks in standing order 8(iii) should also be the minimum period. EEC Directives 71/305 and 77/62 set out the periods that must be allowed for applications to be invited to tender and for the receipt of tenders in those cases which need to be advertised in the Official Journal of the European Communities.

iii. In standing orders 7(iv) and 8(v) it is left to authorities to decide the number of firms to be invited to tender, but for works they are recommended to adopt the range of numbers related to various sizes and types of contract as shown in the NJCC "Code of Procedure for Single Stage Selective Tendering" or "Code of Procedure for Two Stage Selective Tendering", as appropriate. Numbers in excess of these maxima should be avoided, otherwise the resultant increase in abortive tendering costs will inevitably show itself in increased building costs.

5. Monetary thresholds, as in standing order 6, etc, have not been included in the model as it is impracticable to quote figures appropriate for all the varied types of works and supplies contracts undertaken by local authorities. Appropriate levels will depend upon the number, type and size of the contracts of a particular authority and whether they are for works or supplies contracts. It is recommended that monetary thresholds included in standing orders are updated from time to time to keep pace with changing costs.

6. In standing orders 7 and 8 where references are made to the committee or sub-committee, the committee or sub-committee contemplated is the one authorised by the Council to decide what form of tendering should be used for the Council's contracts. This would normally be a general committee or sub-committee rather than a functional committee or sub-committee. However, it need not be the same committee or sub-committee that compiles and maintains the list under standing order 8(ii)(a) or approves names under standing order 8(ii)(b).

7. It would be necessary for a resolution to be passed setting out the manner in which the firms are to be selected, either in the form of a general instruction or in respect of a particular contract or type of contract. It is most important that the method chosen should be a fair one, such as tendering by rotation in the case of firms on their standing lists. Where it is considered appropriate, foreign firms may be included in a standing list. But local authorities cannot advertise for applicants to their lists in the Official Journal of the European Communities.

8. Generally, standing lists of contractors should be kept under continuous review with provision for both deletions and additions at any time. It is important that standing lists should not become rigid and self-perpetuating and that the entry of new and rising firms be encouraged. In reviewing standing lists it is suggested that those firms who have shown interest in local authority contracts and whose performance has been satisfactory should, subject to checks on their current viability, be retained. Those who have failed to show an interest should be dropped.

9. In cases of late receipt of a tender only official postmarks should be accepted as evidence of the day of the posting of a tender. Where such postmarks are illegible the tender should be rejected. The envelopes of admitted late tenders should be endorsed by the official responsible and the envelope retained. Late tenders which are not admitted should be returned to the sender as soon as possible.

10. For highway works where an authority is acting as an agent for the Department of Transport or the Welsh Office, the latter bodies may have special requirements which must be taken into account, eg that selective tendering has to be used for contracts above a certain size.

11. Standing order 15 relates to the selection of sub-contractors or suppliers to be nominated to a main contractor. Its adoption enables an authority to leave control of nominated sub-contracts in the hands of the appropriate chief officer or duly authorised committee or sub-committee if they wish to do so.

12. In standing order 16(i)(c) provision is made for local authorities to require, in appropriate cases, the payment of liquidated damages for failure to complete a contract, exceeding [£   ] in value within the stipulated time. The following points should be borne in mind in connection with this standing order:

i. Where liquidated damages are provided for in a contract, the amount included for them should be a genuine pre-estimate of the loss to the client which delayed completion is likely to cause. Amounts which are likely to be construed as a penalty should not be inserted.

ii. When considering whether it is necessary to provide for liquidated damages in a contract, a local authority should satisfy itself that such damages are applicable to the type of work and the form of contract and that they are enforceable and administratively economic to recover, (eg in the case of standing-offer type contracts (term contracts) where there may be difficulties in genuinely pre-estimating the loss to the client they may not be appropriate). Provision for liquidated damages must however be made in all highway works contracts where an authority is acting as agent for the Department of Transport or the Welsh Office.

iii. Where a contract provides for a phased hand over, liquidated damages should be specified for each phase and authorities should ensure that if any phase of a contract is not finished on time, their entitlement to liquidated damages is considered in calculating the amount due to the contractor under the terms of the contract.

13. Standing order 16(ii) provides that a Council may take security for the due performance of a contract. The most common form of security is the performance bond, the cost of which is inevitably met by the authority. Where proper selective tendering procedures are used, including the investigation of the financial standing of firms, the need for bonds may be reduced. Authorities are therefore recommended to consider each contract on its merits and to dispense with bonds wherever this seems reasonable. It is emphasised, however, that the question of bonding is left entirely to the discretion of individual authorities to be exercised in the light of all relevant circumstances. If no bond is called for, tender documents should state this so that all tenderers are clear as to the basis on which they are tendering. Guidance on the use of performance bonds has been issued by the local authority associations.

14. Standing order 17 has been drawn so as to impose compliance with a standard for goods and materials used, or supplied, and for all workmanship of not less than the British Standard in all cases where an appropriate standard exists. It has the effect of requiring formal steps to be taken, under standing order 3, for any proposal to depart from an existing standard. Local authorities and their agents are strongly recommended to consider the advantage of third party schemes of certification or assessment, such as BSI Kitemark and Registered Firm schemes, or Agrément Board Certification, where such schemes are available.

SPECIMEN FINANCIAL STANDING ORDERS AND FINANCIAL REGULATIONS AS PROVIDED BY THE CHARTERED INSTITUTE OF PUBLIC FINANCE AND ACCOUNTANCY

(The following specimen is reproduced with the kind permission of the Chartered Institute of Public Finance and Accountancy who retain the copyright)

FINANCIAL STANDING ORDERS

General Note

Where regulations contain financial limits a figure has not been inserted. This is a matter on which each authority must make its own decision.

The term finance "committee" denotes the appropriate body of members which depending on local circumstances might be a policy and resources committee, a policy and co-ordinating committee or a finance sub-committee.

"Treasurer" is intended to be synonymous with "director of finance" or any other title which might be given to the officer responsible for finance in accordance with section 151 of the Local Government Act 1972.

(i) FINANCIAL ADMINISTRATION

01 The finance committee is responsible for regulating and controlling the finances of the Council.

02   The treasurer shall, for purposes of section 151 of the Local Government Act 1972 be responsible under the general direction of the finance committee, for the proper administration of the Council's Financial affairs.

03   As the Council's financial and economic adviser, the treasurer shall report to the finance committee with respect to the level of resources proposed to be utilised in each financial year and shall keep that committee informed with respect to the Council's finances and financial performance and other committees informed with respect to the financial implications of their activities.

04   The chairman of the finance committee or his nominee, being a member of the finance committee, is entitled to attend meetings of all spending committees and to speak but not to vote on matters relating to annual or supplementary estimates   or   on   any   proposal   involving   expenditure exceeding (£   ).

05   The finance committee shall appoint from its members a sub-committee the terms of reference of which shall be:

(a)   to select heads of continuing expenditure for review,

(b)   to compare such expenditures with comparable financial standards and trends, and

(c)   to express an opinion whether such expenditures are providing   value   for   money   and   to   report   with recommendations.

06   The finance committee is responsible for making and amending from time to time such financial regulations as it considers necessary and desirable for the supervision and control of the finances, accounts, income, expenditure and assets of the Council, in conformity with these standing orders.

07   Each committee shall be responsible for the observance of the Council's financial standing orders and financial regulations throughout all departments under its control.

08   Each chief officer is responsible for the accountability

and control of staff and the security, custody and control of all other resources including plant, buildings, materials, cash and stores appertaining to his department.

(ii) **FINANCIAL PLANNING**

09   Each committee shall submit to the finance committee a programme of capital expenditure and estimates of income and expenditure on revenue account for such future period(s) and in such form and by such date(s) as the finance committee shall require.

10   The finance committee shall consider the aggregate effect of these programmes and estimates upon the Council's financial resources and, after consultation on any proposed amendment, shall submit them to the Council for approval with a recommendation of the rate to be levied for the ensuing financial year.

11   Each member of the Council shall be provided with a copy of the proposed capital programme and revenue estimates together with a statement by the treasurer of their effect on the Council's finances and the rate to be levied at least . . . days before the meeting of the Council at which such matters will be considered.

(iii) **BUDGETARY CONTROL**

12   It shall be the duty of every committee to monitor and regulate its financial performance during the currency of each estimate period.

13   A committee may not incur expenditure which cannot be met from the amount provided in the revenue estimates under a head of estimate (including any virement made in accordance with standing order 3.3 below) to which that expenditure would be charged or would result in an over-spending in the year on that head of estimate unless a supplementary estimate has been submitted to the finance committee and approved by that committee or by the Council. This standing order shall apply to a reduction in income as to an increase in expenditure.

14 Amounts provided under the several heads of the approved annual revenue estimates shall not be diverted to other purposes by the committee concerned without the approval of the finance committee save that such approval is not required where the amount does not exceed (£   ).

15 A committee proposing to vary its approved programme of capital expenditure by the addition, deletion or material modification of a project in that programme shall submit a recommendation to the finance committee which may approve, but not disapprove, the proposal on the Council's behalf. Such approval shall not be required where a committee wishes to transfer an amount not exceeding £   from one head of the capital programme to another.

16 Nothing in these standing orders shall prevent a committee from incurring expenditure which is essential to meet any immediate needs created by a sudden emergency or which is referable to section 138 of the Local Government Act 1972 subject to their action being reported forthwith to the finance committee.

17 The inclusion of items in approved revenue estimates or capital programmes shall constitute authority to incur such expenditure save to the extent to which the finance committee for the Council shall have placed a reservation on any such item or items. Expenditure on any such reserved items may be incurred only when and to the extent that such reservation has been removed.

18 The finance committee shall from time to time keep the Council informed as to the state of the Council's finances and shall report on the accounts of each financial year as soon as practicable.

19 Where a committee proposes:–

(a)   a new policy; or

(b)   a variation of existing policy; or

(c)   a variation in the means or time-scale of implementing existing policy which affects or may affect the Council's finances, it shall submit a report to the finance committee which shall report thereon to the Council.

(xviii) CANCELLATION

20   In every written contract a clause shall be inserted to secure that the Council shall be entitled to cancel the contract and to recover from the contractor the amount of any loss resulting from such cancellation, if the contractor shall have offered or given or agreed to give to any person any gift or consideration of any kind as an inducement or reward for doing or forbearing to do or for having done or forborne to do any action in relation to obtaining or the execution of the contract or any other contract with the Council, or for showing or forbearing to show favour or disfavour to any person in relation to the contract or any other contract with the Council, or if the like acts shall have been done by any person employed by him or acting on his behalf (whether with or without the knowledge of the contractor) or if in relation to any contract with the Council the contractor or any person employed by him or acting on his behalf shall have committed any offence under the Prevention of Corruption Acts 1889 to 1916, or any amendment of them, or shall have given any fee or reward the receipt of which is an offence under sub-section 2 of section 117 of the Local Government Act 1972.

21   In every written contract for the execution of work or the supply of goods or materials where the work will be executed wholly or in part in the United Kingdom or the goods or materials to be supplied will be manufactured or made wholly or in part in a factory, workshop or a place situate in the United Kingdom the following clause shall be inserted:–

The contractor shall in respect of all persons employed by him (whether in execution of this contract or otherwise) in every factory, workshop or place situate in the United Kingdom and occupied or used by him for the execution of the contract comply with the following conditions, namely:–

(a)

(i) The contractor shall pay rates of wages and observe hours and conditions of labour not less favourable than those established, for the trade or industry in the district where the work is carried out, by machinery of negotiation or arbitration to which the parties are organisations of employers and trade unions representative respectively of substantial proportions of the employers and workers engaged in the trade or industry in the district.

(ii) In the absence of any rates of wages, hours or conditions of labour so established the contractor shall pay rates of wages and observe hours and conditions of labour which are not less favourable than the general level of wages, hours and conditions observed by other employers whose general circumstances in the trade or industry in which the contractor is engaged are similar.

(b) The contractor shall recognise the right of his work people to be members of such trade unions as they may choose.

(c) The contractor shall at all times during the continance of the contract display, for the information of his work people, in every factory, workshop or place situate as aforesaid and occupied or used by him for the execution of the contract a copy of the Fair Wages Resolution passed by the House of Commons on 14 October 1946.

(d) The contractor shall be responsible for the observance of this clause by sub-contractors employed within the United Kingdom in the execution of the contract, and shall if required notify the Council of the names and addresses of all such sub-contractors.

(e)   In the event of any question arising as to whether the foregoing conditions are being observed, the question shall, if not otherwise disposed of, be referred by the Secretary of State for Employment to an independent tribunal for decision.

Provided that any contract made by or on behalf of the Council in the Standard Form of Building Contract (1963 Edition as revised) in which Clause 17A stands without amendment shall be deemed to comply with the provisions of this contract standing order.

22   Before accepting a tender or making a contract for the execution of work or the supply of goods or materials and before placing a contractor on a selected list of contractors under contract standing order 3 the Council shall obtain from the contractor an assurance in writing that, insofar as he has, for the whole or any part of a period of three months immediately preceding the date of his tender or of his application to be placed on such list, employed persons in any factory, workshop or place situate in the United Kingdom, to the best of the knowledge and belief he has in respect of persons so employed complied with the general conditions of the Fair Wages Resolution passed by the House of Commons on 14 October 1946, for the said period of three months or part thereof, as the case may be.

FINANCIAL REGULATIONS

General Note

Where regulations contain financial limits a figure has not been inserted. This is a matter on which each authority must make its own decision.

The term finance "committee" denotes the appropriate

body of members which depending on local circumstances might be a policy and resources committee, a policy and co-ordinating committee or a finance sub-committee.

"Treasurer" is intended to be synonymous with "director of finance" or any other title which might be given to the officer responsible for finance in accordance with section 151 of the Local Government Act 1972.

(i) GENERAL

01 Each chief officer shall consult the treasurer with respect to any matter within his purview which is liable materially to affect the finances of the Council before any provisional or other commitment is incurred or before reporting thereon to a committee.

02 References in these regulations to chief officers are to chief officers as defined by standing order . . . together with the Chief Constable. References to the Council include reference to the Police Authority where the context so requires.

(ii) BUDGET

03 The detailed form of capital and revenue estimates shall be determined by the treasurer consistently with the general directions of the finance committee and after consultation with each chief officer concerned.

04 Estimates of income and expenditure on revenue account and of receipts and payments on capital account shall be prepared by chief officers in consultation with the treasurer who shall collate the estimates approved by committees and report to the finance committee thereon, such report to include compliance with the financial plan(s) approved by the Council and other financial implications.

05 Upon the approval by the Council of a programme of capital expenditure the chief officer concerned shall be authorised:–

(a) To take steps to enable land required for the purposes of the programme to be acquired in due time; and

(b) to prepare a scheme and estimate including associated revenue expenditure for approval by the appropriate committee.

06 Any proposal to a committee which would involve the incurring of expenditure during a period in respect of which the Council has approved a budget or a programme of capital expenditure shall be accompanied by a report of the chief officer concerned indicating the sufficiency or otherwise of the finance provision therefore in the budget and/or programme.

07 Where it appears that the amount of any head of estimate of approved expenditure may be exceeded or the amount of any head of approved income may not be reached, it shall be the duty of the chief officer concerned after consultation with the treasurer, or of the treasurer as the case may require, to inform the committee concerned.

08 The treasurer shall furnish each chief officer with periodical statements of receipts and payments under each head of approved estimate and such other relevant information as he has.

*Where a management team is appointed (under the chief executive), this regulation may require revision.

(iii) **ACCOUNTING**

09 All accounting procedures and records of the Council and its officers shall be determined by the treasurer. Where such procedures and records are maintained in a department other than that of the treasurer he shall, before making any determination, consult the chief officer of the department concerned.

10 All accounts and accounting records of the Council shall be compiled by the treasurer or under his direction.

11   The following principles shall be observed in the allocation of accounting duties:–

(a)   The duties of providing information regarding sums due to or from the Council and of calculating, checking and recording these sums, shall be separated as completely as possible from the duty of collecting or disbursing them;

(b)   officers charged with the duty of examining and checking the accounts of cash transactions shall not themselves be engaged in any of these transactions.

(iv) ADVANCE ACCOUNTS

12   The treasurer shall provide such advance accounts as he considers appropriate for such officers of the Council as may need them for the purposes of defraying petty cash and other expenses. Such accounts shall be maintained in the imprest system.

13   Where he considers it appropriate, the treasurer shall open an account with the Council's bankers or National Giro for use by the imprest holder who shall not cause such account to be overdrawn. It shall be a standing instruction to the Council's bankers that the amount of any overdrawn balance on an imprest holder's banking account shall forthwith be reported to the treasurer.

14   No income received on behalf of the Council may be paid into an advance account but must be banked or paid to the authority as provided elsewhere in these regulations.

15   Payments shall be limited to minor items of expenditure and to such other items as the treasurer may approve and shall be supported by a receipted voucher to the extent that the treasurer may require.

16   An officer responsible for an advance account shall, if so requested, give to the treasurer a certificate as to the state of his imprest advance.

17   On leaving the employment of the Council or otherwise ceasing to be entitled to hold an imprest advance, an officer shall account to the treasurer for the amount advanced to him.

(v)   AUDIT

18   A continuous internal audit, under the independent control and direction of the treasurer, shall be arranged to carry out an examination of accounting, financial and other operations of the Council.

19   The treasurer or his authorised representative shall have authority to:–

(a)   Enter at all reasonable times on any Council premises or land;

(b)   have access to all records, documents and correspondence relating to any financial and other transactions of the Council;

(c)   require and receive such explanations as are necessary concerning any matter under examination: and

(d)   require any employee of the Council to produce cash, stores or any other Council property under his control.

20   Whenever any matter arises which involves, or is thought to involve, irregularities concerning cash, stores or other property of the Council or any suspected irregularity in the exercise of the functions of the authority, the chief officer concerned shall forthwith notify the treasurer who shall take such steps as he considers necessary by way of investigation and report.

(vi)   BANKING ARRANGEMENTS AND CHEQUES

21   All arrangements with the Council's bankers shall be made by or under arrangements approved by the treasurer, who shall be authorised to operate such banking accounts,

including National Giro Accounts, as he may consider necessary.

22 All cheques, including National Giro payment forms, but excluding cheques drawn on authorised imprest accounts, shall be ordered only on the authority of the Treasurer, who shall make proper arrangements for their safe custody.

23 Cheques on the Council's main banking accounts, including National Giro accounts, shall bear the facsimile signature of the treasurer or be signed by the treasurer or other officer authorised to do so.

(vii) CONTRACTS FOR BUILDING, CONSTRUCTIONAL OR ENGINEERING WORK

24 Where contracts provide for payment to be made by instalments, the treasurer shall arrange for the keeping of a contract register or registers to show the state of account on each contract between the Council and the contractor, together with any other payments and the related professional fees.

25 Payments to contractors on account of contracts shall be made only on a certificate issued by the architect, engineer or estates officer (or private architect, engineer or consultant where engaged by the Council) as appropriate or by his deputy or other officer nominated by him in writing for the purpose.

26 Subject to the provisions of the contract in each case every extra or variation, shall, unless otherwise evidenced to his satisfaction, be authorised in writing by the architect, engineer or estates officer (or private architect, engineer or consultant) as may be appropriate or by his deputy or other officer nominated by him in writing for the purpose.

27 Any such extra variation, the estimated additional cost of which exceeds (£   ), shall be reported to the appropriate committee as soon as practicable.

28 The final certificate of completion of any contract shall

not be issued until the appropriate officer, private architect, engineer or consultant has produced to the treasurer a detailed statement of account, and all relevant documents if required.

29 The treasurer shall, to the extent he considers necessary, examine final accounts for contracts and he shall be entitled to make all such enquiries and receive such information and explanations as he may require in order to satisfy himself as to the accuracy of the accounts.

30 Claims from contractors in respect of matters not clearly within the terms of any existing contract shall be referred to the solicitor for consideration of the authority's legal liability and, where necessary, to the treasurer for financial consideration before a settlement is reached.

31 Where completion of a contract is delayed by more than (two-twelfths) of the contract period, it shall be the duty of the technical officer concened to take appropriate action in respect of any claim for liquidated damages and to report his action to the committee concerned.

32 In any case where the total cost of any work carried out under a contract exceeds by more than 5% the approved contract sum a report of such cost shall, after agreement of the final account, be submitted to the appropriate committee.

33 A chief officer regularly undertaking by direct labour work which contractors are able and willing to undertake shall periodically compare the cost of a representative selection of such work with the cost of the same work performed by contractors.

(viii) ESTATES

34 The (estates officer) will maintain a terrier of all properties owned by the Council (except dwellings provided under the Housing Acts) in a form approved by the treasurer, recording the holding committee, purpose for which held, location, extent and plan reference, purchase details,

particulars of nature of interest and rents payable and particulars of tenancies granted.

35   The solicitor shall have the custody of all title deeds under secure arrangements agreed with the treasurer.

(ix) **INCOME**

36   The collection of all money due to the Council shall be under the supervision of the treasurer.

37   Each chief officer shall furnish the treasurer with such particulars in connection with work done, goods supplied or services rendered and of all other amounts due as may be required by him to record correctly all sums due to the Council and to ensure the prompt rendering of accounts for the recovery of income due.

38   The treasurer shall be notified promptly of all money due to the Council and of contracts, leases and other agreements and arrangements entered into which involve the receipt of money by the Council and the treasurer shall have the right to inspect any documents or other evidence in this connection as he may decide.

39   All receipt forms, books, tickets and other such items shall be ordered and supplied to departments by the treasurer, who shall satisfy himself as to the arrangements for their control.

40   All money received by an officer on behalf of the Council shall without delay be paid to the treasurer or, as he may direct, to the Council's banking or National Giro account or transmitted directly to any other body or person entitled thereto. No deduction may be made from such money save to the extent that the treasurer may specifically authorise. Each officer who so banks money shall enter on the paying-in slip a reference to the related debt (such as the receipt number or the name of the debtor) or otherwise indicate the origin of the cheque on the reverse of each cheque, the officer shall enter the name of his department, office or establishment.

41 Personal cheques shall not be cashed out of the money held on behalf of the Council.

42 Every transfer of official money from one member of staff to another will be evidenced in the records of the departments concerned by the signature of the receiving officer.

(x) INSURANCES

43 The (treasurer) shall effect all insurance cover and negotiate all claims in consultation with other officers where necessary.

44 Chief officers shall give prompt notification to the (treasurer) of all new risks, properties or vehicles which require to be insured and of any alterations affecting existing insurances.

45 Chief officers shall forthwith notify the (treasurer) in writing of any loss, liability or damage or any event likely to lead to a claim, and inform the police unless otherwise decided.

46 All appropriate employees of the Council shall be included in a suitable fidelity guarantee insurance.

47 The (treasurer) shall annually, or at such other period as he may consider necessary, review all insurances in consultation with other chief officers as appropriate.

48 Chief officers shall consult the treasurer and solicitor respecting the terms of any indemnity which the Council is requested to give.

(xi) INVENTORIES

49 Inventories shall be maintained by all departments and therein shall be recorded an adequate description of furniture, fittings and equipment, plant and machinery, save that the extent to which the property of the Council shall be so recorded and the form in which the inventories shall be kept is to be determined by the appropriate chief officer with the concurrence of the treasurer.

50 Each chief officer shall be responsible for maintaining an annual check of all items on the inventory, for taking action in relation to surpluses or deficiencies and noting the inventory accordingly.

51 The Council's property shall not be removed otherwise than in accordance with the ordinary course of the Council's business or used otherwise than for the Council's purposes except in accordance with specific directions issued by the chief officer concerned.

(xii) INVESTMENTS, BORROWINGS AND TRUST FUNDS

52 All investments of money under its control shall be made in the name of the Council or in the name of nominees approved by the finance committee; bearer securities shall be reported to the finance committee.

53 All securities the property of or in the name of the Council or its nominees and the title deeds of all property in its ownership shall be held in custody of the (solicitor) (treasurer) (Council's bankers).

54 All borrowings shall be effected in the name of the Council.

55 The treasurer shall be the Council's registrar of stocks, bonds and mortgages and shall maintain records of all borrowing of money by the Council.

56 All trust funds shall wherever possible be in the name of the Council.

57 All officers acting as trustees by virtue of their official position shall deposit all securities, etc, relating to the trust with the (solicitor) (treasurer) unless the deed otherwise provides.

(xiii) ORDERS FOR WORK, GOODS AND SERVICES

58 Official orders shall be in a form approved by the treasurer and solicitor and are to be signed only by officers

authorised by the appropriate chief officer who shall be responsible for official orders issued from his department.

59 Official orders shall be issued for all work, goods or services to be supplied to the Council except for supplies of public utility services, for periodical payments such as rent or rates, for petty cash purchases or such other exceptions as the treasurer may approve.

60 Each order shall conform with the directions of the Council with respect to central purchasing and the standardisation of supplies and materials.

61 A copy of each order shall, if so required, be supplied to the treasurer.

(xiv) **PAYMENT OF ACCOUNTS**

62 Apart from petty cash and other payments from advance accounts (see FR 4.4) the normal method of payment of money due from the Council shall be by cheque or other instrument drawn on the Council's banking account or National Giro account by the treasurer.

63 The chief officer issuing an order is responsible for examining, verifying and certifying the related invoice(s) and similarly for any other payment vouchers or accounts arising from sources in his department. Such certification shall be in manuscript by or on behalf of the chief officer. The names of officers authorised to sign such records shall be sent to the treasurer by each chief officer together with specimen signatures and shall be amended on the occasion of any change therein.

64 Before certifying an account, the certifying officer shall save to the extent that the treasurer may otherwise determine, have satisfied himself that:–

(a) The work, goods or services to which the account relates have been received, carried out, examined and approved;

(b) the prices, extensions, calculations, trade

discounts, other allowances, credits and tax are correct;

(c) the relevant expenditure has been properly incurred, is within the relevant estimate provision;

(d) appropriate entries have been made in inventories, stores records or stock books as required; and

(e) the account has not been previously passed for payment and is a proper liability of the Council.

65 Duly certified accounts shall be passed without delay to the treasurer who shall examine them to the extent that he considers necessary, for which purpose he shall be entitled to make such enquiries and to receive such information and explanations as he may require.

66. Any amendment to an account shall be made in ink and initialled by the officer making it, stating briefly the reasons where they are not self-evident.

67 Each chief officer shall, as soon as possible after 31 March and not later than (30 April) in each year notify the treasurer of all outstanding expenditure relating to the previous financial year.

(xv) PROTECTION OF PRIVATE PROPERTY

68 The (director of social services) shall notify the treasurer in such form as he may require of any case known to him where steps are necessary to prevent or mitigate loss or damage of movable property and shall forward to the treasurer an itemised inventory in each case prepared in the presence of two officers.

69 All valuables such as jewellery, watches and other small articles of a similar nature and documents of title shall unless in any case otherwise decided by the treasurer be deposited with him for safe custody.

(xvi) SALARIES, WAGES AND PENSIONS

70 The payment of all salaries, wages, pensions, compensation and other emoluments to all employees or former employees of the Council shall be made by the treasurer or under arrangements approved and controlled by him.

71 Each chief officer shall notify the treasurer as soon as possible and in the form prescribed by him, of all matters affecting the payment of such emoluments, and in particular:–

(a) Appointments, resignations, dismissals, suspensions, secondments and transfers;

(b) absences from duty for sickness or other reason, apart from approved leave;

(c) changes in remuneration, other than normal increments and pay awards and agreements of general application;

(d) information necessary to maintain records of service for superannuation, income tax, national insurance and the like.

72 Appointments of all employees shall be made in accordance with the regulations of the Council and the approved establishments, grades and rates of pay.

73 All time records or other pay documents shall be in a form prescribed or approved by the treasurer and shall be certified in manuscript by or on behalf of the chief officer. The names of officers authorised to sign such records shall be sent to the treasurer by each chief officer together with specimen signatures and shall be amended on the occasion of any change.

(xvii) SECURITY

74 Each chief officer is responsible for maintaining property security at all times for all buildings, stocks, stores,

furniture, equipment, cash, etc. under his control. He shall consult the treasurer in any case where security is thought to be defective or where it is considered that special security arrangements may be needed.

75   Maximum limits for cash holdings shall be agreed with the treasurer and shall not be exceeded without his express permission.

76   Keys to safes and similar receptacles are to be carried on the person of those responsible at all times; the loss of any such keys must be reported to the treasurer forthwith.

77   The (computer officer) shall be responsible for maintaining proper security and privacy as respects information held in the computer installation or for its use.

(xviii)   **STOCKS AND STORES**

78   Each chief officer shall be responsible for the care and custody of the stocks and stores in his department.

79   Stocks shall not be in excess of normal requirements except in special circumstances with the approval of the committee concerned.

80   Chief officers shall arrange for periodical test examinations of stocks by persons other than storekeepers and shall ensure that all stocks are checked at least once in every year.

81   The treasurer shall be entitled to receive from each chief officer such information as he requires in relation to stores for the accounting, costing and financial records. Surplus materials, stores or equipment shall be disposed of by competitive tender or public auction unless the committee concerned decides otherwise in a particular case.

(xix) TRAVELLING, SUBSISTENCE AND FINANCIAL LOSS ALLOWANCES

82 All claims for payment of car allowances, subsistence allowances, travelling and incidental expenses shall be submitted, duly certified in a form approved by the treasurer, to him, made up to a specified day of each month, within seven days thereof. The names of officers authorised to sign such records shall be sent to the treasurer by each chief officer together with specimen signatures and shall be amended on the occasion of any change.

83 Payments to members, including co-opted members of the Council or its committees who are entitled to claim travelling or other allowances will be made by the treasurer upon receipt of the prescribed form duly completed. All claims for a financial year are to be submitted within one month of 31 March.

84 The certification by or on behalf of the chief officer shall be taken to mean that the certifying officer is satisfied that the journeys were authorised, the expenses properly and necessarily incurred and that the allowances are properly payable by the Council.

85 Officers' claims submitted more than (six) months after the expenses were incurred will be paid only with the express approval of the treasurer.

INDEX

C

M

N